# A Comparative Study of *Jainism* & *Buddhism*

# CONTENTS.

# INTRODUCTION

On reading some Buddhist works in the original Pali, some translations in English and some independently written English books on Buddhism, I found out that old Buddhism resembled Jainism in many points. In order to know Pali Buddhism I went to Ceylon and stayed for a month in the Vidyalankara College, Kelaniya, from the 14th May to 13th June 1932. Also I went to some other famous Buddhist places to know the religious ways and customs. In the College I gained much information on Buddhism from the Buddhist monk Ananda Kausalyayana and Râhula Sankrityayana, the editor of " Buddha Charya."

I thought it advisable to write a book in which I might show the similarities between the Jaina and Buddhist philosophies by quoting passages from the literatures of both ; so that the readers may be convinced of their oneness and of their common source.

So far as I understand, the nature of Nirvâna and its path as shown in the Buddhist Pali Books are not different from the nature of Nirvâna and its path as given in the old Jain Books.

From the description given in this book, the readers will know that Goutama Buddha on leaving his home, adopted the conduct of a naked saint, like a Digambar Jain ascetic for some time. Afterwards he proclaimed his ***middle path*** in which clothes were allowed for the monks. But the philosophy was not changed by him.

Whatever literature in Pali compiled in the 1st Century A.D. is available, specially describes internal conduct. Such questions as depend on inference and logic were not answered by Goutama Buddha to the general public, such as 'what is soul ?, 'what is Nirvâna ?, 'what happens after death ?'. But these questions have been answered and described in such a way that no discussion may arise, while the reasonable men may understand the answers correctly, and may be engaged in making efforts for *Nirvâna*.

Although the Jains acknowledge one philosophy, there have now been two divisions among them, DIGAMBAR AND SVETAMBAR. Similarly the Buddhist Order was established separate from the Jain Order on allowing clothes to monks by Goutama Buddha even at the time of Lord Mahavira, *i.e.*, before Mahavira began to preach in His age of 42 when He became *ârhat* and omniscient. At the time of Mahavira there appears to have existed some rivalry between them, which is proved from some Buddhist sutras which do not speak favourably of some Jain Views ; although this unfavourable description will be found to be incorrect when Jain literature is consulted properly and compared with the Buddhist sayings. I give below the names of some of the Sutras in which Mahavira has been spoken of as *Nigantha Nâtaputta*. These are the instances of rivalry which existed between the Jains and the Buddhists at least at the time when the Buddhist literature was compiled in the first century A.D. in Ceylon.

From " Buddha Charya " the following such sutras are quoted here. (1) P. 91. Jatila sutta (S. N. (3–1–1). Raja Presanajita of Kausala spoke to Goutama, " O Goutama, the Lord of Saints and Brahmans, the leader of saints, the teacher of saints, learned, famous, Tirthankara well-honoured by many people just as Nigantha Nâttaputta."...........

(2) Page 110 Asibandhaka putta sutta (An. N. A. K. 2-4-5) and (S.N. 40-1-9).

" Once the Exalted One Goutama with an assembly of monks went to *Nalinda*, where *Nigantha Nataputta* was staying with a very large assembly of Niganthas (Jain monks)."

(3) Page 148. Siha Sutta (A.N. 8-2-1. 2).

" Once Lord Goutam was at Vesali, then the commander-in-chief Sinh, a layman ***srâvaka*** of ***Niganthas*** was sitting in the assembly.........Sinha went to where *Nigantha Nataputta* was seated......Goutam says, " Sinha, your family has been serving Niganthas for a very long time, when they arrive, you should not refrain from giving them alms."

(4) Page 228 Chula Dukkha Kandha Sutta (M.N. 1-2-4). Goutama says, " Once I was walking on Gridha Kuta hill of Rajagraha and there many Nirganthas (Jain Saints) were suffering strong having a vow of standing on ***Kâla silâ*** of Riṣigiri. Goutama asked, " Niganthas ! why are you suffering ?" Then they said, " Nigantha Nâtaputta (Jain Tirthankara Mahavira) is all-knowing,

all perceiving. He is always in Knowledge and perception...........

(5) Page 265. Maha sukuladai sutta (M.N. 2-3-6).

*Nigantha Nattaputta* has come in Rajagraha for rainy season...........

(6) Page 280. Chula—sukuladai sutta (M.N. 2-3-9).

"Who are claiming to be all-knowing, all-perceiving, knowing all knowledge and perception—? O Lord! *Nigantha Nattaputta*"...........

(7) Page 341. Deva daha sutta (M.N. 3-1-1).

"Those Nigantas told me '*Nigantha Nattaputta* is all-knowing, all-perceiving, having all knowledge and perception."

(8) Page 445. Upali Sutta (M.N. 2-2-6).

At that time *nigantha nattaputta* with a great assembly of Niganthas (Jain Saints) was roaming at Nalinda—"

"Lord Buddha said to Upali," "Your family has been serving the Niganthas for a very long time, when they arrive, you should not refrain from serving them with alms."—

"O Lord! Goutam orders me to give alms to Niganthas."

"A great ascetic went to where *Nigantha Nattaputta* was sitting."

(9) Page 456 Abhaya Raja Kumar Sutta (M.N. 5-1-8).

" Abhayarajakumara went to where *Nigantha Nattaputta* was sitting."

(10) Page 459. Sâmanja phala sutta (M.N. 1-1-2).

" Some one said *Nigantha Nattaputta*."

(11) Page 481. Samagamasutta (M.N. 3-1-4).

Once Goutama Buddha was touring in *Sakya* country, then *Nigantha Nâttaputta* (Jain Tirthankara Mahavira) had his *Nirvana* at Pava.

*Note.* According to " Buddha Charya " (505 V. S.–428). Goutama was then 77 years of age. His full age was 80.

(12) Page 520. Mahâparinibbâna sutta (D.N. 2–3 (16–12).

" The famous dignified Tirthankara *Nigantha Nâttaputta*."...........

(13) Majjhim Nikaya Chulá Saropam Sutta 30.

**" ये इमे भो गोतम समण ब्राह्मण संघिनो गणाचरिया ज्ञातायसस्सिनो तित्थकरा साधुसम्मता बहुजनस्स सेय्यत्थिदं निगंत नाथपुत्तोः. "**

*" Ye ime bho Gotama samana brâhmanâ sangino ganâ chariyâ jnâtâ yasassino titthakar sadhu sammata-bahujanassa seyyathidam nigantha nathputto."*

" O Goutama, those who have an assembly of saints and Brahmans, leader of assembly, knowing, famous, well honoured by many people, just as Nigantha Nathaputta."

(14) Digha Nikaya III 29 Basâdika Suttanta.

" Eka samayam Bhagavâ sakkesu viharati—tena kho pana samayena *Nigantha Nathputta* pâvâyam adhâna kâla kato hoti............"

" Once Lord Goutama was touring in Sakya country, then Nirgrantha Nathputta breathed his last at Pâvâ.............."

(15) Majjhim Nikaya mahasachchikasutta 36.

" Sachchaka Nigganthaputto-mahâvanam upasankâmi.

" Nigantha natha puttam vâden."

" Sachchka, the follower of Nirgrantha went to the great forest. Nirgrantha nathaputra by discussion......"

From the above quotations it also appears that at the time of Goutama Buddha the followers of Nirgrantha were prevalent from a very long time and that Lord Mahavira was recognized as Tirthankara and Omniscient.

Just at the present time we see in India Digambar and Svetambara Jains following their religious duties side by side, but with rivalry, in the same way the Jains and Buddhists were living side by side, but with rivalry in the olden days.

From " Buddha Charya " page 577 it appears that Mahendra, son of Asoka went to Ceylon in V.S. 190, when 236 years had passed after the Nirvâna of Gotama.

It is also known that either Jainism was prevalent in Ceylon, before this time or the preachers of Jainism must have gone to Ceylon along with Mahendra.

The Buddhistic Book Maha-Vansa says that there were Nirgranthas at Anuradhapura in Ceylon.

A Buddhist king was displeased with them and turned them away and in their religious place he constructed a Buddha temple. The Pali words are :—

*Mahavansa chapter 33.*

**"वा सितो व सदा आसी एकवीसाति राजासुतं दिस्वान पलायंतं निगंथो गिरिनामको पलायाति महाकाल सीहलोति भुसंरवितं, सुतान महाराजा सिद्धेमम मनोरथे विहारं एत्थकारेस्सं इच्चेवं चिंतईतदा दाटिकं दमलं हत्त्वा सयं रज्जं अकारई ततो निग्गंथराम तं विद्धंसेत्वा महीपातिः विहारकारई तस्स द्वादस्स परिवेणिकं."**

*"Vâ sito va sadâ âsi eka visati râjasutam dis vâna palâyantam Nigantho Girinâmako palayati mahakala sihaloti bhasam ravi tam sutana mahârâjâ siddhemama mano ratha Viharam ettha karessam ichchevam chintaitadâ Dâthikam damalam hattva sayam rajjam akârai tato nigganthârâmam tam viddhansetva mahi patih vihara kârai tassa dva dasa pariveni kam."*

"The 21st Raja was living (at Anuradhapura) *a Nirgrantha* (Jain whether saint or layman) seeing him fleeing away said loudly that Maha Kala Sinhala was fleeing. Hearing this, Maharaja Sinhala resolved in his mind that when his object would be fulfilled, then he would construct a temple here. He killed *Dâthika* Damila and ascended the throne himself, then he destroyed the shrine of Nirgranthas and constructed (Buddha) temple with twelve *pravinas*."

*Note.* This is said to have occured about 2 centuries B.C.

The above statement shows that there were Jains along with the Buddhists in Ceylon, but they were not in good terms. On reading this book it will be known that whatever philosophy is described in the old Pali books has been explained in details in the Jain Scriptures. On consulting the Jain literature, the glory of the Buddhist Scriptures can be realised better.

The present-day scholars also maintain that old Buddhism was somewhat different from the present Buddhism. Some of their statements are given below:—

I. *Sacred Books of the East Vol. XI* (1881).

Translation by W. Rhys Davids from Pali edited by Max Muller :—

Intro. Page XXI. " It will be acknowledged that the suttas have preserved for us at least the belief of the earliest Buddhists—the Buddhists of India—as to what the original doctrines taught by the Buddha himself, had been."

Page XXII. " The first record we have of the Buddhist Scriptures being reduced into writing is the well-known passage in Dipa Vansa, which speaks of their being recorded in books in Ceylon towards the beginning of the first century before the commencement of our era." The date of Dipavansa may be placed about the 4th century A.D."

Buddhism of the Pali Pitakas is not only a different thing from Buddhism as hither-to commonly received, but is antagonistic to it.

Page XXXIV. No record of his actual words could have been preserved. It is quite evident that the speeches placed in the Teacher's mouth, though formulated in the first person, in direct narrative, are only intended to be summaries, and very short summaries, of what was said on these occasions."

II. "*The Doctrine of the Buddha*" by George Grimm.

Preface page XVI. "The fixing of the Tipitaka in writing followed only a few decades before the beginning of our era under King *Vattagamini* in Ceylon, to which island the Canon had been brought by Mahinda, the son of King Asoka. This definite fixing of the Pali Canon took place about 400 years after the Buddha's death." The present work sets forth the original genuine teaching of the Buddha.

III. *The life of the Buddha* by Edward J. Thomas, M.A., (1927).

Intro—Page XVIII. "As the authoritative teaching represented by the dogmatic utterances and discourses of the Founder were not recorded in writing, but were memorised by each school, differences inevitably began to appear."

Page XXII. "They (the Pali Chronicles of Ceylon) are corroborated in their main out-lines by the Puranic and Jain traditions. The chronological relations with general history have been determined by the discovery of Sir William Jones that the Candagutta (Candragupta) of the Chronicles and Puranas is the Sandrocottos of Strabo and Justin, the Indian King who about 303 B.C.

made a treaty with *Seleucus Nicator* and at whose court Megasthenes resided for some years as ambassador."

Page 204. "They all agree in holding that the primitive teaching must have been something different from what the earliest Scriptures and commentators thought it was."

If the philosophies of the Jains and the old Buddhists were the same with only difference in some external conduct of monks, especially in this that Nirgrantha saints were naked and the Buddhist monks wore clothes, then it is to be found out whether Mahavira began his preaching or not when Goutam Buddha left home and followed external conduct of a Digambar Jain Saint for some time.

Whether Lord Mahavira had commenced his preaching or not it is certain that knowledge of Jainism was prevalent before Lord Mahavira began his sermon. *Buddha Charya* P. 481 Samagama Sutta (M. N. 3-1-4) says "When Goutama Buddha was 77 years of age Mahavira attained Nirvâna in his age of 72. It is evident from the Jain Scriptures that Mahavira did not begin his preaching before his age of 42. He preached during his last 30 years. It means that when Goutama Buddha was of 47 years of age, Maha vira's teachings were commenced. Goutama Buddha left home in his age of 29 and began his preaching after 6 years *i.e.,* at the age of 35. It proves that the Preaching of Mahavira began 12 years after the commencement of the preaching of Goutama Buddha. Then whatever conduct of Digambar Jain Saints was prevalent in India at the time when Goutama left home at 29 and began preaching at 35, was due to the teaching of some one previous to *Mahavira*. The Jaina Saint Devasena writes in his *Darsanasara* that Goutama Buddha became the disciple of Pihitasrava Jain saint, who was in the line of Lord Parsva Nath, the 23rd Tirthankara of the Jains. This proves that Parsvanath flourished before Mahavira. The period of 250 years is the interval time between the Nirvâna of Parsva and that of Mahavira. When Mahavira was born, Parsva had attained nirvâna only 178 years before.

As yet the name of *Parsva* has not been found in many inscriptions or historical records ; therefore he may not be taken as a historical great man ; but it is perfectly proved that Jainism or the old Buddhism was prevalent before Lord Mahavira and Goutama Buddha began their teachings.

In my opinion there is not any difference between Jainism and Buddhism. Whether we speak of Jainism or Buddhism before Gautama Buddha we speak of one and the same thing. Gautama Buddha made easy the external conduct of the monks only. He maintained the same philosophy which was prevalent in Jainism or old Buddhism. This fact will be known to the readers if they study these books carefully. That there was Jainism before the preaching of Buddha was commenced, will be known from some of the opinions of the scholars, given below :—

P. 25. I. *The life of the Buddha* by E. J. Thomas (1927).

Intro. P. XIV. "There were gymnosophists or naked saints in India, but they were not Buddhists."

II. *Ancient India* as described by Magasthenes and Arrian (1887).

Page 104. "Philosophy, then with all its blessed advantages to man, flourished long also among the Indians, the gymnosophists."

P. 105. Sarmanes called Germanes by Strabo and Sumarians by Parphyrius, are the ascetics of a different religion, and may have belonged to the sect of the Jains or to another.

Page 115. When Alexander arrived at Taxila, and saw the Indian gymnosophists (Jain Munis), a desire seized him to have one of these men brought into his presence. The oldest of these sophists with whom the others lived as disciples with a master Daulanus by name, not only refused to go himself, but prevented the others going. He is said to have won over *Kalanus* one of the sophists of the place.

P. 122. Socrates speaks of the soul as at present confined in the body as in species of prison. This was the doctrine of Pythogoras, even in its most striking peculiarities, bears such a close resemblance to the Indians as greatly to favour the supposition that it was directly borrowed from it. There was even a tradition that Pythogoras had visited India.

III. *Science of Comparative religions* by Major General J.G.R. Forlong, F.R.S.E., F.R.A.S.M.A.I. etc. (1877).

This book shows that Jainism and old Buddhism were one and the same religion, and that this religion was prevalent in India and outside of India from a very, very long time and that its influence was impressed upon the Jewish religion and Christianity also.

Intro. P. XIV. "The selection of these Short Studies has enabled us to virtually embrace and epitomize all the faiths and religious ideas of the world, as well as, to lay bare the deep-seated tap root from which they sprang, viz., the crude yatism, jati or asceticism of thoughtful Jatis or Jinas, who in man's earliest ages have in all lands separated themselves from the world and dwelt from pious motives in lone forests and mountain caves."

Intro. P. XIX. "It is clear also that the Gotama of early Tibetans, Mongols and Chinese must have been a Jaina; for the latter say he lived in the 10th and 11th centuries B.C. Tibetans say he was born in 916, became a Buddha in 881, preached from his 35th year and died in 831 B.C. dates which closely correspond with those of the saintly *Parsva*."

Page 2. "Through what historical channels did Buddhism influence early Christianity ?. We must widen the inquiry by making it embrace Jainism—the undoubtedly prior faith of very many millions through untold millenniums—though one little known in Europe except to the few."

Page 20. "So slight seemed to Asoka the difference between Jains and Buddhists that he did not think it necessary to make a public profession of Buddhism till about his 12th regnal year (247 B.C.); so that nearly if not all his Rock inscriptions are really those of a Jaina Sovereign."

P. 29. From Aini-akbari of Abul Fazl it is clear that Asoka supported Jainism in Kashmir when Viceroy of Ujjain about 260 B.C., as had his father Bindusara and grand-father Chandragupta throughout the Magadha Empire. Buddhism was apparently for about a century after Gotama's death thought, by all who did not trouble themselves with details to be a mere form of Jainism. Among and beyond these millions, Asoka laboured assiduously to propagate his mild and kindly Jainism, especially concerning the sacredness of all life, as well as peace, charity, and universal brother-hood. In all his rock-inscriptions he designates himself *by the favourite Jaina title* "*Deva nam piya*," the Beloved of God?

"This then was the theory and practice of the great Jaino-Buddhist religion which flourished in India many centuries *before and after* the teaching of Gotama Sakya Muni.........It was certainly long prior to Parsva and Mahavira...........Whilst India was certainly the fruitful centre of religion from the 7th century B.C., yet Trans Himalaya, Oxiana, Baktria, and Kaspiana seem to have still earlier developed similar religious views and practices; and Indian Jains and Buddhists claim and almost historically show, that about a score of their saintly leaders perambulated the Eastern World long prior to the 7th Century B.C. We may reasonably believe that Jaino-Buddhism was very anciently preached by them from China to the Kaspian......It existed in Oxiana and north of the Himalayas 2000 years before *Mahavira.*

Page 32. In these moves, we see how Baktrian faiths passed West and how in the 7th and 6th centuries B.C. or earlier, Xalmoxis and Pythogoras were preaching and teaching like the *Butha gurus* of Jains and Buddhists.

Strabo says "They were a Thrakian sect who lived without wives. Their brethren the Masi religiously abstained from eating anything that had life."

Homer, of the 7th century B.C. or earlier, called them," most just men......livers on milk......devoid of desire for riches. John the Baptist, Jesus and their disciples are common examples of Essenik life in Asia.

Josephus says the Essenik brethren like the ancient Dacae neither married, drank wine, nor kept servants, living apart. They offer no sacrifices and teach the immortality of the soul as do Jains.

P. 35. He (Zalmoxis) taught more than the Jaina doctrine of the immortality of the soul.

P. 36. "He taught the Indian doctrines of........ transmigration etc..........and considered no animal should be injured—all having souls like men.'

P. 40. "The Savans of Alexander found Jaino-Buddhism strongly in the ascendant throughout Baktria, Oxiana and all the Passes to and from Afghanistan and India."

P. 46. Aristotle saying (about 330 B.C.) that "the Jews of Cæle-Syria were Indian philosophers called in the East Calani and *Ikshvaku* or sugar-cane people and only Jews, because they lived in Judea. These Jews (evidently Essenes) *derived from Indian philosophers wonderful fortitude in life, diet and continence.* They were, in fact Jaina-Bodhists, whom the great Greek confounded with Syrians.

Page 67-202-193 B.C. Rise of Chinese Han dynasty, before which say compilers of Sui dynasty of about 600 A.C. Buddhism was unknown in China, so that all prior to 200 B.C. was Jain-Bodhism.

From the above statements also the readers will know that the philosophy of the Jains and Buddhas is the same and that this Jain-Buddhist religion was prevalent in the world many thousand years before Christ and that the Jewish and the Christian religions were also influenced by it. Both Jainism and Buddhism flourished side by side in many places. There are many old places in India which have old relics of both the religions. Let me enumerate a few.

(1) *Sarnath* (Benares). It is the birth place of 11th Jain Tirthankar *Sri Sreyamnsa Nath.* Still there is a Jain temple and Dharmsala. Jains visit this as a place of pilgrimage. Just opposite to the Jain temple there is an old *Buddhist stupa.*

This is the place where Gautama Buddha preached his first sermon of middle path. On excavations along with many Buddhist images, Jain idols are also found; which are kept outside the museum.

(2) *Rajagraha* (Bihar). Here are five mountains on which there are Jain temples. Here the Buddhists

also visit and generally they pay respect to the Jain images.

(3) *Sravasti* or *Saheth Maheth* (Gonda U.P. in Balrampur State).

This is the birth place of *Sambhava Nath* the third Tirthankara of the Jains. Some Jain images were found here. They are kept in the Lucknow Museum. This is the chief religious place of the Buddhists also.

(4) *Nâsik* (Bombay P.) *Pandulena Caves.* Here are many Buddhist caves with images and stupas. There is also a Jain cave with Jain images.

(5) *Ellora* caves (near Aurangabad, Hyderabad, Nizam state). Here are many caves of the Buddhists and the Jains side by side with their own images.

(6) *Taxila* (Rawalpindi). Here are many Buddha *stupas* and images. Some sites are found out which appear to belong to the Jain temples. Vide Guide to Taxila by Sir John Marshall (1921).

Page 7. At *Jandial* a little to the north of Kachcha Kota are two conspicuous mounds, on one of which is a spacious temple dedicated, there is good reason to believe, to fire worship, and a little beyond these again, are the remains of two smaller stupas which may have been either Jain or Buddhist probably the former.

P. 68. *Sircap city*—Among these buildings is a spacious apsidal temple of Buddhist and several smaller shrines belong either to Jain or to Buddhist.

P. 74. In several houses, is a stupa shrine occupying in each case a court which opens with the high street. The best preserved of these shrines are to be seen in blocks G and F—both probably of Jain origin. The reason for regarding these stupas as of Jain rather than Buddhist origin is that they closely resemble certain Jain stupas depicted in reliefs from *Mathura*.

As far as the old literature of Jainism and Buddhism will be comparatively and minutely studied, so far there would appear similarity in their root principles. I could not read Svetambara Jain literature which is in Prakrit. I have compared Buddhism only with what is known from Digambar Jain literature. If any scholar will take up the task of comparing Buddhism with what is given in the Svetambara Jain literature there will appear a special glory of their similarity. I have made efforts to write this only with the view that the research scholars of philosophy in the world may be able to recognise their oneness.

With my scanty knowledge I have dealt with the subject with a pure heart; if there should be any mistakes the learned may kindly inform me of them; for which I shall ever be grateful to them.

*Saugar C. P.* | BRAHMACHARI SITALPRASAD JAIN,

24—10—1932 | *Chandawadi, Surat.*

# LIST OF WORKS CONSULTED.

## BUDDHIST LITERATURE.


(1) *Buddhist Wisdom*, the mystery of the self....... by George Grimm, Munich, Germany.

(2) Majjhim Nikaya Bhaya bherava sutta chaturtha.

(3) ,, Sati patthan sutta dasamam.

(4) ,, Mula pariyaya sutta dasamam.

(5) ,, Aruja pariyasana sutta 26.

(6) ,, Maha malumba suttam chatutham 64.

(7) *The word of the Buddha* by Nyana Tiloka Mahathera, Dodunduva, (Ceylon).

(8) *The Doctrine of the Buddha* by George Grimm, Germany (1926).

(9) *Some Sayings of the Buddha* according to Pali Canon translated by F. L. Woodward, M.A., Cantab, Ceylon. (1925).

(10) *Dhammapada* translated by F. Max Muller.

Sacred Books of the East Vol. X (1881).

(11) *Sutta Nipata* translated by G. V. Fausbold (1881).

(12) Visuddha Magga of Buddha Ghosha translated by P. Maung Tue.

(13) *The Life of the Buddha* by Edward J. Thomas, M.A., D. Litt (1927).

(14) Sacred Books of the East Vol. XVIX by F. Max Muller.

Buddha Charita by Asvaghosha.

(15) Buddha Chariya Hindi by Monk Rahula Sankrityayana (1985 v).

(16) Samyutta Nikaya avakata samyutta (10).

(17) Do. Chando (13).

(18) Majjhim Nikaya algaddipama sutta 22.

(19) Samyutta Nikaya (4) Salayalam Vaggo.

(20) Sacred Books of the East Vol. XI (1881).

*Maháparinibbânasutta* translated by T. W. Rhys Davids.

(21) Tuvataka Sutta of Sutta Nipata by Fausbold (1881).

(22) Sacred Books of the East III by T. W. Rhys Davids.

Dialogues of the Buddha from D.N.P.II (1910).

(23) Majjhim Nikaya Sammiditthi Sutta 9th.

(24) Manuscript Remains of the Buddhist Literature in Eastern Turkestan by A. F. Rudolf Hoernle (1916).

(25) Majjhim Nikaya Savvasava sutta dutiyam.

(26) Digha Nikaya Sangita suttanta 3; 33.

(27) *Samsara* by Bhiksu Narada (Ceylon) 1930.

(28) Bodhisatta Ideal by do.

(29) Majjhim Nikaya Sallekha Sutta athamam.

(30) Digha Nikaya (3) Singalo Vada Sutta 37.

(31) Anguttara Nikaya 5-177.

(32) Sutta Nipata Dhammika Sutta.

(33) Majjhim Nikaya Vatthapanna sutta (7).

(34) Lankavatara Sutta published by Bunyin Nanjio, M.A., Otam University, Kyoto (Japan).

(35) Majjhim Nikaya Maha Siha Nada Sutta (12).

*Note.* These Buddhist books can be had at the Mahabodhi Society, Saranath Benares; Mahabodhi Society, 4 A, College Square, Calcutta and the Imperial Library, Calcutta.

JAINA LITERATURE.

(1) *Samaya Sâra* Prakrit by Kunda Kunda Acharya of 49 V. S. (1st Cent. B.C.)

(2) *Asta Pâhuda* by do.

(3) *Panchâstikâya* by do.

(4) *Niyamasâra* by do.

(5) *Tattvartha Sutra* by Uma Swami Acharya of 81 V.S. (1st Cent. A.D.).

(6) *Ratna Karanda Sravakachara* by Samanta Bhadra Acharya (1st Cent. A.D.).

(7) *Sarvartha Siddhi* by Pujyapada Acharya of the 4th Cent. A.D.

(8) *Samâdhi Sataka* by do.

(9) *Purushartha Siddhiupaya* by Amrit Chandra Acharya of the 10th Cent. A.D.

(10) *Tattvârtha Sâra* by do.

(11) *Samaya Sâra Kalasâ* do.

(12) *Sravakachara* by Amitagati Acharya of the 10th Cent. A.D.

(13) *Ekatva Bhavana* by Padmanandi of the 10th Cent. A.D.

(14) *Siddha Stuti* by do.

(15) *Ekatva Saptati* by do.

(16) *Apta Svarupa*

(17) *Sâru Samuchchaya* by Kulabhadra Acharya.

(18) *Tattvânusâsana* by Nagasena Muni.

(19) *Istopadesa* by Pujyapada Acharya 4th Cent. A.D.

(20) *Atmânusasana* by Gunabhadra Acharya 9th Cent. A.D.

(21) *Laghu Samayika Patha* by Amitigati Acharya of 10th Cent. A.D.

(22) *Nischaya panchâśat* by Padmanandi Acharya of 10th Cent. A.D.

(23) *Yogasâra* by Yogindrâcharya.

(24) *Paramatma prakasa* by Yogindrâcharya.

(25) *Tattva Sâra* by Devasena of the 9th Cent. A.D.

(26) *Dravya Sangraha* by Nemichandra Siddhanta Chakravarti of the 9th Cent. A.D.

(27) *Vairagya Mâla* by Chandra of 16th Cent. A.D.

(28) *Brahat Sâmâyika* by Amitagati Acharya of the 10th Cent. A.D.

(29) *Sadbotha Chandrodaya* by Padmanandi Acharya of the 10th Cent. A.D.

(30) *Svayambhu Stotra* by Samantabhadra Acharya of the 1st Cent. A.D.

31) *Jnanalochana Stotra* by Vadiraja Acharya.

(32) *Subhasita Ratna Sandoha* by Amitagati Acharya.

(33) *Gomat Sara* by Nemichandra Siddhanta Chakravarti of the 9th Cent. A.D.

(34) *Mulachara* by Battakera.

(35) *Jnanarnaua* by Subbachandra Acharya of 11th Cent. A.D.

*All these books are printed and can be had from*—

(1) The Digambar Jain Publishing House, Chandawadi, Surat.

(2) The Jain Grantha Ratnakar Office, Hirabag, Girgaum, Bombay.

*Note.*—Nos. 13, 14, 15, 22, and 29, are included in one book *Padmanandi Pancha Vimsatika.* Nos. 16, 17, 23, 28, and 31 are only in Sanskrit and are included in *Siddhanta Saraadi Sangraha*, Manekchand Grantha Mala No. 21. Nos. 18, 21, 25, and 27 are in Sanskrit and are included in *Tattvanusasanadi Sangraha*, Manekchand Grantha Mala No. 13.

Nos. 1, 3, 4, 5, 6, 9, 19, 20, 21, 24, 26, and 33, are translated into English also and can be had from (1) The Jain Publishing House, Ajitashram, Lucknow (Oudh). (2) Jain Publishing House, Bijnor (U.P.) (3) The Jaina Mission Society, 436, Mint Street, Madras.

# JAINISM AND BUDDHISM

## CHAPTER I

### Nirvana, Moksha or Liberation

THE meaning of the word *Nirvâna* is extinction, while the word *Moksha* means "liberation." Extinction of the mundane condition is *Nirvâna;* and liberation from the same is *Moksha.* Both the terms thus contain and express the same idea. It is generally supposed that Buddhism preaches the philosophy of "transitoriness" or "destruction;" that it does not believe in the indestructibility of the soul or in the permanence of *Nirvâna.* It is this supposition which has led to the general notion that the word *Nirvâna* means total destruction or annihilation. The old Pali books of Buddhism, however, show that the *Nirvâna* of Buddhism is not "annihilation," but is a positive condition of the soul. As a result of elucidative discussions with the Principals of the Vidyalankar College, Kelaniya, and the Vidyodaya College, Colombo, (Ceylon) and with the English-educated Buddhist Monk, Narad Maitreya of Vajrarama Bambalpitiya (Ceylon), as well as with other Buddhist monks of Ceylon, I have come to know that *Nirvâna* is neither annihilation nor non-existence of the soul, but that it is an indescribable condition. Relying on the description of Nirvâna, as given in the Pali books, they strongly maintain that *Nirvâna* is not annihilation.

The "Hindu Organ," Jaffna, (Ceylon) dated the 19th May, 1932, contains an article on the subject of Nirvana by the Buddhist Monk B. Anand Maitreya, Belangoda, (Ceylon). Therein says the learned monk :—

*Nirvâna is not nothingness. As regards those things which do not tend to freedom from sorrow, the Buddha was silent. This is because his only aim was to lead the suffering world to real happiness. Nirvâna is holiness. Though it is neither this nor that, Nirvâna is not nothingness, yet it is a third possibility.*"

In "Buddhist Wisdom, The mystery of the self" George Grimm (Munich, Germany, akademiestrasse 19/II) says :—

"*It is characteristic of modern materialism to have chosen the first alternative, that of absolute annihilation, despite the Buddha's repeated assurances that he does not teach annihilation, but on the contrary, shows a way to the Imperishable, the Deathless.*" (Page 86). Again he says :—

"The Buddha further explains and teaches that extinction applies only to the three "flames" of lust, hate and delusion (the three kinds of thirst for sensation) and for this reason he defines *Nibbânam*, the goal of sainthood, as *Tanha Nibbânam*, literally, the extinction of thirst. The holy life with the sublime one is lived for the extinction of craving." (Page 57.)

In *Majjhima Nikâya Bhaya Bhairava Sutta 4th*, in the Pali language, we find that Goutam Buddha has shown how he advanced himself and then declared that *Nirvâna* is not extinction, but is a blissful condition. The Pali text is :—

* "*So evam samâhite chitte pari-suddhe pariyodâte anangame vigatupakkilese mudubhute kammaniye thite ânijjapatte âsavânâm khaya ṇâṇâya chittam abhininnamesim so :—iyam dukkhanti yathâ bhutam abhannasim... ayam dukkhasamudayoti yathabhutam abhannasim, ayam dukkha nirodho ti yathabhutam abhannasim, ayam dukkha-nirodha-gamini patipada ti yathabhutam abhannasim ; ime âsava ti yathabhutam abhannasim, ayam âsava-samudayoti yathabhutam*

---

*"सो एवं समाहिते चित्ते परिसुद्धे परियोदाते अनंगमे विगतूपक्किलेसे मुदुभूते कम्मनिये थिते अनिज्जप्पत्ते आसबानां खय णाणाय चित्तं अभिनिन्नमेसिं सोः...इयं दुक्खांति यधाभूतं अभण्णासिं—अयं दुक्खसमुदयोति यथाभूतं अभण्णासिं...अयं दुख्खनिरोधोतियथाभूतं अभण्णासिं, अयं दुख्खनिरोधगामिनी पटिपदातियथाभूतं अभण्णासिं, इमे आसवान्ति यथाभूतं अभण्णासिं, अयं आसब समुदयोति यथाभूतं अभण्णासिं, अयं आसव निरोधोति यथाभूत अभण्णासिं, अयं आसव निरोधगामिनी पटिपदाति यथाभूतं अभण्णासिं, तस्समे एव जानतो एवं पस्सतो कामासवापि चित्तं विमुच्चिथ विमुत्तस्मिं विमुत्तं इति

*abhannasim, ayam asava-nirodho ti yathabhutam abhannasim, ayam asava-nirodha-gamini patipada ti yathabhutam abhannasim; tassa me evam jânato evam passato kamasavapi chittam vimuchchitha vimuttasmin vimuttam iti nanam ahosi; khîna jâti, vusitam brahmchariyam, katam karaniyam nâparam itthatthayati abhannasim, ayam kho me brahmana rattiya pachhime yame tamo vihato aloko uppanno, yatha tam appamattassa âtâpino pahitattassa viharto."*

An English rendering of the text would be as follows. "Having thus pacified the mind, purified it, made it dirtless, having got rid of miseries, having become blissful, having brought the mind under control, on the destruction of *âsavâs* or impure thoughts, I realized thus:—It is misery, its true nature is known; it is the cause of misery, its true nature is known; it is the preventing of misery, its true nature is known; it is the way leading to prevention of misery, its true nature is known; these are the *âsavâs*, now truly known; these are the causes of *âsavâs*, now truly known; this is the prevention of *âsavâs* now truly known; this is the way of prevention of *âsavâs*, now truly known. When thus I knew, and thus I realised, thought activities

---

**णाणं अहोसि; खीणा जाति, वुसितं ब्रह्मचरियं, कतम करणीयं, नापरं इत्थत्थायाति अभण्णास्सिं, अयं खोसे ब्राह्मण मे रत्तिया पच्छिमे यामे तमो विहतो आलोको उप्पन्नो, यथातं अप्पमत्तस्स मातापिनो पहितत्तस्स विहरतो"**

of desire left my mind, I became free from desires. It was realized by me, that my birth is destroyed, my chastity is fulfilled, whatever I had to do I had done, nothing remained for me to be done. Thus I knew. In this way O Brahman, I procured this third knowledge in the last quarter of the night. Then ignorance fled away, knowledge appeared, darkness was removed, the Light burst forth, just as is possible to a wandering monk who is free from carelessness, is alert and absorbed in meditation of the Truth."

The above description shows that when the thought of *Nirvâna*, full or partial, is awakened, knowledge shines forth, desires cease to be, the causes of impure thought activity or *âsavâs* are removed. It further shows, that *Nirvâna* is not extinction, but a blissful condition, free from attachment and full of knowledge.

The words *âsava and apramatta* found here frequently occur in Jain Literature, where lust, hate and delusion are included in the term *âsavâs*, and it is stated that a monk without carelessness is capable of being liberated.

In "Samayasara," the Jain Saint Kunda-Kundacharya, says in the chapter on *Āsavâ*:—

** Râgô dôsâ môhôya âsavâ ṇatthi sammadiṭṭhisa,*
*Tahma âsâva bhávêṇa, viṇa hêdû ṇa pachchayâ hônti.*

* रागो दोसो मोहो य आसवा णत्थि सम्मदिट्ठिस्स ।
तह्मा आसव भावेण विणा हेदू ण पच्चया होंति ॥ १९८ ॥

"Lust, hate and delusion, impure thoughts, causing the inflow (of karmas) are not found in a right-believer, therefore in the absence of these Inflow-causing thoughts, the material karmas, in existence with a soul, can never be the cause of bondage."

The Jain Saint Kula-bhadra-âcharya says in his "Sârasamuchchaya":—

* *Jnan bhâvanayâ siktâ nibhritenantarâtmana. Apramattam guṇam prāpya, labhantê hitamâtmanah.*

"Those who are engaged in meditation of true knowledge, come to know the inner self, and having got rid of carelessness acquire the goal of the soul."

*Majjhima-nikâya, sattipatthana suttam (the tenth)*, describes four kinds of concentrated meditations as helpful to *Nirvâna*, (1) meditation upon the transitory and impure nature of the body, (2) indifference to pleasure or pain, (3) meditation for getting rid of lust, hate and delusion, and for acquisition of non-attachment, (4) meditation on the different natures of things, such as, upon the nature of the causes of troubles and *âsrava*, upon the nature of the impurity caused by sensual enjoyment, and upon the nature of self absorption. In the last part of this Sutra, the following words show the result of such meditations.

---

* ज्ञान भावनया सिक्ता निभृतेनान्तरात्मनः ।
अप्रमत्तं गुणं प्राप्य, लभन्ते हितमात्मनः ॥ २१८ ॥

* " *Yohi kochi Bhikkhuve ime chattârô sati-patthâ-nê evam bhâveyya sattâham, tassa duvinnam phalânam annataram phalam patikankham: ditthe va dhamme Annâ, sati va upâdhi sese anâgâmitâ...evam ayam bhikkhuve maggo sattânan visuddhiya sakapariddavanam samatikkamaya dukkha-domanassavam atthagamâya nâyassa adhigamâya, nibbanassa sachchhikiriyaya yadidam chattaro satipatthanati, iti yam tam vuttam iyametam patichcha vuttanti idamavocha Bhagawa, attamanâ ti bhikkhu bhagawato bhâsitam abhinandunti.*

" Any monk who thus dwells upon these four meditations even for seven days, will achieve either of the two results: he may realise *Nirvâna* while residing in this body, or if the practice is deffective he will not suffer transmigrations. O monks! This is a way for purification of beings, for removal of sorrow and weeping, for freedom from misery and impure mind, for realization of Truth, for direct per-

---

* योहि कोचि भिक्खवे इमे चत्तारो सतिपट्ठाने एवं भावेय्य सत्ताहं, तस्स द्विन्नं फलानं अण्णतरंफलं पटिकंखं दिट्ठे वा धम्मे अण्णा, सति वा उपाधिसेसे अनागामिता एवं अयं भिक्खवे मग्गो सत्तान विसुद्धिया सोकपरिद्दवानं समतिक्कमाय दुक्ख-दोमनस्सानं अत्थगमाय णयस्स अधगमाय ।निब्बानस्स सच्छि-किरयाय यदिदं चत्तारो सति पट्ठानाति इति यं तं वुत्तं इयमेतं पटिच्छ वतंति। इदमवोच भगवा अत्त मना ते भिक्खू भगवतो भासितं अभिनंदुन्ति ॥

ception of *Nirvâna*—such are these four meditations. They should be believed in as stated. So spoke the Lord. The monks greeted the saying of the Lord with joy."

The above statement clearly shows that *Nirvâna* is not annihilation but is self-realization. It is the direct perception of the self, it is full and complete pure thought activity.

*Majjhima-nikâya, Mula pariyâya sutta, 1st.*

This *sutra* says:—"I am apart from all worldly objects." It removes delusion. The following extract from it will show that *Nirvâna* is something positive, not annihilation.

* *Yopi so bhikkhave bhikkhu araham khînasavo vusitava katakaraniyo ohitabharo anuppatta sadattho*

---

* यो पि सो भिक्खवे भिक्खु अरहं खीणासवो वुसित वा कतकरणीयो ओहितभारो अनुप्पत्त सदत्थो परिक्खीण भव संयोजनो सम्मद अण्णा विमुत्तो सोपि पथविं पथवितो अभि- जानाति......पंथविं मेति न मण्णति......आपं......तेजं......मे न मण्णति...तं किस्स हेतुः...खया मोहस्स वीत मोहिता...... तथागतोऽपि भिक्खवेअरहं सम्मासंबुद्धो पथविं पथवितो अभि- जानाति...पथविं मेतिन मण्णति...तं किस्स हेतुः नंदी दुक्खस्स मूलं ति इति विदित्वा भवाजाति भूतस्स जरामरणंति तस्मादिह भिक्खवे तथागतो सब्बसो तन्हान खया निरागा निरोधा चागा पटिनिस्सग्गा अनुत्तरं सम्मा संबोधिं अभिसंबुद्धोति वदामीति, इदम बोच भगवा...अत्तमनाते भिक्खू भगवतो भासितं अभि- नुंदुंति "॥

*parikkhinabhava sanyojano sammad anna vimutto sopi pathavim pathavito abhijanati......pathavim meti na mannati......apam......tejam......me na mannati ; tam kissa hetu:......khaya mohassa vitamohatta. Tathagatopi bhikkhave araham samma sambuddho pathvim pathavito abhijanati......pathavim me ti na mannati......tam kissa hetu : nandi dukkhassa mulam ti iti viditva bhava jati bhutassa jara-marananti, tasmadih bhikkhave Tathagato sabbaso tanhanam khaya niraga nirodha chaga pati-nissagga anuttaram samma sambodhim abhisambuddhoti vadamiti-idamavocha Bhagawa, attamanate bhikkhu Bhagavato bhasitam abhinundunti.*

" O Monks ! The monk who is worshipful, who has destroyed *âsavas*, is fully chaste, has done what had to be done, has thrown away the burden, has attained truth, has destroyed the bondage of birth, has become rightly learned, is non-attached, knows earth to be earth, and does not maintain that earth to be his own. In the same way, he knows water as water, fire as fire, he does not maintain that water is his and fire is his. Because he has become delusionless, on destruction of delusion. In the same way, Tathagata (Gotam Buddha) is also worshipful, has right knowledge, he also knows earth as earth ; he does not maintain earth to be his own. He knows that Thirst is the root-cause of misery. Becoming is cause of birth. The living being suffers old age and death."

"O monks! This is the reason why Tathagata on destruction of all thirst, being non-attached from it, having prevented it, having removed it, being freed from it, becomes the right knower, having gained the highest right knowledge. Thus I say. The Lord spoke thus. The monks greeted His saying with joy."

The above statement refers to one who has acquired the liberated condition, even when residing in the body. The words *Arahanta, khînâsrava, vîtamôha*, are found in Jain Literature also. The qualities of *arahanta*, have been described by Nemichandra, a great Jain Saint in his work "Dravya Samgraha" as below:—

* *Naṭṭha chadu ghâikammo daṃsaṇa suha ṇâṇa vîriya maîo,*
*Suha dehattho appâ suddho ariho vichintijjo.*

"The soul which has destroyed the four destructive Karmas, Knowledge-obscuring, Conation-obscuring, Deluding and Obstructing Karmas and has attained infinite Conation, infinite Knowledge, infinite Happiness and infinite Power, is residing in a fine body, and is pure; He should be meditated upon as *arahanta*."

The Jain Saint Amritchandra-acharya in his *Tattvartha-sara*, uses an expression similar to *khînâ srava*.

---

* णट्ठ चदु घाइ कम्मो दंसण सुह णाण वीरिय मईओ ।
सुह देहत्थो अप्पा सुद्धो आरिहो विचिंतिज्जो ॥ ५० ॥

* *Jậnataḥ pasyataschordhvam jạgat kâruṇyataḥ punaḥ,*
*Tasya bandhaprasango na sarvâsarva pari kśayât.*

"On the destruction of all the *âsavâs*, one who knows and sees the world does not become liable to bondage."

*Vitamoha*, which means the same thing as kshînamôha, is used by him in *Samayasara* :—

*Jidamôhassa du jaiyâ khínô môhô havijja sâhussa*
*Taiyâ du-khîna môhô bhaṇṇadi so nichchhaya vidûhiṃ.*

"When delusion is destroyed in a saint who has already conquered delusion, then he is called delusionless by the knowers of reality."

*Majjhima-nikâya, Ariya-pariyesana suttam* · *26*. This sutra shows that Goutam Buddha on leaving home had the company of Alara Kalama, Uddaka Ramputta and on reaching *Uruvela* he attained knowledge. The last part refers to *Nirvâna*, which he searched after.

---

* जानतः पश्यतश्चोर्ध्वं जगत् कारुण्यतः पुनः ।
तस्य बंध प्रसंगो न सर्वास्रव परिक्षयात् ॥

† जिदमोहस्स दु जइया खीणो मोहो हविज्ज साहुस्स ।
तइया हु खीणमोहो भण्णंदि सो णिच्छयविदूहिं ॥ ३८ ॥

* "*Nibbânam pariyesâmnam ajâtam anuttaram, yogakkhemam, nibbânam ajjhagamam, ajaram, avyâdhim, amatam, ashokam, asanklittham, adhigatô khô me ayam dhammo gambhîro, duddaso, duranuvodho, santo, panîtô, atakhavacharo, nipuno, pandita vêdanîyô.*"

"That *Nirvâna* which is to be searched after, is uncreated, unrivalled, realizable through concentration, free from oldness, devoid of diseases, deathless, sorrowless, painless. I have really known this nature of it. It is deep, hard to see, peaceful, highest, beyond argument or logic, and realizable only by the highly learned."

In the face of the above statements about *Nirvâna*, how can it be taken to mean extinction. Really speaking *Nirvâna* is the pure essence of the soul which is uncreated, immortal, realizable through concentration, and cognizable by itself.

*Majjhim Nikâya, Mahâmâlumba Suttam 64.*

† "*So yadeva tattha hoti vedanâgatam sannâgatam sankharagatam vinnanagatam te dhamme anichhto*

---

* "निब्बानं परियेसमानं अजातं अनुत्तरं योगक्खेमं निब्बानं अज्झगमं, अजरं, अब्याधिं, अमतं, अशोकं, असंक्लिट्ठं...अधिगतो खो मे अयं धम्मो गंभीरो, दुद्दसो, दुरनुवोधो, संतो, पणीतोः अतक्कावचरो, निपुणो, पंडित वेदनीयो ॥

† "सो यदेव तत्थ होति वेदनागतं संण्णागतं संखारागतं वि–

*dukkho, rogato, gandato, sallato, aghato, abadhato, parato, palokato, sunnato, anattatto, samanupassati so tehi dhammehi chittam pativâpeti, so tehi dhammehim chittam patavapetva amatâya dhatuyya chittam upasanhati : Etam santam etam panitam yaditam savvasankharasamatho, savvupadhipatinissago tanha-khayo virâgo nirodho nibbananti so tattha thito âsavânam khayam pâpunâti.*"

"He sees the nature of feeling, perception, contact and (impure) consciousness as transitory, painful, diseased, wounded, pricking, demeritorious, miserable and foreign, and finds himself free from them. He removes his mind from them. Being thus unattached, he carries his mind to the immortal. That *Nirvâna* is peaceful, highest, where all contacts are dissolved, where all defects are removed, where thirst is destroyed, non-attachment has risen, non-self is prevented—that is *Nirvâna*. He who is absorbed in it destroys *âsavas*."

"The Word of the Buddha" by Nyaya tiloka

---

ण्णानागतं ते धम्मे अनिच्छतो, दु:खो, रोगतो, गंडतो, सल्लतो, अघतो, आबाधतो, परतो. पलोकतो. सुन्नतो, अनत्तत्तो समनु पस्सति । सो तेहि धम्मेहि चित्तं पटिवापेति, सो ते हि धम्मेहिं चित्तं पटिवापेत्वा अमताय धातुय्य चित्तं उपसंहाति एतं संतं एतं पणीतं यदितं सब्बसंखारसमथो सब्बुपाधिपटि-निस्सग्गो, तन्ह-खयो विरागो निरोधो निब्बानंति सो तत्थायि-ता आसवानं खयं पापुणाति ॥"

Mahathera Buddhist monk of Dodundawa (Ceylon) late Professor Tokyo University, Udân 8 varga, describes *Nirvâna* thus :—

"There is an unborn, unoriginated, uncreated, unformed. If there were not this unborn, this unoriginated, this uncreated, this unformed, escape from the world of the born, the originated, the created, the formed, would not be possible. But since there is an unborn, unoriginated, uncreated, unformed, therefore is escape possible from the world of the born, the originated, the created, the formed."

The Pali text is as follows :—

* *Atthi bhikkhave ajâtam abhûtam akatam asankhatam noched bhikkhave abhavissa ajatam abhutam akatam asankhatam na ida jâtassa bhûtassa katassa sankhatassa nissaranam pajnaya, yasma cha kho bhikkhave atthi ajâtam abhûtam akatam asankhatam tasma jâtassa bhûtassa katassa sankhatassa nissaranam pajnâyâti.*

This clearly shows that *Nirvâna* itself is such, or there is some thing in "Nirvâna" condition which is uncreated. And it cannot be anything else than

---

* "अत्थि भिक्खवे अजातं अभूतं अकतं असंखतं नो चेद् भिक्खवे अभविस्सा अजातं अभूतं अकतं असंखतं न इद जातस्स भूतस्स कतस्स संखतस्स निस्सरणं पञ्ञायां यस्मा च खो भिक्खवे अत्थि अजातं अभूतं अकतं असंखतं तस्मा जातस्स भूतस्स कतस्स संखतस्स निस्सरणं पञ्ञायाति ॥"

a pure soul. When all the impure thought activities are removed, all the bodies and formations are rid of, all the varied notions are gone, all the pleasant and painful feelings are vanished, then that pure soul, devoid of all the transitory and foreign elements, remains as ever existing. This is "Nirvâna." And this is the belief of the Jains also.

The learned Buddhist monk Shri Dharmananda, the Principal of the Vidyalankara College, Kelaniya, (Ceylon), on being asked about Nirvâna declared, "It cannot be said to be quite extinction or non-existing. There is bliss." His actual words are:—

"शून्यं वक्तुं न शक्यते, सुखं च अस्ति"

"*Sûnyam vaktum na sakyate, sukham cha asti.*"

The learned Principal consulted a Pali Dictionary and gave me a note about the different synonyms of Nirvâna, as found in the Buddhist Pali Scriptures. They are as follows:—

**मुखो, निरोधो, निब्बाणं, दीपं, तण्हक्खय, तानं, लेनं, अरूपं, सांतं, असंखतं, सिवं, अमुत्तं, सुदुद्दसं, परायनं, सरणं, निपुणं, अनन्तं, अक्खरं, दुःखक्खय, अव्यापज्झ, अनालयं, विवट्ठ, खेम, केवल, अपवग्गो, विरागो, पणीतं, अच्चुतंपदं, योगखेमं, पारं, मुत्ति, विसुद्धि, विमुत्ति, असंखधातु, सुद्धि, निब्बुत्ति ॥"**

*Mukhō*, special, *Nirōdhō*, prevention, *Nibbānam*, the extinguishing of mundane life, *Dîpam*, island. *Tanhe-kkhaya*, destruction of thirst, *Tānam*, safe place, *Lenam*, absorption, *Arûpam*, without form.

*Santam*, peaceful, *Asankhatam*, uncreated, *Sivam*, blissful, *Amuttam*, incorporeal, *Sududdasam*, difficult to realize, *Parâyanam*, highest way, *Saranam*, place of refuge, *Nipunam*, knowledge, *Anantam*, infinite, *Akkharam*, indestructible, *Dukkhakkhaya*, cessation of miseries, *Avyâpajjha*, truth, *Anâlayam*, highest home, *Vivatta*, mundaneless, *Khēma*, safe, *Kēvala*, independent, *Apavaggô*, above worldly engagements, *Viragô*, without attachment, *Panîtam*, best, *Achchutam padam*, unshakeable position, *Yogakhêmam*, realizable by concentration, *Param*, beyond the world, *Mutti*, liberation, *Visuddhi*, purity, *Vimutti*, freedom, *Asankhadhatu*, uncreated substance, *Suddhi*, purity, *Nibbutti*, liberation.

Some extracts are given below from "The Doctrine of the Buddha" by George Grimm, published by Verlag W. Drugulin, Leipzig, Germany

" Page 212. " Unshakeable is my deliverance, *this is the last birth*, there is no more becoming anew " (Majjhima-Nikaya, page 167).

Pages 350—351. " Whoso once has experienced this state within himself, is lost to the turmoil of the world, even if he again awakes to it : " His mind inclines to solitude, bends towards solitude, sinks itself in solitude." For to him, this is highest blessedness (M. I. page 330). Thus Nibbāna shows itself to be *eternal rest*, eternal stillness (M. II. page 110.) The great peace (Angutta N. I. page 132), whose realm the delivered one enters even during his lifetime, and which he completely realizes at death, and in which he has taken possession for ever of everything that is true and real. " Bliss is Nibbâna, bliss is Nibbâna, Sâriputta exclaims (A. V. page 414). Hunger is the worst disease; the activities of senses are the worst suffering. Having recognized this, verily one reaches *Nibbâna—highest bliss* (Dhammapada V. 203).

Page 475. " Liberated from what is called corporeality, Vachha, the Perfected One is indefinable, inscrutable, immeasurable, like the ocean " (M. I. page 487).

Extracts from "Some sayings of the Buddha" (according to the Pâli Canon translated by F. L. Woodward, M.A., Cantab, Ceylon, 1925).

Pages 2, 3, 4. Search after the unsurpassed, perfect security, which is Nibbâna. Goal is incomparable security which is Nibbâna. (M. I. page 170). This reality (Dhamma) that I have reached is profound, hard to see, hard to understand, excellent, pre-eminent, beyond the sphere of thinking, subtle, and to be penetrated by the wise alone. Destruction of craving, Passionlessness, Cessation, which is Nibbâna (D. N. II. page 312.)

Page 118. And *I*, friend, by the destruction of the *âsavas* have entered on and abide in that emancipation of mind, which is free from the *âsavas*, having realized it by mine own super-knowledge even in this present life (Samyutta Nikaya, ii. 220).

Page 188. Impermanent, alas, are all compounded things. Their nature is to rise and fall. When they have risen they cease. The bringing of them to an end is Bliss (D. N. ii, 198).

Page 204. Nibbâna is the resort of release. Plunged in Nibbâna is the holy life lived, with Nibbāna for its goal, and ending in Nibbāna (S. N. v. 217—19).

Page 321. *Foot-note.* Nibbāna is a state beyond mind—consciousness.

Page 326. The delightful stretch of level ground is a name for Nibbāna (S. N. iii, 106).

Page 327, The destruction of craving is Nibbāna (S. N. iii, 188).

Page 328. Release means Nibbāna. Rooted in Nibbāna the holy life is lived.

P. 331. *Possessing naught and cleaving unto naught—*
That is the Isle, th incomparable isle.
That is the ending of decay and death.
Nibbāna do I call it, Kappa, (said
The Exalted One), that is the Isle. (Sn. v. 1093).

Dhammapada (Sacred Books of the East Vol. X translated by Max Muller 1881), page 55.

Chapter 15. " Health is the greatest of gifts, contentedness the best of riches, trust is the best of relationships, *Nirvâna the highest happiness,*"

*Sutta Nipata* translated by G. V. Fausbold 1881).

(1) Vijaya sutta 1, 12/203. Such a Bhikkhu who has turned away from desire and attachment and is possessed of understanding in the world, has (already) gone to the immortal place, the unchangeable state of *Nirvâna.*

(2) Hemak Mânava-pukkhâ 3/1085. In this world (much) has been seen, heard and thought, the destruction of passion and of wish for the dear objects that have been perceived, O Hemanka, is the imperishable state of *Nibbâna.*

(3) Kappa-Manava-pukkha 3/1093. This matchless island, possessing nothing (and) grasping after nothing, I call *Nibbâna*, the destruction of decay and death.

The Pâli terms are :—

**अकिंचनं, अनादानं - एतं दीपं अनापरं, निब्बानं इति नंब्रूमि - जरामिच्चुपरिक्खयं ॥**

***Akinchanam, anâdânam, Etamdipam, anâparam. Nibbânam iti nambrūmi, Jarâmichchu parikkhayam.***

(4) Pinjaya Mânava—pukkhâ 26/1148. To the insuperable, the unchangeable (Nibbâna) whose likeness is no where, I shall certainly go, in this (Nibbana) these will be no doubt (left) for me, to know (me to be) a dispossessed mind.

The Pâli terms are :—

**असंहीरं असंकुत्यं - यास्स नत्ति उपमा कुचि - अद्दा गमिस्सामि न मेत्त कंखा - एव पधारेहि अवितच्चित्तं ॥**

*Asamhîran Asankutyan, yâssa natthi upamā kuchi*

*addhâ gamissâmi na mettha kankhâ, evapadhârêhi avitachittam.*

*Vissuddha Maggha*—Path of purity of Buddha Ghosh, translated by P. Maun Tui, Parts, I and II.

Page 57. Virtue is abstention, Volition, restraint, non-transgression in regard to all things. Such kind of virtue conduces to absence of mental remorse, to gladness, rapture, tranquillity, joy, practice, culture, developement, adornment, requisites of concentration, fulness, fulfilment, certain disgust, dispassion, cessation, quiet, higher knowledge, perfect knowledge, *Nibbâna.*

Page 248. *Nibbâna* with its intrinsic nature of eternity, deathlessness, refuge, shelter and so on is well proclaimed.

Page 338. Nibbâna is ageless (and) permanent.

The life of the Buddha by Edward J., Thomas M.A., D. Litt, (1927).

Page 197. *Nirvâna*—The state to which the monk has now attained is the other shore, the immortal (*i.e.*, permanent) fixed state. The word *Nirvâna* blowing out, extinction, is not peculiarly Buddhistic. For the Buddhist, it is, as is clear, the extinction of craving.

From lust and from desire detached,
The Monk with insight here and now
Has gone to the immortal peace,
The unchangeable Nirvâna state.

It is unnecessary to discuss the view, that Nirvâna means the extinction of the individual, no such view has ever been supported from the texts and there is abundant evidence as to its real meaning, the extintion of craving in this life.

Page 191. *Amalam Padam*—Nirvâna they implied some state inconceivable to thought, inexpressible by language. F. N. (Professor Radhakrishna admits the silence of Buddha and speaks of his "avoidance of all metaphysical themes"; but he holds that "Buddha evidently admitted the positive nature of Nirvana.")

Sacred Books of the East Vol. XLIX by F. Max Muller.

*Buddha Charita* by Asvaghosh.

Book XIV. Page 156. After accomplishing in due order the entire round of the preliminaries of perfect wisdom, I have now attained that highest wisdom, and I am become the all-wise *arhat* and *Jina*. My aspiration is thus fulfilled; this birth of mine has borne itself fruit, the blessed and immortal knowledge which was attained by former Buddhas is now mine. Possessing a soul now of perfect purity, I urge all living beings to seek the abolition of worldly existence through the lamps of the Law.

Page 157. There has arisen the greatest of all beings, the omniscient all-wise *arhat*—a lotus, unsoiled by the dust of passion, sprung up from the lake of knowledge.

Page 178. When these effects of the chain of causation are thus one by one put an end to, he at last, being free from all stain and substratum, will pass into a ***blissful Nirvana.***

Buddhist Mahayan text P. II *Sukhavati Vyuha.*

Page 29. " Hence, O Anand for that reason that Tathagata is called *amitâbha* (possessed of infinite light), and is called *amitprabha* (possesssd of infinite splendour), *amitaprabhâs* (possessed of infinite brilliancy, *asamâptaprabhâ* (whose light is never finished) *asangataprabhâ* (whose light is not conditioned)."

Buddhacharya Hindi by Sadhu Rahula Sankrityayan 1988 S. V.

Page 36. Adittapariyaya sutta (S. N. 43-3-6) Defectless--realisable not by any other help—*nirvana* --seeing it, I became disattached from the seen and the destroyable.

I have given above some extracts about Nirvâna, from the Buddhist works which I could find for study. I shall hereafter show that authoritative Jain books declare *nirvâna* to be a similar condition.

According to the Jains, Nirvâna is a condition of soul, free from all bondage of Karmas, all impure thought activities bringing inflow of Karmas, devoid of all kinds of fine and gross bodies, being cessation of all the worldly miseries, fully blissful, peaceful, enlightened and eternal, without fall.

To show this, I proceed to give some references from authoritative Jain works.

(1) *Samayasâra* by Kunda Kundâchârya.

वंदित्तु सव्वसिद्धे, धुवममलमणोवमं गदिं पत्ते ।
वोच्छामि समयपाहुड मिणमो सुदकेवलीभणिदं ॥ १ ॥

*Vandittu savva siddhe dhuvamamal manovamam gadimpatte,*
*Vochchhâmi samaya-pâhuda minamo sudakevali-bhanidam.*

" I shall describe the Sâmayasâra book as uttered by saints with complete scriptural knowledge, after bowing down to all the liberated ones who have attained to a condition which is eternal, pure and unrivalled."

(2) *Ashta-Pâhuda* by the same author.

दंसण अणंत णाणं मोखो णट्ठट्ठ कम्मबंधेण ।
णिरुवम गुणमारूढो अरहंतो एरिसो होई ॥ २ ॥

*Damsana anantanana mokkho natthattha Kamma-bandhena!*
*Niruvama gunamârûdo, arahanto eriso hoio.*

" The worshipful in Nirvâna is possessed of infinite conation, infinite knowledge, has destroyed the eight kinds of Karmas and is full of unrivalled attributes."

जर वाहि जम्म मरणं चउ गइगमणं च पुण्णपावं च ।
हंतेण दीणकम्मं हइ णाणमयं च अर्हंत ॥ ३ ॥

*Jara-Vâhi Jamma-maranam changai gamanam cha punna pavanchan*

*Hantena dîna kammam hai- namnaayan ha archanta.*

" The worshipful has destroyed old age, disease, birth and death, and wandering in the four conditions of life, as well as merit and demerit, and the Karmas, and is full of enlightenment."

भावेह भाव सुद्धं, अप्पा सुविसुद्ध णिम्मलंचैव ।
लहु चङ्गइ चइऊणं - जइ इच्छय सासयं सुखं ॥ ६ ॥

*Bhâveh bhâva suddham, appâ suvisuddha nimmalam chaiva*

*Lahu changai chaûnam Jai ichchhaya sâsayam sukkham.*

" If you desire immediate eternal bliss, and freedom from the four worldly conditions, then meditate upon the utmost pure and defectless soul with pure thought activities."

जेसिं जीव सहावो - णत्थि अभावो य सब्बहातस्स ।
ते होंति भिण्णदेहा - सिद्धावच गोयर मदीदा ॥ ६३ ॥

*Jesim Jiva sahâvo, natthi abhavo ya sabbahâ tassa,*
*Te houti Bhinnadeha, siddhâ Vachagoyar madidâ.*

" They are the perfect liberated ones who are full of their own nature, never become devoid of that, quite free from bodies and are indescribable."

जं जानिऊण जोई - जोअत्तो जोइ ऊण अणवरयं ।
अब्बाबाह मणंतं - अणोवमं हवइ णिब्बाणं ॥ ३ ॥ मो.

*Jam Jâniûna Joî-Joattho Joiûna anavarayam,*
*Abbâbâha manantam, anovamam havai nibbânam*

"The saint, who having known Him—(the pure soul) continually realizes Him, deeply absorbed in concentration, attains *Nirvâna* which is painless, eternal and unrivalled."

मलरहि ओ कल चत्तो - अणादि ओ केवलो विसुद्धप्पा ।
परमपदो परमजिणो, सिवं करो सास ओ सिद्धो ॥ ६ ॥
*Malarahio Kalachatto, anadio kevalo visuddhappa,*
*Paramapado paramajino sivamkaro sâsao siddho.*

"The perfect liberated one is pure, bodiless, without beginning, independent, sacred, the highest situated, the highest conqueror, blissfull, and eternal."

*Panchâstikâya* by the same author.

उवसंत खीणमोहो मग्गं जिणभासिदेण समुवगदो ।
णाणाणुमग्गचारी णिब्बाणपुरं वजदि धीरो ॥ ७६ ॥
*Uvasanta khîna mohô maggam Jinabhasidena samuvagado,*
*Nânânumaggachârî nibbânapuram vajadi dhîrô.*

"A fearless one, who having followed the path, declared by the Conqueror, has subsided (and then) destroyed delusion, walking on the way of Light, goes to the city of *Nirvâna*."

*Niyamasâra* by the same author.

अब्बाबाह मणिंदिय मणोवयं पुण्णपाव णिम्मुक्कं ।
पुणरागमण विरहियं णिच्चं अचलं अणालम्बं ॥ १७७ ॥
णविदुक्खं णविसुखं णविपीडा णव विज्जदे बाहा ।

णवि मरणं णवि जणणं तत्तेवइ होइ णिब्बाणं ॥ १७८ ॥
णवि इंदिय उवसग्गा णवि मोहा विंहियो ण णिद्दाय ।
णवि तण्हा णेव छुहा तत्तेवइ हवदि णिब्बाणं ॥ १७९ ॥
णवि कम्मं णोकम्मं णविचिंता णेवअत्त रुद्दाणि ।
णवि धम्म सुक्कझाणे तत्तेवइ हवदि णिब्बाणं ॥ १८० ॥

*Abbābāhahamaṇindiya*
*maṇovamam puṇṇa pāva ṇimmukkam*
*Puṇarâgamaṇa Virahiyam ṇichcham*
*achalam aṇâlamham* (177)
*Navidukkham Navi sukkham*
*ṇavi piḍa ṇeva Vijjade Bâhá,*
*Navi marṇam ṇavi jaṇaṇam*
*tatthevaya hoi ṇibbâṇam* (178)
*Navi indiya uvasaggâ ṇavi mohâ*
*Vimhiyo ṇa ṇiddâya.*
*Navi tanhâ ṇeva chhuhâ tatthevai*
*havadi ṇibbâṇam* (179)
*Navi Kammam ṇokammam ṇavi*
*chintâ ṇeva attaruddâṇi*
*Navi dhamma sukkajhṅe ttatthevai*
*havadi ṇibbaṇam* (180)

"Nibbâna is without obstruction, not cognisable by the senses, unrivalled, devoid of merit and demerit, not liable to rebirth, eternal, steady, independent," (177.)

"Where there is neither pain, nor pleasure, nor misery, nor obstruction, neither death, nor birth, there only is Nirvâna." (178).

" Where there are not sense organs, nor any afflictions, neither there is delusion, nor wonder, nor sleep, neither thirst, nor hunger, there only is Nirvâna." (179).

" Where there are neither material Karmas, nor any bodies, neither anxiety, nor painful nor wicked concentration, neither even good nor pure concentration, there only is Nirvâna." (180)

*Tattvârthasūtra* by Umaswami.

**बन्धहेत्वभावनिर्जराभ्यां कृत्सनकर्मविप्रमोक्षो मोक्षः ॥**

*Bandahêtvâbhâva nirjarâbhyâm Kritsna Karma Vipramôkṣô môkṣah.*

" Liberation is freedom from all the Karmas on account of cessation of causes of bondage and shedding off of all the Karmic matter."

*Ratnakaranda Sravakâchâra* by Smantabhadra Acharya.

**शिवमजरमरुजमक्षयमव्याबाधं विशोकभयशङ्कम् ।**
**काष्ठागतसुखविद्याविभवं विमलं भजन्ति दर्शनशरणाः ॥४०॥**

*Sivamajara maruja makṣaya mavyâbâdham*
*vîṣoka bhayaṣankam*
*Kâṣṭhagata sukha vidyâ vibhavam vimalam*
*bhajanti darṣana saraṇah.* (40).

" Those who are purified in right belief enjoy Nirvâna which is blissful, devoid of old age, disease, destruction, obstruction, sorrow, fear and doubt, and is pure and full of the glory of highest happiness and enlightenment."

The introduction to *Sarvârtha Siddhi* by Pûjyapâda.

**निरवशेष निराकृत कर्ममल कलंकस्य अशरीरस्य आत्मनः अचिन्त्य स्वाभाविक ज्ञानादि गुणं अव्याबाध सुखं अत्यन्तिकं अवस्थांतरं मोक्षः ॥**

*Niravaṣësa nirâkrita Karmamala Kalankasya aśarirasya âtmanah achintya svâbhâvika jṇanâdi gunam avyâbâdha sukham atyantikam avasthântaram mokṣah.*

" Liberation is the extremely highest condition, full of unthinkable inherent attribute of knowledge and unobstructed bliss, of a soul which becomes, totally free from the defect of Karmic dirt and is liberated from body."

*Samâdhi Sataka* by the same author.

**निर्मलः केवलः सिद्धो विविक्तः प्रभुरक्षयः ।**
**परमेष्ठि परात्मेति परमात्मेश्वरो जिनः ॥ ६ ॥**

*Nirmalah Kevala siddho viviktâh prabhurakṣayah*
*Parmeṣthi parâtmeti paramâtme śvaro Jinah.*

" The liberated One is pure, independent, perfect, free, lord, indestructible, in the highest position, the greatest soul, the highest soul, glorified and Conqueror."

**मुक्तिरेकान्तिकी तस्य चित्त यस्याचलाधृतिः ।**
**तस्य नैकान्तिकी मुक्तिर्यस्यनास्त्यचला धृतिः ॥**

*Muktirekântikî tasya chitta yasyâchalâ dhritih*
*Tasya naîkântikî muktiryasya nâstyachalâ dhritih*

" The highest Nirvâna is His who has unshakeable steadiness of mind, and Nirvâna is not his, who has not unshakeable steadiness of mind."

*Purushârtha siddhiupâya* by Amritchandra Acharya.

नित्यमपि निरूपलेपः स्वरूप समवस्थितो निरूपघातः ।
गगनमिव परमपुरुषः परमपदे स्फुरति विशदतमः ॥२२३॥

कृतकृत्यः परमपदे परमात्मासकलविषय विषयात्मा ।
परमानन्द निमग्नो ज्ञानमयो नन्दति सदैव ॥ २२४ ॥

*Nittyamapi nirupalepah svarupa samavasthito nirupaghâtah,*

*Gaganamiva parama puruṣah paramapade sphurati Viśadatamah* (223).

*Kritakrityah paramapadê paramâtmâ sakalaviṣaya Viṣayatmâ*

*Paramânanda nimagnô jnanamayô nandati sadaiva.* (224)

" (The liberated one in Nirvâna), is always dirtless, rightly fixed in one's own nature, without obstruction, quite pure like the sky, the greatest soul, enlightening itself in that highest position." (223).

" He has done what was to be done ; He always glorifies himself in that highest position, being the greatest soul, penetrating to all the knowable objects, full of knowledge and absorbed in highest bliss."

(10) *Tattvârthasâra* by the same author.

**पुण्यकर्मविपाकाच्च सुखमिष्टेन्द्रियार्थजम् ।**
**कर्मक्लेशविमोक्षाच्च मोक्षे सुखमनुत्तमम् ॥ ४९ ॥**
**लोकेतत्सदृशोह्यार्थ कृत्स्नेप्यन्यो न विध्यते ।**
**उपमीयेत तद्येन तस्मान्निरुपमं स्मृतम् ॥ ५० ॥**

*Punyakarmavipâkâchha sukhamiṣṭendriyârthajam,*
*Karmaklesh Vimokshâchcha Mokse sukha manuttamam.* (49)
*Loke tatsadraśô hyarthah Kritsnê pyanyo na vidyaté,*
*Upami:yeta tadyêna tasmânnirupamamsmritam.*

" Pleasure due to agreeable sense object is enjoyed on account of the ripening of meritorious Karmas, while the Highest Bliss in Nirvana is due to freedom from the miseries of karmas. There is no such object in the whole universe which can be compared with Nirvâna; therefore it has been said to be unrivalled."

*Samayasâra Kalasa* by the same author.

**बन्धच्छेदात्कलयदतुलं मोक्षमक्षय्यमेतन् ।**
**नित्योद्योत स्फुटित सहजावस्थ मेकांत शुद्धं ॥**
**एकाकार स्वरस भरतोऽत्यन्तगंभीर धीरं ।**
**पूर्णंज्ञानं ज्वलितमचले स्वस्यलीनं महिम्नि ॥**

*Bandhachchhedâtkalaya datulam môksa maksayya mĕtana,*
*Nittyôdyôta sphutita sahajâvastha mêkânta śuddham,*

*Ekâkâra svarasa bharatô atyanta gambhîra dhîram,*

*Pûrṇam jṇânam jvalita machalê svasya lînam mahimni.*

"On destruction of bondage, shines forth, Nirvâna which is incomparable and indestructible. It exposes itself eternally enlightened in its own nature. It is purest, full of unique self produced nectar, very deep, contented, full of knowledge; unshakeable and absorbed in its own glory."

*Srâvakâchâra* by Sri Amitagati Acharya.

नाकिनि कायस्तुत पद्कमलो
दीर्णदुरुत्तर भवभयदुःखम् ।
याति स भव्योऽमितगाति रनघां
मुक्ति मनश्वर निरुपम सौख्याम् ॥

*Nâkinikâyastuta pada kamalô dîrṇa duruttara bhava bhayadukkham,*

*Yâtî sa bhavyômitagati ranaghâm mukti manas-vara nirupama saukhyam.*

"The deserved enlightened one at whose lotus feet bow the assembly of celestials, attains *Nirvâna* which is beyond the unbearable and deep mundane fears and miseries, is sinless, and full of eternal and unrivalled bliss."

*Ekatva Bhâvana* by Padmanandi.

**मोक्ष एव सुखं साक्षात्तच्च साध्यम् मुमुक्षुभिः ।**
**संसारेऽत्र तु तन्नास्ति यदास्तिखलुतन्नतम् ॥ ६ ॥**

*Moksa êva sukham sâksâttachcha sâdhyam mumuksubhih,*
*Samsârêtratu tannâsti yadasti khalu tannatam.*

"Nirvâna itself is Bliss, which should be procured by those desirous of liberation. That is not found in this world; what is here verily is not that."

*Siddhastuti* by the same author.

**ते सिद्धाः परमेष्ठिनो न विषयावाचामतस्तान्प्रति ।**
**प्रायोवच्मि यदेवतत्खलुनभस्यालेख्यमालिख्यते ॥**
**तन्नामापि मुदे स्मृतं तत इतो भक्त्याथ वाचालित ।**
**स्तेषां स्तोत्रमिदं तथापि कृतवानम्भोजनंदी मुनिः ॥**

*Tê Siddhâh paramêsthinó Visayâ Vâchâmatastân prati:*
*Prâyô vachmi yadêva tatkhalu nabhasyâ lêkhya mâlikhyatê,*
*Tannâmapi mudê smritam tata itô bhaktyâtha vâchâlitâ*
*Stesâm stôtra midam tathâpi Kritawânambhôja nandî munih.* (29)

"Those perfect liberated ones are not objects of speech; whatever description is given about them is like drawing a picture in the sky; but as their name ever procures happiness, therefore Padmanandimuni has has praised them on account of devotion."

"*Ekatva saptati*" by the same author.

यदव्यक्तमबोधानां व्यक्तं सद्बोध चक्षुषाम् ।
सारं यत्सर्ववस्तूनां नमस्तस्मै चिदात्मने ॥ ३ ॥

*Yadavyaktamabôdhânâṃ Vyaktam sadbodha chakṣuṣâm,*
*Sâram yat sarva bastūnâm namastasmai chidâtmane.* 3.

"I bow to that pure soul which is the best of all the substances and can be realised by the wise but can not be realised by the unwise."

विकल्पोर्मिभरत्यक्तः शान्तः कैवल्यमाश्रितः ।
कर्माभावे भवेदात्मा वाताभावे समुद्रवत् ॥ २६ ॥

*Vikalpormi bharatyâktah śântah kaivalyaniaśritah,*
*Karmâbhâve bhavedâtma vâtâbhâve samudravat.* 26.

"The soul, on the destruction of the Karmas becomes peaceful and independent, being freed from the variety of thoughts, like a sea free from winds."

संसारघोरधर्मेण सदा तप्तस्य देहिनः ।
यंत्र धारागृहं शांतं तदेव हिमशीतलं ॥ ४७ ॥

*Samsâra ghora gharmeṇasadâ taptasya dehinah,*
*Yantra dharâgraham śântam tadeva himaśîtalam.* 47.

"To those who are ever scorched by the intense heat of the world, *nirvâna* is a peaceful place cool like the snow."

निश्शरीरं निरालम्बं निश्शब्दं निरुपाधियत् ।
चिदात्मकं परंजोतिरवाङ्मानसगोचरम् ॥ ६० ॥

*Nissarîram nirâlambam nissabdam nirupâdhi yat,*
*Chidâtmakam param jyotir avângmânasa gocharam* 60.

" (The liberated one), is bodiless, independent, soundless, defectless, full of Knowledge, the greatest light, not realisable by mind, and indescribable."

" *Āpta svarupa.*"

**शिवं परमकल्याणं निर्वाणं शांतं मक्षयं ।**
**प्राप्तं मुक्तिपदं येन स शिवः परिकीर्तितः ॥ २४ ॥**
**सर्वद्वन्द्वविनिर्मुक्तं स्थानमात्मस्वभावजं ।**
**प्राप्तं परमानिर्वाणं येनासौ सुगतः स्मृतः ॥ ४१ ॥**

*Śivam parama Kalyânam nirvâṇam śânta maksayam,*
*Prâptam muktipadam yêna sa sivah parikîrtitah*
*Sarvadvanda vinirmuktam sthâna mâtma svabhâvajam*
*Prâptam parama nirvânam yenâsau sugatah smritah.*

" He is praised as Siva, when he has acquired the state of liberation, which is peaceful, blissful, and indestructible. He is remembered as Sugata, when he has attained the highest nirvâna, which is devoid of all misfortunes and is a natural condition of the soul."

" *Sâra samuchchaya* " by Sri Kulabhadra Acharya.

**इन्द्रियप्रसरं रुदुध्वा स्वात्मानं वशमानयेत् ।**
**येन निर्वाणसौख्यस्य भाजनं त्वं प्रपत्स्यसे ॥ १३४ ॥**

*Indriya prasaram rududhva svâtmânam vasamânayet*

*Yena nirvâna saukhyasya bhâjanam tvam*
*prapatsyase.*

"After having checked the spreading of sense desires, have control over thyself, then thou shalt enjoy the happiness of *nirvâna.*"

(18) *Tattvânuśâsana* by Acharya Nâgasena.

आत्यंतिकः स्वहेतोर्यो विश्लेषा जीवकर्मणोः ।
स मोक्षः फलमेतस्य ज्ञानाद्याःक्षायिका गुणाः ॥ २३० ॥
स्वरूपावस्थितिः पुंसस्तदा प्रक्षीणकर्मणः ।
नाभावो नाप्यचैतन्यं न चैतन्यमनर्थकम् ॥ २३४ ॥
त्रिकालविषयं ज्ञेयमात्मानं च यथास्थितम् ।
जानन् पश्यंश्च निःशेषमुदास्ते स तदा प्रभुः ॥ २३८ ॥
अनंतज्ञानदृग्वीर्यवैतृष्ण्यमयमव्ययं ।
सुखं चानुभवत्येष तत्रातींद्रियमच्युतः ॥ २३९ ॥
आत्मायत्तं निराबाधमतींद्रियमनश्वरं ।
घातिकर्मक्षयोद्भूतं यत्तन्मोक्षसुखं विदुः ॥ २४२ ॥

*Âtyantika svahêtôryô viślêshô jîva karmanôh*
*Sa moksahphalamêtasya jnanâddhyâ kshayikâ gunâh 230.*

*Svarûpâvasthiti pumsastadâ prakhṣiṇa karmaṇah*

*Na bhâvô napyachâitanyam na chaitânya manarthakam 234.*

*Trikâla viṣayam jneyamâtmânam cha yathâ sthitam,*

*Jnanan pasyancha nissêshamudastê sa tada prabhu 238.*

*Ananta jnana drig vîrya vai trisnya maya mavyayam*

*Sukham chânubhavatyesha tatrâtîndriya machchutam 239.*

*Atmâyattam nirâbâdhamatîndriya manasvaram*

*Ghati karmaksayôd bhutam yattan môksa sukham viduh : 242.*

"Complete separation of the soul from Karmas and their causes is Liberation ; it results in the attainment of pure attributes (such as) knowledge etc." 230

"When Karmas are destroyed, the Self becomes steady in its own nature ; there is neither annihilation, unconsciousness, nor useless consciousness." 234.

"The Lord in that condition perceives and knows Himself and the other knowables, as they are, with reference to their past, present and future conditions but remains unattached." 238.

"There that Self realizes the eternal bliss which is full of infinite knowledge, perception and power, is independent of sense enjoyment, free from craving, and is never destroyed." 239.

"The bliss in *nirvâna* is independent, unobstructed, above sense gratification, eternal, sprung up on the destruction of the destructive Karmas." 242.

The above quotations with reference to nirvâna from the Jain scriptures, will clearly show, that the description of nirvâna is similar in the Jain and Buddhist scriptures.

The Buddhistic literature describes nirvâna as enlightenment, eternal, immortal, peaceful, blissful, unshakeable, devoid of birth and death, out of mind and speech, free from âsavâs, free from craving unattached, defectless, painless, pure, independent, non-material, birthless, the highest condition, island, best, deep, realizable by the wise etc. The same attributes are applied to nirvâna in the Jain literature also.

All defects, delusion and ignorance found in mundane life are completely destroyed. Only the indestructible nature shines out. From the philosophical point of view the nirvâna of both the systems is the same. In the Jain scriptures it is further said that the liberated and perfect souls go upward and stay on the top of the universe eternally and their extent is a little less than that of the last body in the meditative posture. This statement has not been found by me in the Buddhistic literature. But the real inherent nature of nirvâna in both the systems appears to be the same without any difference whatsoever.

# CHAPTER II

## EXISTENCE OF THE SOUL

Although the Buddhistic literature does not contain an explicit description of the soul, still, if it is minutely searched, it will be found to contain enough to show that the Buddhistic conception of the nature of the soul is the same as is described in the Jain literature.

We have shown in the preceeding Chapter that the *nirvâna* of the Buddhists is not annihilation, not total non-existing, but it is something positive. When it is something, the next point to decide is whether it is matter without consciousness or something possessed of inherent consciousness. It cannot be matter; it is not a material substance devoid of consciousness because nirvâna is attainable only by one who has right enlightenment, through *Prajna*, self analysis, or self discernment. It must therefore be a conscious substance. *Rupa* (form), *sanjna* (sensation), *vedana* (feeling), *samskâra* (contact) and *vijnâna* (impure consciousness) are the causes of mundane wanderings. When these causes are all destroyed, what remains is nothing else than the pure Self or the Soul. Whatever qualifications of the pure soul are mentioned in the Jain Scriptures, are the same as are in the Buddhist scriptures attributed to the state of nirvana. Nirvâna is synonymous, identical with the pure soul. As in the Buddhist literature so in the Jain scriptures also, it is said that in respect of the attainment of nirvâna, or the ultımate purity of the soul argument cannot find it, mind cannot reach it, speech cannot describe it. The pure soul is only realizable by the Self.

In "*Samâdhi Sataka*" the Jain author Pujya pada Swami says:—

**यत्परैः प्रतिपाद्योहं यत्परान् प्रतिपादये ।**
**उन्मत्तचेष्टितं तन्मे यदहं निर्विकल्पकः ॥ १९ ॥**

*Yatparaih pratipâdyôham yat parân pratipâdaye,*
*Unmatta chêṣṭitam tanmê yadaham nirvikalpakah.*

"The notion that, "I can be known by the others" or that "I shall make it known to others" is the uttering of a mad man like me, because 'I' am beyond thinking. (I am only realizable by myself.)"

In the Jain literature, the description of the soul is given in a direct manner. In the Buddhist literature though no direct mention of the soul is found, it is described in an indirect way, in the enunciation of Nirvâna. In the Jain Literature also indirect mention of the soul has been made in many places. The same author Pujyapada Swami says elsewhere in "*Samâdhi Śataka*" thus.

**सर्वेन्द्रियाणि संयम्यास्तिमितेनान्तरात्मना ।**
**यत्क्षणं पश्यतो भाति तत्तत्वं परमात्मनः ॥ ३० ॥**

*Sarvêndriyâṅi sayyamyastimitênântarâtmanâ,*
*Yatksaṇampaśyatôbhâti tattattvam paramâtmanah.*

" After having brought under control all the senses, and after a steady internal insight, whatever is then realized is the true nature of the pure soul."

This worldly being grasps different objects through the five senses and the mind, and is plunged in delusion, lust and hate and is therefore always away from its own Self. If he restrains himself from attending to these six organs, then what is realizable within, is nothing but the pure soul or the *nirvâna*. Take the case of a man living in a house with six windows. He always looks outside through one or more of those windows, but never looks within. If he would divert his attention away from the windows, and look inside he would see all that is within. In the same way when one becomes non-attached to the six organs and attends within, he finds his own Nirvâna or the pure soul within himself. In the Buddhistic Literature, such indirect description is made with the purpose of diverting attention from the Non-self to the Self. There, one is asked to relinquish all the causes of *âsavâs*, i.e. impure thought activities, to get rid of delusion, lust and hate, to follow full chastity, to practise perfect concentration, to have perfect equanimity, to be totally non-attached, and to have perfect meditation. He is asked to have no attachment to transitory conditions which rise and fall. To be non-attached to all the flittering objects, is to be absorbed in one's own Self.

I shall show by quotations from Buddhist Literature,

how one has been advised to be non-attached to the other, the non-self, and to be bent on reaching the goal of Nirvâna.

Another fact which appears in the Buddhist Literature is that it has not taken up the subtle questions of metaphysics, which stand on the basis of intellect or argument, and has avoided all controversial points. It has mostly dealt with matters, that may be easily understood by the ordinary public, so that they may easily understand, and try to walk on the Path. It has mostly described four things; (1) What is pain? (2) What is the cause of pain? (3) What is cessation of pain? (4) What is the means of cessation of pain? The utility of such description is this that the student is saved the difficulty of discussing different views of different systems of philosophy, and easily engage himself in following the path, with the result that he reaches the same goal, which would have been reached also through subtle metaphysics. On giving deep thought, he gradually understands the subtle philosophy also. We shall take some examples from Buddhist Literature.

*Patthapâda Sutta of Digha Nikâya. 1 : 9.*

The translation and purport of which has been given in the Hindi book "Buddhacharya" see pages 189 to 199.

"Patthapadâ asked the following questions of Gautam Buddha (1) Is the universe indestructible?

(2) Is the universe destructible? (3) Is the universe finite? (4) Is the universe infinite? (5) Is the soul same as the body? (6) Is the soul another, and the body another? (7) Is Tathagata born again after death? (8) Is Tathagata not born after death? Buddha replied that these questions were not to be discussed. Gautama says in these words, "Paṭṭhapâda, they are not useful; they do not lead to virtue; they are not causes of chastity, or self-absorption, nor do they bring non-attachment, nor cessation of miseries, nor they lead to Nirvâna; and therefore I do not describe them." Again Paṭṭhapâda asks: "What has the Lord Buddha described:" Then Buddha says, "Paṭṭhapâda: It is misery which I have described; the cause of misery, the cessation of misery, the means of the cessation of misery; this I have described. Paṭṭhapâda, this is useful, leading to Virtue, procuring chastity or self-absorption, bringing non-attachment, causing cessation of pain, leading to passionlessness, providing knowledge, making intellectual, and leading to nirvâna; therefore I have described."

Although, Jain Literature has given a very fine description of the substances, still it is said that the description is of three kinds *Heya*, avoidable, *Upadeya*, adoptable, *Jneya*, knowable. Out of these three, he who is desirous of liberation, should pay his deep attention first to the former two. He should know what are the causes of misery, and what lengthens worldly wanderings, and then after having understood them properly and without vacillation try to avoid those causes ; and he should also know the means which bring destruction of mundane conditions and lead to ***nirvâna*** and after having understood them properly and assuredly try to adopt those rules.

The knowables, he may try to know according to his common sense and intellect. If any subtle matters are not capable of being grasped by his understanding, he should not be sorry or uneasy on that account. Necessary it is to know the avoidable and the adoptable as Saint Nâgasena says in his " *Tattvânusâsana.*"

तापत्रयोपतप्तेभ्यो भव्येभ्यः शिवशर्मणे ।
तत्त्वं हेयमुपादेयमिति द्वेधाभ्यधादसौ ॥ ३ ॥
बंधो निबंधनं चास्य हेयमित्युपदर्शितं ।
हेयं स्याद्दुःखसुखयोर्यस्माद्बीजमिदं द्वयं ॥ ४ ॥
मोक्षस्तत्कारणं चैतदुपादेयमुदाहृतं ।
उपादेयं सुखं यस्मादस्मादाविर्भविष्यति ॥ ५ ॥

*Tapatrayôpa taptebhyô Bhavyêbyah siva sarmanê*
*Tattvam hêyamūpâdeyamiti dvedhabhyadhadasau 3*
*Bandho nibandhanam châsya heyamitvūpa darśitam,*
*Heyamsyadduhka sukhayor yasmadbîjamidam dvayam 4.*
*Moksastatkâranam chaita dupadēya mudâhritam,*
*Upadêyam sukham yasmâdasmâdâvirbhavisyati 5.*

" In order that the deserved ones who are afflicted

with the three afflictions of birth, decay and death, may attain the bliss of *Nirvâna* the principles to be observed are said to be of two kinds, avoidable and adoptable." 3.

" Bondage and its cause, are said to be avoidable, because these two are the seeds of the avoidable. pain and pleasure." 4.

" Liberation and its cause are said to be adoptable, because from them will arise the adoptable bliss." 5.

To show what Buddhist Literature has directly or indirectly said about the soul, let us take a few examples.

(1) Sanyukta nikâya No. 4, page 400.

*Avâkata sanyuktam No. 10.*

**अथ खो बच्छगोत्तोपरिब्बाजको येन भगवा तेनुपसंकामि, उपसंमित्वा भगवता सद्दिं सम्मोदि । सम्मोदनीयं कथं सारनीयं बीतिसारेत्वा एकं अन्तं निसीदि । एकं अन्तं निसिन्नो खो बच्छ-गोत्तो परिब्बाजको भगवन्तं एद्वोच-किं नु खो भोगोतं अत्थ-त्ताति-एवं उत्ते भगवातुण्ही अहोसि. किं पनभोगोतम नत्थ-त्ताति – दुतियंपि भगवा तुण्ही अहोसि । अथ खो पच्छगोत्तो परिब्बाजको उत्थयासना पक्कामि. अथ खो आयस्मा आनंदो अचिरपक्कंतोबच्छगोते परिब्बाजके भगवन्तं एतद्वोच कीं नु खो भंते भगवा बच्छगोतस्स परिब्बाजकस्स पण्हं पुट्ठं न व्याकसीति. अहं आनंद बच्छगोत्तस्स परिब्बाजकस्स अत्थ-त्ताति पुट्ठो समानो अत्थत्ताति. व्याकरेय्यं-येते आनंद समणा ब्राह्मणासस्सुबादा तेसं एतं सद्धि अभविस्स. अहंचानंद बच्छ-गात्तस्से परिब्बाजकस्से नत्थत्ताति पुट्ठा समानो नत्थत्ताति व्याकरेय्यं येते आनंद समणा ब्राह्मणा उच्छेदवादा तेसं एतं सद्धि अभविस्स.**

**अहंचानंद बच्छगोत्तस्स परिब्बाजकस्स अत्थत्ताति पुट्ठो समानो अत्थत्ताति व्याकरेय्यं अपि तुमे तं अनुलोमं अभविस्स णाणस्स उपादाय सब्बेधम्मा अनत्ताति. नोहेतं भंते अहं चानंद बच्छगोत्तस्स परिब्बाजकस्स नत्थत्ताति पुट्ठो समानो नत्थत्ताति व्याकरेय्यं – सम्मुदस्स आनंद बच्छगोत्तस्सभीय्यो सम्मोहाय अभावस्स अहमेनून पुब्बो अत्ता सो एतर्हि नत्थीति.**

*Atha Kho Bachchagotto paribhâjako yena bhagawâ tenupasankami, Upa sanka mitvâ bhagavâ saddhim sammodi, sammodanîyam Kaṭham sâra nîyam Bitisâratvaekam antam nisidi, ekam antam nisinno kho Bachchhagotto paribhâjoko Bhagavantam etadavocha—Kim nu Kho bho Gotam, Atthattâti. Evamutte Bhagavâ tuṇhi ahosi. Kim pana bho Gotama nattahattâti dutiyampi Bhagavâ tuṇhi ahosi. Atha kho Bachchha gotto pâribhâjako uṭṭhayâsanâpakkâmi. Atha Kho âyasma Ānando achirapakkanto Bachchhagotte paribhâjake Bhagavantam etadavocha Kim nu Kho Bhante Bhagava Bachchhagottassa Paribhâjakassa paṇhan puṭṭham na Vyakasiti aham ananda Bachchhagottassa paribhâjakassa atthattati puṭṭho samano atthattati Vyâkareyyam ye te Ananda Samaṇâ Brahmaṇâ sassada vâdâ tesam etam saddhim abhavissa. Aham Bachchhagottassa paribhajakassa natthattati puṭṭho samano natthattati Vyakareyyam ye te Ānanda samaṇâ Brahmaṇâ Uchchheda vâdâ tesâm etam saddhim abhavissa,*

*Ahamchananda Bachchha gottassa Paribhajakassa atthattati puṭṭho samanô atthattati vyakareyyam api tu me tam anulomam abhavissa ṇaṇassa upâdâyạ savve dhamma anattâti nohe tambhante Ahamchânanda Bachchhagottassa Paribhajakassa Natthattati puṭṭho samano natthattati Vyakareyyam. Sammudhassa Ananda Bachchhagottassa bhiyyo sammohâya abhavissa ahame nûna pubbe attâ so etarhi natthiti.*"

" Once a Bachchagotta Paribrajaka went to Buddha, met Him and after talking pleasantly, sat aside and asked the question, " Gotam, Is there a soul ?" On this Gotam did not reply, but remained silent. Again he asked, " Gotam ! Is there no soul." Then even he remained silent. Then, Bachchhagotta got up and went away. Just after his departure the Bhikṣu Ananda asked the Lord, " Why did you not reply to the questions of Bachchhagotta." Then Lord Gotama said " Ananda, if in reply to the question of Bachchhagotta 'Is there a soul,' I told him, 'there is soul,' then O Ananda I would have sided with those saints and Brahmans who maintain things (totally) indestructible : and Ananda ! if I had replied to the question of Bachchhagotta 'Is there no soul' that 'there is no soul,' then I would have sided with those Saints and Brahmans who maintain that every thing is transitory and destructible. Ananda ! if I would have replied to the question of Bachchhagotta that there is soul, then would that saying of mine be correct when I had said that for acquisition of Truth all things are not the soul. Ananda said it would have gone contrary to that.

And Ananda! if I would have replied to the question of Bachchhagotta that there is no soul then he would have been perplexed thinking that he maintained the soul which is denied now."

The above conversation requires a careful and deep thinking. The reason why Gotam Buddha did not reply to the questions of Bachchhagotta, and remained silent, appears to be, that he avoided a discussion on these points, and further his mode of silence showed to Bachchagotta that the soul cannot be known by talking, but has to be realized.

His first reply to his near disciple Ananda shows that Gotam did not take a one-sided view, did not maintain that the soul was absolutely indestructible or destructible. As stated in Jain Philosophy, the soul according to him had both the attributes of permanent existence, and changeability. From the point of view of its nature, the soul is indestructible, while at the same time from its liability to change it is destructible. This is true of every existing substance in the universe. If it be totally indestructible, no change is possible, if it is totally destructible, it cannot exist. We see that substances are ever existing and still changing. To maintain both the predicates is the real Truth. The Jain Saint Samantabhadra, in his book "Aptamîmâmsa" says on this point as below:—

नित्यत्वैकान्तपक्षेऽपि बिक्रिया नोपपद्यते ।
प्रागेव कारकाभावः क्व प्रमाणं क्व तत्फलम् ॥ ३७ ॥
क्षणिकैकान्त पक्षेऽपि प्रेत्यभावाद्यसंभवः ।
प्रत्यभिज्ञाद्यभावान्न कार्यारम्भः कृतः फलम् ॥ ४१ ॥

*Nittyatve Kântâpaksepi Vikriyâ nopapadyate, Prâgeva Kârakâbhâvah Kva pramâṇam Kva tatphalam (37)*
*Ksanikaikantapaksepi pretyabhavadyasambhavah, Pratyabhijṇâdyabhâvanna Kâryârambhah Krutahphalam (41)*

"If a substance be said to be totally indestructible, than no condition or change is possible. There cannot be any action, as there cannot be then the doer or object of any action. Neither can it be proved nor can it be believed in because there will be no modification even in knowledge. And if a substance is maintained to be totally destructible, then there can't be rebirth, and no recognition: neither can any action be commenced, nor can any result be achieved."

A substance is to be understood by the many-sided view of *Syadvâda* Logic (syad—from some point of view Vâda-speaking). Soul is indestructible as well as destructible, is the view to be inferred from Buddha's first reply to Ananda. His reply to Ananda further shows that all the worldly conditions of the soul are transitory. If Bachhagotta had been told in reply that 'there was soul,' he might have taken the fleeting conditions to be the soul and may not have thought further, and if the reply had been that there was no Soul, he might have been bewildered and might have turned a materialist or an atheist.

This description of Samyutta Nikâya clearly shows that Gotama believed in the soul, just in the same way as the Jains did. To take an illustration. As regards its composition, gold is indestructible, but as regards its modifications or conditions, it is destructible. Its own inherent attributes are permanent, but it may be moulded into any form, or changed into any alloy.

*Samyutta Nikâya of Sutta Pitaka* "Chando 13."

The Pâli words are :—

**तस्मांदिह आनन्द अत्तदीपा विहरथ अत्तसरणा अनण्ण सरणा धम्मदीपा धम्मसरणा अनण्ण सरणा.**

*Tasmâdih ânanda attadîpa Viharatha attasaraṇâ anaṇṇa saraṇâ dhamma dîpâ dhamma saraṇâ anaṇṇa-saraṇâ.*

"Therefore, O, Ananda, walk in the Isle of Self: Self is the safe refuge, there is no other place of safety. Dharma (Path of Nirvâna) is the Isle. Dharma is the place of security. There is no other place of safety."

These above words show that one's own pure soul should be taken to be an Island or a right resort, and the nature of soul which is *Dharma* should be taken as an Isle or a place of safety.

Majjhima Nikâya sutta pathana *Mula pariyâya sutta.*

The whole sutta being carefully read would show that he who maintains that anything other than the true self is the soul, is ignorant, while he who believes all the non-self to be the non-self is the wise. Let us give a quotation.

**भगवा एतद्वोच—अरियधम्मस्स अकोविदो...... पथवीं पथवितो संजानाति, पथविं पथावितो संज्ञत्वा पथविं मण्णति, पथवियां मण्णति, पथवितोअपरिज्ञातंपथविंमेति मण्णति, पथविं अभिनंदति: तं किस्सहेतु, अ ज्ञातं तस्साति वदामि. आपं... तेजं....वायं...भूतै....देवे....आकांसानंचायतनं...विज्ञानंचाय-तनं....दित्तं....सुतं......अभिनंदति त किस्स हेतु अपरिज्ञातं तस्साति वदामि.**

**योपि सो भिक्खवे भिक्खु अनुत्तरं योगखेमं पक्षयमानो विहरति सोपि पथविं पथावितो अभिज्ञानाति, पथविं पथवितो अभिज्ञाय पथविं मा मण्णि, पथविथा मा मण्णि, पथवितो मा मण्णि, पथविं मेति मा मण्णि, पथविं मा अभिनंदति; तं किस्सहेतु: परिज्ञेयं तस्साति वदामि...आपं तेजं. .वायं...भूते ...देवे...आकासानंचायतनं...विज्ञानंचायतनं....दिट्ठ....सुतं... ता अभिनंदति: तं किस्सहेतु: परिज्ञेय्यं तस्साति वदामि.**

*Bhagawa etadavocha-ariyadhammassa akovido...... pathavim pathavito sanjanati, pathavim pathavito sanjnatva pathavim mannati, pathaviyam mannati, pathavito mannati, pathavim meti mannati pathavim abhinandati ; tam Kessahetu* aparijnâtan*tassati Vadami âpam...tejam...Vâyam...bhūti,...deve...âkâsanan châ* *yatanam......Vijnânânchaytanam.....dittham....sutam....abhinandati tam Kissa hetu-aparijnâtam tassâti vadâmi. Yopi so bhikkhave bhikkhu anuttaram yogakhemam patthayamano viharati sopi pathavim pathavito abhijânati : pathavipathavito abhijnaya pathavim mâ manni, pathaviya ma manni, pathavito ma manni ; pathavim meti mâ manni, pathavim ma abhinandati, tam kissa hetu ; parijneyyam tassâti vadami apam...tejam...vâyam ...bhute...deve....akasanancha yatanam...dittha...sutam ...ma abhinandati tam kissa hetu ; pari jneyyam tassati vadâmi*

Bhagavan Gotam said, "He who is not learned in Arya Dharma (The Truth) knows earth as earth ; Knowing earth as earth, he maintains earth (as himself), he maintains (himself) in the earth, he maintains (his use) from the earth, he maintains that earth belongs to him, he welcomes earth. In this way he deals with water, fire, air, all the worldly beings, celestials, space, consciousness (derived through senses and mind), all objects capable of being seen or heard. He welcomes them all ; because he is ignorant, thus I say. And again O Monks! That Saint, who walks after having known that Nirvâna is the best and realisable by concentration, also knows earth as earth ; and having known earth as earth, he does not maintain earth (as himself), does not maintain (himself) in the earth, does not maintain (his use) from the earth, does not maintain earth to be his own, he does not welcome earth, because he is the Knower, thus I say. In the same way he does not welcome water, fire, air, all the living beings, celestials, space, consciousness (impure), all objects seen and heard; because he is the Knower, so I say."

The above statement clearly declares that the pure Soul is what is *Nirvâna*. All else than Nirvâna or pure Soul is non-Soul. This is called ***Prajna Vivêka, bheda vijnâna*** i.e. Self-analysis or Self-discrimination. This is the way to Liberation.

The Jain saint *Kunda Kunda Ācharya* also says the same in his ***Samayasâra*** :

**सव्वे करेदि जीवो अज्झावसाणेण तिरियणेरेइए ।**
**देवमणुवेपि सव्वे पुण्णं पावं अणेयविहं ॥ २९१ ॥**
**धम्माधम्मं च तहा जीवाजीवे अलोगलोगं च ।**
**सव्वे करेदि जीवो अज्झ वसाणेण अप्पाणं ॥ २९२ ॥**
**जा संकप्पवियप्पो ता कम्मं कुणइ असुहसुहजणयं ।**
**अप्पसरूवा रिद्धी जाव णहियए परिप्फरइ ॥ २९४ ॥**

*Savve karedi Jîvâ ajjhavasâṇeṇa tiriya neraiye,*
*Deva manuvepi savve puṇṇam pâvam aneyaviham, (291)*
*Dhammadhammam chataha Jîvâjîva alogalogamcha*
*Savve Karedi Jivo Ajjhavasânena appanam, (292).*

*Jâ sankappa viyappo ta Kammam Kuṇai asuh suhajaṇayam, appasaruva riddhi jâva nahiyaé parip-pharai.* (294).

"On account of wrong attachment, this (ignorant) being, maintains all the sub-human, hellish, celestial, and human beings and different kinds of merit and demerit to be is own. (291).

The (ignorant) being on account of wrong attachment maintains medium of motion and medium of rest, all the souls and non-souls, non-universe and the universe as his own. (292).

So long as there are wavering thoughts, he performs actions bringing merit and demerit so long as the glory of the nature of the soul has not been effulgent within him." (294).

These Jain passages also show that all else besides his own pure self is not his own self. To maintain all the others as himself or belonging to him is ignorance and wrong belief.

*Majjima nikâya alagaddupama sutta, 22.*

This Sutta also very nicely declares that all the other conditions are not the soul.

All those impure thought—activities, feelings of pleasure and pain, perception and knowledge which arise on account of five senses and mind and the bodies formed owing to their effects are included in the five *skandhas* of the Buddhists i.e., *Rupa* (body), *Vedana* (feeling pleasure and pain), *Sanjna* (perception through senses and mind), *Samskâra* (mental activities) *Vijnâna* (consciousness through senses and mind). This sutta very beautifully contradicts the belief of self in these five *skandhas*.

We give below a portion of this Sutta containing conversation between Gautam and his disciples.

Gautam Says :—

तं किं मन्नाथ भिक्खवे रूपंनिच्चं वा आनिच्चं वाति अनिच्चं-भंते यं पन अनिच्चं दुःखं वा तं सुखं वाति ; दुःखं भंते ; यं पन्न अनिच्चं दुःखं विपरिणामि धम्मं कल्लं नुतं समनुपास्सितुं : एतं मम, एसोऽहं अस्मि, एसो मे अत्तोति नोहि एतंभंते ; तं किं मन्नाथ भिक्खवे वेदना निच्चा वा अनिच्चा वा ति...संज्ञानिच्चावा अनिच्चावाति संखार निच्चावा आनच्चावाति...विज्ञानं निच्चं वा अनिच्चंवाति...तस्मादिः भिक्खवे यं किंचि रूपं अतीतानागत पच्चुप्पन्नं अज्झत्तं वा बहिद्दावा ओतारीकंवा सुखमं वा, हीनं वा पणितं वा, यं दीरे संतिके वा, सव्वं रूपंः—न एतं मम, न एसोऽहं अस्मि, न मे सोअत्ताति-एवं एतं यधा भूतं सम्मप्प-ज्ञाय-दट्ठव्वं. या काचि वेदना...या काचि संज्ञा......ये केचि संखारा ..यं किं च विज्ञानं...दत्तव्वं.

एवं पस्सं भिक्खवे सुतवा अरिय सावको रूपास्मिन् निव्विदंति, वेदनाय निव्विदंति संज्ञाय निव्विदंति, संखारेसु निव्विदंति, विज्ञानस्मि निव्विदंति ; निव्विदं विरज्जति, विरजा-विमुंचति, विमुत्तस्मि विमुत्तं इति ज्ञानं होति ; खीणाजाति, वुसितं ब्रह्मचारियं, कतं करणीयं, नापरं इत्थत्थायाति, पज्ञानाति तस्मादिह भिक्खवे यं न तुम्हाकं तं पजाहथ तं वो पहीनं दीघा-रत्तं हिताय सुखाय भविस्सति ; किं च भिक्खवे न तुम्हाकं रूपं भिक्खवे ने तुम्हाकं....वेदना....न तुम्हाकं....संज्ञा....न तुम्हाकं..संखारा ..न तुम्हाकं....विज्ञानं....न तुम्हाकं....तं किं मन्नाथ भिक्खवे : यं इमस्मि जेतवने तिणकट्ठ साखा पलासं तं जनोहरेय्यं वा दहेय्य वा यथापच्चयं करेय्य ; अपि नु तुम्हाकं

एवं अस्सः—अम्हेजनो हरति वा दहति वा यथा पच्चयं वा करतितिः नोहि एतं भंते तं किस्सहेतु-नहि नो एतं भंते अत्ता व अत्तनीयं वाति. एवं खो भिक्खवे यं नो तुम्हाकं तं पजाहथ... सुखाय भविस्सति. एवं स्वाकखातो भिक्खवे मयाधम्मो.

*Tam kim mannâtha bhikkhave: rupam nichcham va anichcham vaté, anichcham bhante; yam pana anichcham dukkham va tam sukham vati, dukkham bhante; yam pana anichcham dukkham viparinami dhammam Kallam nutam samanupassitum: etam mama, esoham asmi; eso me attati, no hi etam bhante; tam Kim mannâtha bhikkhave Vedanâ nichcha va anichcha vati sanjne nichchâ va anichcha vâtê...Sankhârâ nichcha va anichchavati...Vijnanum nichcham Va anichcham vâti tasmadih bhikkhave yam Kinchi rupam atitanagata pachchuppannam ajhattam va bahiddha va, otarikam va. sukhumam va hinam Va panitam va, yam dire santike va. savvam rupam:—na etam mama, na eso ham asmi na me so attati evam etam yatha bhutam sammappajanaya datthavvam. Yâ kâchi vedanâ ya kachi sanjna. Ye Ke chi sankhara-Yam Kinchi Vijnanam...datthavvam.*

*Evam passam bhikkhave sutava ariya sâvako rupasmin nivvindati, Vedanaya nivindati, sanjnaya nivvindati, sankharesu nivindati. Vijnanasmin nivvindati; nivvidam virajjadi, Viraja Vimunchati, Vimuttasmin Vimuttam iti jnanam hoti; Khina Jati, Vusitam Brahmchariyam, Katam Karaniyam, naparam itthatta yati, pajanati.*

*Tasmadih bhikkhave yam na tümmhakam tam pajahath tam Vo pahinam digharattam hitaya sukhaya Bhavissati; Kincha bhikkhave na tumhâ kam: rûpam bhikkhave na tumhakam vedanâ...na tumhakam...sanjnâ ...na tumhakam...Vijnânam...no tumhakam...tam Kîm mannâtha bhikkhave:—Yam imasmin Jetavane tiṇa-kaṭṭha sâkhâ palasam tam jano hareyyam Va da heyya va yathapachchayam Kareyya; apime tumhakam evam assa:—ambejano harati; va dahatti va yathapach-chayam vá Karatiti: noh etem bhante tam Kissa hetu —yami no tumhakam tam pajahath:—Sukha ya bhavîssati. Evam svakkhato bhikkhave mayê dhammo.*

Gotam—"O Monks, which do you maintain, whether the body is indestructible or destructible?

Monks—O Lord, it is destructible.

G.—Is that which is destructible, painful or pleasing?

M.—O Lord, it is painful.

G.—Should we say of that which is destructible, painful, changeable, that it is mine, or that my soul is this?

M.—O Lord, not.

G.—Is feeling indestructible or destructible? Is perception indestructible or destructible? Are mental activities indestructible or destructible? Is (impure) consciousness indestructible or destructible?

M.—O Lord, destructible.

G.—Therefore, O Monks, whatever body past, future, or present, external or internal, gross or fine, low or high, far or near, all this body—this is not mine, nor I am its, nor this is my soul. Thus should one see rightly to arrive at the best discrimination. In the same way all these feelings, perceptions, mentalities, consciousness (of past, present and future) should be thought of. O Monks, The *Aryasravaka* well versed in scriptures seeing thus, becomes non-attached from the body, feelings, perceptions, mentalities and consciousness. Being unattached, he gives up affection, becomes free from them through non-attachment, having thus freed mentally he realizes that he is freed—his birth is destroyed, his Brahmacharya (chastity or self absorption) is complete, whatever was to be done has been done, here nothing else is mine, he knows this. Therefore, O Monks, give up that which is not yours. By this means you will be happy and contented for a long time.

O Monks—What objects do not belong to you? This body, this feeling, this perception, these mentalities, this consciousness, all this is not yours.

O Monks! If in this *Jetavana* forest, one may steal or break or destroy any grass, any stem, any branch, or any leaf, would you maintain that one has stolen you, broken you or destroyed you.

M.—O Lord, no, we cannot maintain so.

G.—Why will you not feel so?

M.—They are not we, not ours.

G.—O Monks, in the same way, give up all what is not yours.

You will happily live for a long time.

Thus O Monks! This is my declared *Dharma* or Path.

A consideration of the above description of self analysis or self discrimination, will make it clear that only that pure soul which exists in Nirvâna after destruction of all the non-soul objects is "I" or "my Soul." A wise man should realize this. He should give up attachment with all the other thought-activities, objects, ideas, fleeting different kinds of consciousness, pleasure and pain and all the other beliefs or conjectures about the Soul.

The above statement clearly proves the existence of the pure soul, or of the Nirvâna or of the one who is in Liberation. The great Jain Saint *Kunda Kundacharya* has also described the way to Self-analysis in the following verses in his Samayasâra:

अहमेदं एदमहं अहमेदस्सेव होमि मम एदं ।
अण्णं जं परदव्वं सचित्ताचित्तमिस्सं वा ॥ २५ ॥
आसि मम पुव्वमेदं अहमेदं चावि पुव्वकालह्मि ।
होहिदि पुणोवि मज्झ अहमेदं चावि होस्सामि ॥ २६ ॥
एयत्तु असंभूतं आदवियप्पं करेदि संमूढो ।
भूदत्थं जाणंतो ण करेदि दु तं असंमूढो ॥ २७ ॥

*Ahamêdam edamaham aha-mêdassêva hômi*
*mama êdam,*

*Aṇṇam jam paradavvam sachittachittamissam vâ, 25.*
*Āsi mama puvvamêdam ahamêdam châvi puvva Kâlamhi,*
*Hôhidi punovi majjham ahamêdam châvi hôssâmi, 26.*
*Ēyattu asambhūdam âdaviyappam karedi sammuḍho*
*Bhūduttham Jânanto na karedi du tam asammuḍho, 27.*

"It is an ignorant person who says of living, non-living, mixed or any other object (other than I), I am this, this is I, I am its, it is mine; this was mine in past time, I was this in past time; it will be mine in future, I will be this, expresses untrue thought activities. While a wise man never does this. He knows the Truth."

Here living objects are women, children, pupils, lust and hate etc. impure thought activities; non-living objects are gold, silver, books and material Karmic, electric and outward bodies and all the five substances matter, medium of motion, medium of rest, space and time which the Jains believe to be other than the soul substance. The mixed objects are women and children with clothes and ornaments, students with books, four conditions of life, hellish, celestial, sub-human, human, sense-pleasure, impure knowledge, etc. The purport is that all the worldly things, thoughts, conditions or other existing souls or other substances all these are other than myself, they were and will remain other than myself. In reality, I am alone, free from all this. I am only a pure soul or one which is positive in Nirvâna. Such realization is Self-discrimination.

(5) Samyutta Nikâya (4) Satayâtana Vaggo (1) Anichcham.

Gotam says:—

**चकक्कुं भिक्खवे अनिच्चं यदनिच्चं तं दुःखं यं दुःखं तद अनत्तायद अनत्ता तं न एतं मम नेसोऽहं अस्मि न मे सो अत्ताति यवं एतं यथाभूतं सम्मप्पञ्ञाय दट्टव्वं सोतं अनिच्चं घानं अनिच्चं जिहवा अनिच्चं कायो अनिच्चो मनो अनिच्चो.**

"*Chakkum bhikkhave anichcham, yadanichcham tam dukkham, yam dukkham tad anatta-yad anatta tam na etam mama ne so ham asmi na me so attâti evam etam yathabhutam sammapajnâya datthavvam. Satam anichcham, ghânam anichcham, Jihvâ anichcham, Kâyo anichcho, mano anichcho.*"

"O Monks, this eye is destructible, that which is destructible is misery; that which is misery is non-soul; that which is non-soul is not mine, nor I am such; nor it is my soul. Such realization is right knowledge. In the same way ear, nose, tongue, body, and mind are all destructible."

The above statement also clearly declares that 'I' am something else; 'I' am not the five senses and the mind. Discrimination or ***Prajna*** is only possible, when there is something other than the destructible and painful objects. That which is other than the five senses and mind is the *Nirvâna* or the Pure Soul.

The Jain Saint Pujyapâda Swami says in his *Samâdhi Sataka* :

**सर्वेन्द्रियाणि संयम्यस्तिमितेनान्तरात्मना ।**
**यत्क्षणं पश्यतो भाति तत्तत्वं परमात्मनः ॥ ३० ॥**

*Sarvendriyâni samyamyastimitenântarâtmanâ—*
*Yatkṣanam pasyatô bhâti tattattvam paramât-manah, 30.*

" Having brought under control all the senses (and the mind), when that which is lighted there is internally seen, it is the nature of the pure soul."

(6) Majjhima Nikâya Bhaya-Bhairava Suttam Chatuttham.

Some sentences are as below :—

**पण्णाए संपन्नोहं स्मि येहि वो अरिया पण्णा संपन्ना अरण्णे ...तेसं अहं अण्णतमो एतं अदं ब्राह्मणा पण्णसंपदं। अत्तनि संपस्समानो भिय्यो पल्लोमं अरण्णे विहाराय.**

*Paṇṇâye sampanno ham smi, ye hi vo arîyâ paṇṇâ sampannâ araṇṇe......tesam aham aṇṇatamo-etam aham brahmaṇa paṇṇa sampadam attani sampassamâno bhiyyo pallomam araṇṇe vihârâya.*

" I am full of self-discrimination. All those ***Aryas*** who walk in the forest with self-discrimination, I am one of them. O Brahmana, thus seeing the wealth of self-discrimination within myself I walk fearless in the forest."

Here *Prajna* means the realization that I am other than non-self, senses, and all that which is destructible and painful. 'Seeing the wealth of self-discrimination within myself' clearly shows that one is seeing his own nature as it is in his own pure soul. Had there been no existence of the soul or had there been no soul in Nirvâna, then the above statement would have had no meaning at all. *Prajna* is called that intellect which discriminates self from non-self. The Great Jain Saint says in *Samayasâra* :—

पण्णाए घितव्वो जो चेदा सो अहं तु णिच्छयदो ।
अवसेसा जे भावा ते मज्झपरित्त णादव्वा ॥ ३२५ ॥

*Paṇṇâye ghitavvô jô chedâ so aham ta ṇichchhayado*
*avasêsâ je bhâvâ te majjha paritta nâdavvâ, 325.*

"That which should be grasped by self-discrimination is 'I' from the real point of view; all the other conditions should be known as other than 'I'."

*Some Sayings of the Buddha* by F. L. Woodward, M.A., 1925. Some quotations from the above book which show the existence of the soul are given below :—

Page 188.—Impermanent, alas! are all compounded things. Their nature is to rise and fall. When they have risen they cease. The bringing of them to an end is bliss. (D. N. II 198).

P. 190. Then make thyself *an island of defence* :
Strive quick : be wise : when all thy taints
Of dirt and dust are blown away, the Saints
Shall greet thee entering the Happy Land.
(Dhammapada vv 236).

P. 300. Rouse thou the self by self, by self examine self :
Thus guarded by the self, and with thy mind
Intent and watchful, thus, O mendicant,
Thou shalt live happily.
(Dhammapada vv 378).

The Jain Saint says the same thing in *Samayasâra* :

**एदह्मि रदो णिच्चं संतुट्ठो होहि णिच्चमेदहि ।**
**एदेण होहि तित्तो तो होहदि उत्तमं सोक्खं ॥ २२२ ॥**

*Ēdamhi rado nichcham santuṭṭho hohi ṇichchamêdamhi,*
*Edêṇa hohi titto tô hohadi uttamam sôkkham.* 222

"Always be absorbed in this (soul) ; always be contented in it, be satisfied with it ; then you will have the highest bliss."

*The doctrine of the Buddha* by George Grimm 1926.

P. 119. "Which is of greater importance, O youths, to search for this woman or to search for your '*I*' ?"
(Mahavagga I. 14).

P. 120-124. "It must, from the outset, inspire us with confidence in the Buddha that he prefers the safer indirect way. 'This belongs not to me ;' 'This am I not ;' 'This is not myself.' The Buddha has drawn this dividing line between *attâ* and *anattâ*, between "I" and "not I" with great exactness."

" What I *perceive* originating and perishing, that cannot be my *I*, my Ego. On one side stands I ; on the other, the whole gigantic cosmos, the duration, origination, dissolution of which I recognize in and through my personality."

P. 138. "This thought, wisely considered, also must make it clear that I am something standing behind life, behind the five groups, something only adhering, only clinging to life and to the five groups constituting personality, as to something alien which I think desirable."

P. 139. " The soul is an immaterial and therefore spiritual, therefore simple, therefore imperishable, substance. Notions are therefore nothing originally real, but an artificial product of reason distilled from the world given in perception."

Jain literature also says that the pure and true nature of the soul appears in its reality in the Nirvâna condition. The Jain Saint Amritachandra says in *Samayasâra Kalasa* :

आत्मस्वभावं परभावभिन्नमापूर्ण माद्यन्त विमुक्तमेकं ।
विलीन संकल्पविकल्पजालं प्रकाशयन् शुद्ध नयोऽभ्युदेति॥

*Ātma swabhâvam parabhâva bhinnamâpūrṇa mâ*
*dyanta vimukta mekam*
*Vilîna sankalpa vikalpa jâlam prakâsayan suddha*
*nayo bhhyudeti.—10/1.*

अनाद्यनंतमचलं स्वसंवेद्यमिदं स्फुटम् ।
जीवः स्वयंतु चैतन्यमुच्चै श्चकचकायते ॥

*Anâdyanantamachalam swasamvedya midam sphutam,*
*Jîvah svayamtu chaitanya muchchai śchaka chakâyate.*—*9/2.*

" The nature of the soul is distinct from the nature of the non-soul ; it is full of its own attributes, is eternal, independent, devoid of different notions. The soul is realized through the real point of view."—10/1..

" The soul is without a beginning or an end. It is steady, realizable by its own self ; is itself conscious and quite apparent to the wise."—9/2.

This is the nature of Nirvâna also.

Page 178 of *The Doctrine of the Buddha :*

" No eye can see it, no ear hear it, no nose smell it, no tongue taste it, no touching touch it, no brain think it any more ; because the subjective within us thus lies beyond all perception.—" There is a refuge beyond this sensual world." (M. I. 38).

Sacred Books of the East, Vol. XI (1881) by T. W. Rhys Davids. Mahaparinibbhana Sutta Ch. II S. 33.

" Therefore, O Ananda, be ye lamps to yourselves. Be ye refuge to yourselves. Be take yourself to no external refuge. Hold fast as a refuge to the Truth. Look not for refuge to any one besides yourself."

S. 35.—" Whoever shall be a lamp unto themselves, shall reach the very topmost height."

These passages also show the pure nature of the soul.

The Jain Saint Sri Yogindra Acharya says in *Yogasara* :

**अप्पा अप्पउ जउ मुणहि तउ णिव्वाणु लहेहि ।**
**पर अप्पा जउ मुणिहि तुहं तहु संसार भमेहि ॥ १२ ॥**

*Appâ appau Jau muṇahi tau nivvanu lahehi,*
*Para appâ jau munihi tuhum tahu sansara*
*bhamêhi 12.*

" If you will realize yourself, then you will have Nirvâna, but if you consider yourself as something else, you will roam about in the world."

Sacred Books of the East, Vol X, 1881 by F. Max Muller

Dhammapada, Chap. XII, Self.

S. 160. " Self is the lord of Self, who else could be the Lord? With self well-subdued, a man finds a lord such as few can find."

S. 165. " By oneself the evil is done, by oneself one suffers; by oneself evil is left undone, by oneself one is purified. Purity and impurity belong to oneself, no one can purify another."

Here also the soul is referred to. It becomes pure on the removal of all the impurities of the five *skandhas.* The soul is itself responsible.

The same idea has been expressed by the Jain Saint Pujyapâda Swami in his *Samâdhi Sataka* :

**नयत्यात्मानमात्मैव जन्मनिर्वाणमेव च ।**
**गुरु रात्मात्मनस्तस्मान्नान्योऽस्ति परमार्थतः ॥ ७५ ॥**

*Nayatyâtmânàmâtmaiva janma nirvâna meva cha,*
*Guru rätmâtmanastasmân nänyosti-paramarthatah 75.*

"The Self carries itself to births and also to Nirvâna; therefore really the self is the lord of the self; in reality, there is no other lord of the self."

Dhammapada Chap. XVIII. Impurity.

S. 238. "Make thyself an island, work hard, be wise! When thy impurities are blown away, and thou art free from guilt, thou wilt not enter again into birth and decay."

Chap. XXV. The Bhikshu.

S. 369. "O Bhikshu, empty this boat! if emptied, it will go quickly; having cut off passion and hatred, thou wilt go to Nirvâna."

S. 379. "Rouse thyself by thyself, examine thyself by thyself, thus self-protected and attentive wilt thou live happily, O Bhikshu!"

S. 380. "For self is the lord of the self, self the refuge of the self; therefore curb thyself as the merchant curbs a good horse."

*Tuvataka Sutta of Sutta Nipata* by Fausbold. (1881).

2/916. "Let him completely cut off the root of what is called *Papancha* (delusion) thinking "I am wisdom," so said Bhagavata—" all the desires that arise inwardly; let him learn to subdue them, always being thoughtful."

The above refers to the soul.

***Pinjaya mânava pukkhâ.***

11/1133. "As the bird, having left the bush, takes up his abode in the fruitful forest, even so, I having left men of narrow views, have reached the great sea, like the *Hansa*."

The Pâli words are:—

दिजो यथा कुव्वनकं पहाय
बहुक्कलं काननं अवसेय्य ।
एवं वि अहं अप्पदस्से पहाय
महोदधिं हंसोरिव अज्झपत्तो ॥

*Dijo yathá kuvvanakam pahâya*
*Bahukkalam kânanam avaseyya*
*Evam vi aham appa dasse pahâya,*
*Mahodadhim hansoriva ajjha patto.*

Path of Purity by Buddha Ghosh. Translated by P. Maung Tui XX P. I & II P. 342:

The whole wide world we traverse with our thought,
And nothing finds to me more dear than soul
Since, aye, so dear the soul to others is,
Let the soul-lover harm no other man.

*Note.*—This passage also refers to the soul.

*The Life of the Buddha* by Edward J. Thomas (1927).

P. 188. The ascetic Malimkaya Putta is said to have asked many questions, one of which was whether a Tathâgata exists after death. Buddha refused to say whether he exists, whether he does not exist.

The silence proves that what remains in Nirvâna is only realizable, not describable.

P. 189. Dialogue between the nun Khema (wife of Srenika) and King Pasenadi :

She says, " Reverend one, the ocean is deep, immeasurable, unfathomable, even so, king, that body by which one might define Tathâgata is relinquished, cut off at the root, unrooted like a palm tree, brought to nought, not to rise in future. Freed from designation of body a Tathâgata is deep, immeasurable, and unfathomable like ocean."

This passage also proves that the pure soul in Nirvâna is out of mind and speech and is only realizable.

Sacred Books of the East Vol. XLIX. Buddhist Mahayana Text.

*Prajna paramita.*

P. 148. " When the envelopment of consciousness has been annihilated, then he becomes free from all fear, beyond the reach of change, enjoying final Nirvâna. All the Buddhas of the past, present and future, after approaching ***Prajna Paramita***, have awoke to the highest knowledge."

P. 149. " O wisdom, gone, gone, gone, to the other shore, landed at the other shore."

This also shows that discrimination between soul and non-soul is ***prajna***. This leads to purity of soul in Nirvâna. It also proves the existence of the soul.

Sacred Books of the Buddhists Vol. III by T. W. Rhys Davids L.L.D.

Dialogue of the Buddha—Pali D. N. P. II. (1910).

P. 64. " Moreover, Anand, happy feeling is impermanent, a product, the result of a cause or causes, liable to perish, to pass away, to become extinct, to cease, so too is painful feeling, so too is neutral feeling. If when experiencing a happy feeling one thinks " this is my soul "—when that same happy feeling ceases, one will also think :—my soul has departed, so too when the feeling is painful or neutral. Thus he who says : " my soul is feeling " regards as his soul something, which in this present life is impermanent, is blended of happiness and pain, and is liable to begin and to end. Wherefore, Ananda, it follows that this aspect : " my soul is feeling " does not commend itself.

Herein, again Anand, to him who affirms, nay, my soul is not feeling, my soul is not sentient, answer should thus be made :—my friend, where there is no feeling of anything, can you then say I am. You cannot, Lord. Wherefore, Ananda, it follows that this aspect :—nay, my soul is not feeling, my soul is not sentient, does not commend itself.

My friend, when feeling of every sort or kind to cease absolutely, then there being, owing to the cessation, thereof, no feeling whatever could one then say—I myself am ?

No lord, one could not.

Wherefore, Ananda, it follows that this aspect :—nay, my soul is not feeling, nor it is not sentient ; my soul has feeling, it has the property of sentience, does not commend itself.

P. 65. Now, when a brother, Ananda, does not regard soul under these aspects either as not feeling or having feeling, then he, thus refraining from such views, grasps at nothing whatever in this world, and not grasping he trembles not, and trembling not, he by himself attains to perfect peace. And he knows that birth is at an end, that the high life has been fulfilled, that what had to be done had been accomplished, and that after this present world, there is no beyond.

The above dialogue, if deeply thought of, will show that, that which is free from all kinds of thoughts, is only realizable and is fully peaceful, is the pure soul itself.

When all attachment to all the objects, thoughts, impure natures and all lust and hate etc. are given up, then there is nothing to relinquish and nothing to grasp —that is the condition of soul's perfect equanimity or self-absorption. Really it is the way to *Nirvâna* and it is the *Nirvâna* itself.

The Jain Saint Amritachandra says in *Samayasâra Kalasa :*

अन्यैभ्यो व्यातिरिक्तमात्म नियतं विभ्रत पृथक वस्तुता ।
मादानोज्झन शून्य मेतदमलं ज्ञानं तथावास्थितम् ॥
मध्याद्यन्त विभागमुक्त सहज स्फार प्रभा भासुरः ।
शुद्ध ज्ञान घनोयथास्य महिमा नित्योदयास्तिष्ठति ॥
उन्मुक्त मुन्मोच्य मशेषतस्त तथात्त मा देय मशेषस्तद् ।
यदात्मना संहृत सर्वशक्तेः पूर्णस्य संधारण मात्मनीह ॥

*Annyêbhyô vyatiriktamâtma niyatam vibhrat pri-thak vastutâ,*
*Mâdânôjjhana sunya metadamalam jnânam tathâ vasthi tam.*
*Madhyâdyanta vibhâga mukta sahaja sphara prabhâ bhâsurah*
*Śuddha jnâna ghano yathâsya mahimâ nittyodayastiṣṭhati.*
*Unmuktā munmochaya maśeṣatas tat tathâtta mâdeya maśeṣatas tat,*
*Yadâtmanâ sanhrita sarva śakteh purṇasya sandhârana mâtmanîha.*

"When the knowledge of the soul, being freed from else-where, steadfast in the soul, having its substance freed from others, above giving up or grasping anything, assumes its own nature, then its grandeur bursts forth without any distinction of beginning, end and middle and he remains eternal, full of the pure mass of knowledge. One who has kept one's full power within oneself has given up all that was to be given up and has taken in all that was to be taken in."

The Jain Saint Pujyapada Swami says in *Samâdhi Sataka :*

स्वबुद्ध्या यावद्गृह्णीयात्कायवाक् चेतसां त्रयम् ।
संसारस्तावदेतेषां भेदाभ्यासे तु निर्वृतिः ॥ ६२ ॥

*Svabuddhya yâvad grihnî yât kâya vak chetasâm trayam,*
*Sansârastâvadetesâm bhedâbhyâse tu nirvritih 62.*

"So long as the three (things) body, speech and mind, are taken to be the Self, there is wandering; on acquiring discrimination from them, there is Nirvâna."

When notions like "I am," "I am not," "What is I?," disappear, then only there is true knowledge, grasp and realization of the soul.

*Hindi Buddha Charyâ* by Saint Rahula.

(1) Sela sutta Page, 165.

Gotam is saying to ***Saila***: "I have known what should have been known, I have meditated upon what should have been meditated upon, I have given up what should have been given up; therefore, O Brahmana! I am ***Buddha***."

In such words does Gotam declare that he has known himself which is realizable, and has given up all non-soul.

(2) Mahali sutta P. 247. Gotam says:—"Mahali! once I was roaming in Ghoṣitârama of ***Kausambi.*** Then Mandissa Paribrajaka and Jaliya, disciples of Dârupâtrika came to me and stood aside after greeting me. They asked "Gotam, are the soul and the body the same? or are the soul and the body both different?" Then I told them to hear patiently and said, "That monk who is full of right conduct obtains the first concentration and he knows and perceives this. He has no necessity of saying, "Are the soul and the body the same or are they different?" In the same

way he who obtains the second, the third and the fourth concentration and fixes his mind in perception and knowledge, has no necessity of saying "The soul and the body are the same" or "They are different." I know this, even then I do not say "The soul and the body are the same" or "they are different."

This statement proves that soul is different from the body and can be realized.

(3) Sandakasutta Page. *264*. Gotama says "O Sandaka! just as a man whose hands and feet are cut off, knows that his hands and feet are cut off, even when walking, sitting, sleeping and awakening, so the monk who is Arhat and whose ***Āsavâs*** are destroyed, always realizes that he is the destroyer of Āsavâs".

This shows that there is a pure soul, freed from Āsavâs.

(4) Mahasukuldai sutta P. *372*. Gotama says "I have shown the path...Udai! just as some one may separate culm from the grass, then he knows that this is culm, this is grass; culm is separate and grass is separate....Just as a man may take away sword from a sheath, then he knows that this is sword, this is sheath, sword is separate, sheath is separate, although sword has come out of the sheath....Just as a man may bring out a serpent from a basket-thus I have shown the way."

These passages show that the soul is distinct from the body.

(5) Raṭṭhapâla sutta P. 354.

The Monk Rastrapala controlled in self has obtained the best *Brahmacharya* in this very life after knowing and relizing himself.

This also shows realization of the soul.

(6) Page. 358. Ratthapath sutta (M. N. 2. 4. 2).

King! That Lord who is knower and perceiver, *Arhat*, and well-learned have preached 4 paths; knowing them, I have been homeless. They are (1) this world is destructible (2) this world is unsafe (3) this world is not mine, I have to go leaving all, (4) this world is a slave to craving.

Here also the soul is referred to.

I have thus shown such passages as prove the existence of the soul, selected by me from such Buddhistic literature as was available to me.

## SOUL IN JAIN LITERATURE.

Now I shall give some passages about the existence of pure soul from Jain literature.

It should be remembered that the Jain literature describes soul from two stand-points, the real and the practical. The real stand-point speaks of the true and the real nature of the soul as it is free from all Karmic bondage or anything else. The practical point of view shows all the impure and incomplete conditions of the soul, which are caused on account of Karmic bondage, or contact with body and other objects. First of all I shall quote those passages which describe the soul from the real stand-point, so that the nature of the pure soul may be known. The nature of the pure soul is the nature of *Nirvâna*. The Buddhistic literature mainly describes the soul in an indirect way, showing all that is foreign to its nature, but the nature of Nirvâna has been clearly described in a direct way. The Jain literature also has described the soul in an indirect way, showing the absence of that which does not belong to it. The following passages will show both the direct and indirect mention about the soul in the Jain literature :—

(1) *Samayasâra* by Kunda Kunda Acharya.

**अहमिक्को खलु सुद्धो दंशणणाणमइओ सयारूवी ।**
**णवि अत्थि मज्झ किंचिव अण्णं परमाणुमित्तंवि ॥ ४३ ॥**

***Ahamikkô khalu suddhô damsana ṇâṇa maio sayâ-rûvî, ṇavi atthi majjha kinchiva aṇṇam paramânu mittamvî (43).***

"I (am) one, (i.e. myself) really pure, full of perfect knowledge, ever non-material. Another (i.e. the non-self) is never mine in any way, even to the extent of an atom."

**जीवस्स णात्थिवण्णो णवि गंधो णवि रसो णवि य फासो ।**
**णविरूवं ण सरीरं ण वि संठाणं ण संघदणं ॥ ५५ ॥**
**जीवस्स णत्थि रागो णवि दोसो णेव विज्जदे मोहो ।**
**णो पच्चया ण कम्मं णोकम्मं चावि से णत्थि ॥ ५६ ॥**

*Jîvassa natthi vanno navi gandhô navi raso naviya phâsô.*
*Navi rûvam na sarîram navi sanṭhanam na sanghadanam.*
*Jîvassa natthi râgô navi dôsô nēva vijjadē môhô.*
*Na pachchaya na kammam no kammam chăvisē natthi 56.*

"In the soul, there is no colour, no smell, no taste, not even touch, not any material form, nor body, neither material figure nor any kind of bones." 55.

"In the soul, there is no attachment, no hatred, no delusion, neither causes of *âsavâs,* nor Karmaṣ and not the no-Karmas (materials forming outer body)."

(2) *Niyamasâra* by the same author.

णाहं णारयभावो तिरियत्थो मणुवदेवपज्जाओ ।
कत्ता ण हि कारइदा अणुमंता णेव कत्तीणं ॥
णाहं बालो बुड्ढो ण चेव तरुणो ण कारणं तेसिं ।
कत्ता ण हि कारइदा अणुमंता णेव कत्तीणं ॥
णाहं कोहो माणो ण चेव माया ण होमि लोहो हिं ।
कत्ता ण हि कारइदा अणुमंता णेव कत्तीणं ॥

*Nâham ṇâraya bhâvô tiriyattho manuva deva pajjâo,*
*Katta ṇahi kâraidâ anumanta neva kattînam 78.*
*Nâham Bâlo buḍḍho na cheva taruṇo na kâranam tesim.*
*Katta ṇahi Kâraidâ anumanta neva Kattînam 79.*
*Nâham Koho mâno na cheva mâya na homi loho him*
*Katta ṇahi Kâraidâ aṇumaṇta ṇeva Kattiṇam 81.*

"I am neither hellish, nor sub-human, nor human, nor am I in the celestial condition. I am neither the doer, nor do I induce others to do, nor am I the approver of the doers." 78.

"I am neither a child, nor old, nor a young man, nor the cause of any of them. I am neither the doer, nor do I induce others to do, nor am I the approver of the doers." 79.

"I am neither anger, nor pride, nor deceit, nor greed. I am neither the doer, nor do I induce others to do, nor am I the approver of the doers." 81.

**केवलणाणसहावो केवलदंसण सहाव सुहमइओ ।**
**केवलसत्तिसहावो सोहं इदि चिंतए णाणी ॥ ९६ ॥**
**णियभावं णवि मुच्चइ परभावं णेव गेण्हए केइं ।**
**जाणदि पस्सदि सव्वं सोहं इदि चिंतए णाणी ॥ ९७ ॥**

*Kevala nâna sahâvo Kevala damsana sahâva suha maiô,*
*Kevalasatti sahâ vô sôham idi chintaê nâni* 96.
*Niyabhâvam navi muchae para-bhavam neva gênhe Keyim*
*Jânadi passadi savvaṁ sôhaṁidi chintaê nani* 97.

"A Right-Knower meditates that that which has the nature of independent knowledge, independent perception, is blissful and has the nature of independent power is 'I'." 96.

"A Right-Knower meditates that that which does not give up its nature and does not adopt another's nature, but knows and perceives all is 'I'." 97.

एको मे सासदो अप्पा णाणदंसणलक्खणो ।
सेसा मे बहिरा भावा सव्वे संजोगलक्खणा ॥ १०२ ॥

*Ekô mê sâsadô appâ nâna damsana lakkhanô,*
*Sêsâ mê bahirâ bhâvâ savvê sanjôga lakkhanâ 102.*

" My soul is ever one, eternal, having Knowledge and perception as (its) differentia. All the other thought-activities are foreign to me, due to connection with (non-soul)."

जाइजरमरणरहियं परमं कम्मट्ठवज्जियं सुद्धं ।
णाणाइचउसहावं अक्खयमविणासमच्छेयं ॥ १७६ ॥

*Jâi Jaramaranarahiyam paramam Kammattha vajjiyam suddham*
*Nânâe chau sahâvam akkhayamavinâsa machchêyam 176.*

" A pure soul is devoid of birth, old age and death, is supreme and free from the eight Karmas, pure, having the four kinds of qualities of knowledge, perception, power and bliss, is indestructible. eternal and unbreakable."

Such is the nature of Nirvâna also in Jainism.

(3) *Samâdhi sataka* by Pujyapada.

येनात्मनाऽनुभूयेऽहमात्मनैवात्मनात्मनि ।
सोऽहं न तन्न सा नासौ नैको न द्वौ न वा बहुः ॥ २३ ॥
यदभावे सुषुप्तोऽहं यद्भावे व्युत्थितः पुनः ।
अतीन्द्रियमनिर्देश्यं तत्स्वसंवेद्यमस्म्यहम् ॥ २४ ॥

*Yênâtmanâ anubhûyê aham âtmanaivatmanât-mani,*

*Sôham na tanna sâ nâsau naikô na dvau na vâ bahu 23*

*Yadbhâvê suṣuptô ham yad bhâve Vyutthitah punah,*

*Atîndriyamanirdes'yam tat svasamvêdya masmy-aham 24.*

"I am that which is realizable by me, in me, as it is, I am not 'it,' not 'she,' nor he, not one, nor two, not many."

"In the absence of which I was sleeping, in the presence of which I am awakened, that is 'I' which is supra-sensual, indescribable and realizable by myself."

(4) *Istopadesa* by the same author.

स्वसंवेदनसुव्यक्तस्तनुमात्रो निरत्ययः ।
अत्यंतसौख्यवानात्मा लोकालोकविलोकनः ॥ २१ ॥

*Svasamvedana suvyaktastanumâtrô niratyayah,*
*Atyanta saukhyavanâtmâ lôkâlôka vilôkanah 21.*

"The soul has the highest bliss, it knows the universe and the non-universe, is indestructible, is of the size of the body it occupies, and is realizable by the self only."

(5) *Ātmânusâsanâ* by Sri Gunabhadra Acharya.

ज्ञानस्वभावः स्यादात्मा स्वभावावाप्तिरच्युतिः ।
तस्मादच्युतिमाकांक्षन् भावयेज्ज्ञानभावनाम् ॥ १७४ ॥
मामन्यमन्यं मां मत्त्वा भ्रान्तो भ्रान्तौ भवार्णवे ।
नान्योहमहमेवाहमन्योन्वोन्योहमास्ति न ॥ २४३ ॥
अजातोऽनश्वरोऽमूर्तः कर्ता भोक्ता सुखी बुधः ।
देहमात्रो मलैर्मुक्ता गत्वोर्ध्वमचलः प्रभुः ॥ २६६ ॥

*Jnânasvabhâvah syadâtmâ svâbhâvâvâpti rachutih,*
*Tasmâdachyuti ma kânkshan bhavâyej Jnana bhâ-*
*vanâm* 174.
*Mâmanyamanyam mâm matvâ bhrântê bhavârnavé*
*Nânyô hamahamevahamanyônyô nyohmasti na* 243.
*Ajâtônasvarô murtah Kartâ bhoktâ sukhî budhah;*
*Dehamâtrô malairmuktô gatvordhva nachalah*
*prabhuh: 266.*

"The soul has the nature of knowledge, and the realisation of this nature is Nirvâna; therefore one who is desirous of Nirvâna must meditate upon self-knowledge." 174.

"Having maintained myself as another, and another as myself, and being deluded, I have wandered in this Ocean of Worldly existence (Samsara); (really) I am not the other, I am the I, another is another, another is not I." 243.

"This unshakeable Lord (soul) is uncreated, eternal, non-material, doer and enjoyer of one's own self, blissful, knower, free from impurities and is of the size of the body it occupies."

*Tatvârthasâra* by Sri Amritchandra Acharya.

**पश्यति स्वस्वरूपं यो जानाति च चरत्यपि ।**
**दर्शनज्ञान चारित्र त्रयमात्मैव स स्मृतः ॥**

*Paśyati svasvarūpam yo jânâti cha charatyapi*
*Darśanajnâna châritra trayamâtmâiva sa*
*smrutah.*

11

" He, who believes in his own nature, knows it and acts up to it, is said to be soul, an embodiment of the three, belief, knowledge, and conduct."

*Samayasâra Kalasa* by the same author.

अचिन्त्य शाक्तिः स्वयमेवदेवश्चिन्मात्र चिन्तामणिरेषयस्मात् ।
सर्वार्थसिद्धात्मतया विधत्ते ज्ञानी किमन्यस्य परिग्रहेण ॥

*Achintya śaktih svayameva devaśchin mâtra chintâmaṇireṣa yasmât*

*Sarvârtha siddhâtmataya vidhatta jṇâni Kimanyasya parigraheṇa* 12/7.

" Because the self is itself God, having unthinkable power and the unrivalled gem of consciousness and because all the purpose is served by its realization, therefore there is no use in grasping anything else."

ज्ञानी करोति न न वेदयते च कर्म
जानाति केवलमयं किलतत्स्वभावम् ।
जानन्परं करणवेदनयोरभावात्
शुद्धस्वभाव नियतः स हि मुक्त एव ॥

*Jnâni karoti na na vedayate cha karma jânâti kevalamayam kila tatsvabhâvam*

*Jânanparam karaṇa vedanayorabhâvâchchuddha svabhâva niyatah sa hi mukta eva* 6/10.

The one who knows neither performs nor enjoys any action. He only knows the nature of both, therefore not being the doer or enjoyer, but only knowing all else, he is fixed in his pure nature and is liberated in reality.

*Laghusâmâyika pâth by* Sri Amitagati Acharya.

**योदर्शनज्ञान सुखस्वभावः समस्तसंसारविकारभाह्यः ।**
**समाधि गम्यः परमात्मसंज्ञः सदेवदेवोहृदये ममास्तां ॥**

*Yo darśanajnâna sukhasvabhâvah samasta samsâra vikârabâhyah,*

*Samâdhi gamyah paramâtma sanjnah sa deva devo hridye mamâstam 13.*

"May that Lord of Lords, who has the nature of perception, knowledge and bliss, is beyond all the worldly defects and is named the highest soul, be enshrined in my heart."

**एकः सदा शश्वतिको ममात्मा विनिर्मलः साधिगमस्वभावः ।**
**बहिर्भवा संत्यपरे समस्ता न शाश्वता कर्मभवाः स्वकीया ॥**

*Ekah sadâ śaśatiko mamâtmâ vinirmalah sâdhigama svabhâvah,*

*Bahirbhavâh santyapar samastâ na śâśvatâh karmabhavâh svakîyah. 26.*

"My soul is always independent, eternal, pure and has the nature of consciousness, all the others (conditions) beyond me are not eternal, due to Karmic effects only."

*Srâvakâchâra* by the same author.

**ज्ञानदर्शनमयं निरामयं मृत्युसंभवविकारवर्जितम् ।**
**आमनंति सुधियोऽत्र चेतनं सूक्ष्ममव्ययमपास्तकल्मषम् ॥**

*Jnânadarsanamayam nirâmayam mrityusambhava vikâra varjitam.*

*Amananti sudhiyôtra chêtanam sukṣmamavyaya mapasta kalmaṣam 89/15.*

"The wise men maintain the conscious being as the embodiment of knowledge, and perception, disease-less, devoid of defect, of death and birth, fine, eternal and free from dirt."

*Ekatva Saptati* by Padmanandi.

एकमेव हि चैतन्यं शुद्धनिश्चयतोऽथवा।
कोऽवकाशो विकल्पानां तत्राखंडैक वस्तुनि ॥
अजमेकं परं शांतं सर्वोपाधिविवर्जितम्।
आत्मानमात्मना ज्ञात्वा तिष्ठेदात्मनि यस्थिर ॥
स एवामृतमार्गस्थ स एवामृत मश्नुते।
स एवार्हन जगन्नाथः स एव प्रभुरीश्वरः ॥
केवलज्ञान दृक् सौख्यस्वभावं तत्परं मह।
तत्रज्ञातेन किं ज्ञातं दृष्टेदृष्टं श्रुतेश्रुतं ॥
शुद्धं यदेव चैतन्यं तदेवाहं न संशयः।
कल्पनया नयाप्येतद्धीन मानन्द मंदिरं ॥

*Ēkameva hi chaitanyam suddhanischayato-thava,*
*Kovakáso vikâlpánám tatrâ khandaika vastuni* 15.
*Ajamekam param śántam sarvopâdhi-vivarjitam,*
*Ātmánamátmaná jnátva tisthe dâtmani yah sthirah* 18.
*Sa evâmrita márgastha sa evamrita-maśnute,*
*Sa evárhan Jagannathah sa eva prabhurîśvarah* 19
*Kevalajnana drik saukhyasvabhâvam tatparam mahah,*
*Tatrajnátena kim jnâtam driṣṭe driṣṭam śrute śtrutam* 20

*Śuddham yadeva chaitanyam tâdevâham na sanśayah,*
*Kalpanayâ nayâpyetaddhina mânanda mandiram* 22.

" From the pure, real point of view, it is one conscious being, there is no room for any other notions in that unbroken substance." 15.

" He, having known the soul, by himself as one, uncreated, highest, peaceful and devoid of all defects, remains steady in himself." 18.

" The same (self-absorbed) is staying in the path of immortality, the same enjoys the nectar of bliss, the same is the worshipful lord of this universe and the same is Almighty God." 19.

" That highest light has the nature of independent knowledge, perception and bliss ; on knowing it, nothing remains to be known ; on seeing it nothing remains to be seen, on hearing it nothing remains to be heard." 20

" That which is pure consciousness is undoubtedly 'I,' really it is devoid of even this notion. It is the home of bliss."

*Niśchaya Panchâśata* by the same author.

मनसोऽचिन्त्यं वाचामगोचरं यन्महस्तनोभिन्नं ।
स्वानुभवमात्रगम्यं चिद्रूपममूर्त मव्याद्वः ॥
नैवात्मनो विकारः क्रोधादि किन्तुकर्मसंबधात् ।
स्फटिक मणेरिव रक्तत्व माश्रितात्पुष्पतो रक्तात् ॥

*Manasochintayam vâchâmagocharam yanmahasta-*
*norbhinnam,*
*Svânubhava mâtragamyam chidrûpamamûrta mav-*
*yâdvah* 2.
*Naivâtmano vikârah krodhâdih kintu karma sam-*
*bant hât,*
*Sphaṭika maṇeriva raktatva mâsritat puṣpato*
*raktât* 25.

"May that soul which is not thinkable by mind, not describable by speech, bodiless, realizable by self-absorption only, conscious and non-material, protect us." 2.

"Anger etc. are not the soul's own real modifications, but are caused by karmas, just as redness in a crystal piece is due to its contact with the red flower." 25.

*Yogasâra* by Sri Yogindra Acharya.

सुद्ध सचयणे बुद्ध जाणु केवल णाणसहाउ ।
सो अप्पा अणुदिण मुणहु जइ चाहउ सिवलाहु ॥
पुग्गल अण्णुजि अण्णुजिउ अण्णुवि सहुववहारा ।
चयाहेवि पुग्गल गहइजिउ लहु पावहि भवपारु ॥
जेहउ सुद्ध आयासु जिय तेहउ अप्पा उत्तु ।
आयासुवि जड जानि जिय अप्पा चेयणवंतु ॥
इक्कलउ इंदिय रहिउ मणवयकाय ति सुद्धि ।
अप्पा अप्प मुणेइ तुहुं लहुपावहि सिवसिद्धि ॥

*Suddha sacheyaṇa buddha Jiṇu kevala ṇâṇa*
*sahâ-u,*

*So appâ aṇudiṇa muṇahu jai châhau siva lahu* 26.
*Puggalu aṇṇuji annu Jiu annuvi sahuvavahâru,*
*Chayaḥivi puggala gahahi Jiulahu pavâhi bhava-pâru.* 54.
*Jehau suddha Āyâsu Jiya teham appâ uttu*
*Ayâsuvi Jaḍa Jâni Jiya appâ cheyaṇavaṇtu* 58.
*Ikkalau indiya rahiu maṇa vaya kâva ti suddhi,*
*Appâ appa muṇei tuhun lahu pavahi siva siddhi* 85.

" The soul is pure, conscious, Buddha (enlightened), *Jina* (conqueror), having the attribute of independent knowledge; if you desire the acquisition of Nirvâna, then meditate upon it day and night." 26.

" Matter is another, soul is another, all practical conditions are another, give up matter etc., grasp soul only: then thou shalt cross the Ocean of the world soon." 54.

" Just as the sky is pure, so the soul has been said; know space to be unconscious but your own soul to be full of consciousness." 58.

" This soul is independent, super-sensual, devoid of mind, body and speech; if you concentrate upon it by yourself, then you will have the acquisition of Nirvâna very soon." 85.

*Paramâtmaprakâsa* by the same author.
अप्पा गोरउकिण्हु णवि अप्पा रत्तुण होइ ।
अप्पा सुहमवि थूल णवि णाणिउ णाणेजोइ ॥
अप्पा बंमणु वइसुणवि णविखत्तिउ णविसेसु ।

पुरिसु णउंसउ इत्थि णवि णाणिउ मुणइं असेसु ॥
पुण्णविपावि कालणहु धम्माधम्मवि काउ ।
एक्कुवि अप्पा होइ णवि मेल्लिवि चेयण भाउ ॥
अप्पा झायंहि णिम्मलउ किं बहुए अण्णेण ।
जो झायंतह परमपउ लब्भइ एक्क खणैण ॥
मुत्ति विहुणउ णाणमउ परमाणंद सहाउ ।
णियमिं जोइय अप्प मुणि णिच्चुणिरंजणु भाउ ॥
जो परमप्पा णाणमउ सोहउं देउ अणंतु ।
जोहउं सो परमप्पुपरु एहउ भावि णिभंतु ॥

*Appâ Gorau kiṇhu ṇavi appâ rattu ṇa hoi,*
*Appâ suhamavi thûlạ ṇavi ṇâṇiu nâne Joi 87.*
*Appâ bamhaṇa vaisu ṇavi navi khattiu navi sesu,*
*Purisu ṇa unsau itthi ṇavi ṇaṇiu muṇain asesu 88.*
*Puṇnavi pâvâvi kâla nahu dhammâ dhammavi kâ u,*
*Ekkuvi appâ hoi navi mellivi cheyana bhâ u 93.*
*Appâ Jhâyahi nimmalau kim bahue aṇṇena,*
*Jo jhâ yantâh parampau, labbhaye ekka khaṅena 98.*
*Mutti vihunau nâna mau parmânanda sahâ u,*
*Niyamin Joiya appa muni nichchu nîranjanu bhâ u 144.*
*Jo paramappâ nâna mau so haun deu aṇantu,*
*Johaun so paramappuparu ehau bhâvi ṇibhantu. 306.*

"The soul is neither white nor black, the soul is not red, the soul is neither fine nor gross. The learned know it through knowledge." 87.

"The soul is neither *Brahmanā* nor *Vaisya*, nor *Kshatriya*, nor any other, neither it is man nor woman, nor of a commensex. The learned know it thoroughly." 88.

"The soul is neither merit nor demerit, nor time, space, medium of motion or rest, and neither body. It is nothing except the (pure) conscious thought-activity." 93.

"Meditate upon the soul as pure; what will be the gain otherwise; by meditating upon that, the highest position can be procured in a moment." 98.

"O Monk, really realize the soul as non-material, full of knowledge with the nature of highest bliss, eternal and defectless." 144.

"As the perfect soul is full of knowledge, so I am the infinite God; as I am, so the perfect soul, meditate on this without any doubt." 306.

*Sâra Samuchchaya* by Sri Kulabhadrâcharya Acharya.

**ज्ञान दर्शनसम्पन्न आत्मा चैको ध्रुवोमम ।**
**शेषा भावाश्च मे बाह्या सर्वे संयोगलक्षणाः ॥ २४९ ॥**

*Jnâna darsana sampanna âtmâ chaikô dhruvô mama,*
*Śêsâ bhâvâscha me bâhyâ sarvê samyogalaksanah 249.*

"My soul is full of knowledge and perception, is one, independent and eternal; all the other conditions outside me are due to connection with another."

*Tattvânusâsana* by Sri Nâgasena Muni.

तथा हि चेतनोऽसंख्यप्रदेशो मूर्तिवर्जितः ।
शुद्धात्मा सिद्धरूपोऽस्मि ज्ञानदर्शनलक्षणः ॥ १४७ ॥
नान्योऽस्मि नाहमस्त्यन्यो नान्यस्याहं न मे परः ।
अन्यस्त्वन्योऽहमेवाहमन्योन्यस्याहमेव मे ॥ १४८ ॥
अचेतनं भवे नाहं नाहमप्यस्त्यचेतनं ।
ज्ञानात्माहं न मे कश्चिन्नाहमन्यस्य कस्यचित् ॥ १५० ॥
सद्द्रव्यमस्मि चिदहं ज्ञाता द्रष्टा सदाप्युदासीनः ।
स्वोपात्तदेहमात्रस्ततः पृथग्गगनवदमूर्त्तः ॥ १५३ ॥
स्वयमिष्टं न च द्विष्टं किन्तूपेक्ष्यमिदं जगत् ।
नोऽहमेष्टा न च द्वेष्टा किन्तु स्वयमुपेक्षिता ॥ २५७ ॥

*Tathâhi chetanôasankhya pradêsô mûrtivarjitah,*
*Suddhatmâ siddha ruposmi jnâna-darsana laksanah 147.*

*Nânyôsmi nâhamastyanyô nanyasyaham na me parah,*
*Anyastvanyô hame vahamanyô-nya syâha mêva mê 148.*

*Achêtanam bhave nâham nahamapyastya-chêtanam,*
*Jnânâtmâham na me kaschinnâha-manyasya kasyachit 150.*

*Saddravyamsmi chidaham jnâta drista sadâpyudâsînah,*
*Svopâttadehamâtrastatah prathag-gagana vadamurtah 153,*

*Svayamistam nacha dvistam kintu-pêksyamidam jagat,*
*Nôhamesta nacha dvesta kintu svaya mupeksita 157.*

"I am the pure soul, conscious, having innumerable spacial units (in size), non-material, in the nature of the perfect soul and with the differentia of knowledge and perception." 143.

"'I' am not the other, nor the other is 'I', neither 'I' belong to another, nor another belongs to me; another is another, I am the 'I', another belongs to another, I belong to me." 148.

"I never become unconscious, nor unconsciousness becomes 'I', I am full of knowledge, nothing belongs to me, nor I belong to any other." 150.

"I am always an existing substance, conscious, knower, perceiver, and also unattached, I have the size of the body I reside in, even then free from the body, and non-material like the sky." 153.

"This universe neither loves nor hates me, nor is attached to me; I neither love nor hate it, but myself remain unattached to it." 157.

*Tattvasâra* by Sri Dêvasêna.

दंसणणाणपहाणो असंखदेसो हु मुत्तिपरिहीणो ।
सगहियदेहपमाणो णायव्वो एरिसो अप्पा ॥ १७ ॥
जस्स ण कोहो माणो माया लोहो य सल्ल लेसाओ ।
जाइणरामरणं विय णिरंजणो सो अहं भणिओ ॥ १९ ॥
फासरसरूवगंधा सद्दादीया य जस्स णत्थि पुणो ।
सुद्धो चेयणभावो णिरंजणो सो अहं भणिओ ॥ २१ ॥
णोकम्मकम्मरहिओ केवलणाणाइगुणसमिद्धो जो ।
सोहं सिद्धो सुद्धो णिच्चो एक्को णिरालंबो ॥ २७ ॥

*Damsananânapahânô asamkhadêsohu muttiparihînô,*
*Sagahiyadêhapamâno nâyavvo erisô appâ 17.*
*Jassa na kôhô mâno mâyâ lôhô ya salla lêsaô,*
*Jâijâramaranam viya niranjanô so aham bhaṇiô 19.*
*Phâsarasarûvagandhâ-saddâdîya ya jassa natthi punô,*
*Suddhô chêyana bhâvô niranjanâ so aham bhaniô*
*Nokammakammarahio kêvalananaigunasamiddho jo,*
*Sôham siddhô suddhô nichchô ekko nirâlambô, 27.*

"This soul should be known to be having special qualities of perception and knowledge, with innumerable spacial units (like the universe), non-material, having size of the body it occupies." 17.

"That which has not anger, pride, deceit, greed, thorn in thought, thought-paints, birth, old age, death, and any defect is 'I.'" 19.

"That which has not touch, taste, colour, smell, sound etc., but is a pure, conscious and defectless being is 'I.'" 21.

"I am devoid of no-karmas (body etc.) karmas, and full of independent knowledge and other attributes: I am perfect, pure, eternal, one, and independent." 27.

Thus some quotations of Jain Literature have been given above in order to show how the soul is described in them from the real point of view. This is the pure soul and this is what is called *Nirvâna.* There is no difference between pure soul and *Nirvâna* at all.

## THE SOUL FROM THE PRACTICAL POINT OF VIEW.

From the practical point of view, the soul is described in connection with bondage of the material karmas. All the attributes and conditions which do appear through karmas are described. All this description of the soul from the practical stand-point does almost agree with that of the five *Skandhas* of the Buddhists. This impure condition of the soul is not its real nature. When this condition is destroyed, then *Nirvâna* is procured. This is what the Buddhist Literature says that when these skandhas which are destructible and are caused in connection with others are altogether destroyed, then *Nirvâna* is attained.

The Jain saint, Sri Nemichandra Acharya describes the nature of the soul in his *Dravya Samgraha* thus :—

**जीवो उवओगमआ अमुत्ति कत्ता सदेहपरिमाणो ।**
**भोत्ता संसारत्थो सिद्धो सो विस्ससोड्ढगई ॥ २ ॥**

*Jîvo uvaogamas amutti kattâ sadehaparimâno,*
*Bhattâ saṃsârattho siddho so vissasoḍḍha ai* (2).

The soul has nine characteristics. It is (1) living (2) has conscious attentiveness (3) is non-material (4) is the doer of actions (5) enjoyer of the fruits of actions (6) has the size of the body it occupies (7) wanders in the world (8) can become liberated (9) has the natural tendency to go upward.

We may describe these nine characteristics with some details, I. *Living*—The soul exists in any body on account of material vitalities, *Dravya Prana*, and dies when they are destroyed. They are ten in number, five senses, of touch, taste, smell, sight and hearing; three powers of body, speech and mind; age and breathing. They are found in different degrees in the different kinds of mundane beings as below :—

(1) One-sensed, beings such as earth-bodied, water-bodied, fire-bodied, air-bodied, and vegetable-bodied. They have got only one sense namely that of touch and have in all four vitalities, touch, physical power, age and breathing.

(2) Two-sensed beings such as insects of rice shell and conches etc. They have senses of touch and taste, and have six vitalities in all. Sense of taste and speech-power are added to the four of the one-sensed.

(3) Three-sensed beings such as ants, bugs, lice, etc., have three senses of touch, taste and smell and have seven vitalities. Sense of smell is added to the six of the former class.

(4) Four-sensed beings such as flies, wasps, bees, moths etc., have four senses of touch, taste, smell, and sight and have eight vitalities. Sense of sight is added to the seven of the former class.

(5) Five-sensed irrational beings such as some species of serpents which live in water; they have got all the five senses, and have nine vitalities, sense of hearing is added to the eight of the former class.

(6) Five-sensed rational beings such as human beings, celestial beings, hellish beings; four-legged animals like cows, buffaloes, deer, dogs, cats; birds, such as pigeons, peacocks, crows, parrots, and fishes, crocodile, tortoise, etc. They have got mind also in addition and thus have all the ten vitalities.

As the soul is really indestructible, injury to any of these vitalities is called *Himsa*. As a substance, matter is also indestructible, only dis-arrangement of material vitalities is the material injury. Passionate thought-activity is the internal cause of causing hurt to external vitalities. The number and value of vitalities injured, means lesser or greater sin. The least injury is caused in the destruction of one-sensed beings.

From the practical point of view, the soul is living on account of these vitalities. Really consciousness is the vitality which never leaves the soul.

II. Conscious-attentiveness—It is of two kinds :—Conation or perception and knowledge.

Conation is of four kinds :—(1) Conation through the eye (2) Conation through any sense other than the eye or mind, (3) Clairvoyant conation, (4) Infinite conation.

Knowledge is of eight kinds (1) *Mati Jnâna* is knowledge derived through the senses and mind

(2) *Śruta Jnâna* is knowledge derived through objects known by sensitive knowledge or the knowledge of the books.

(3) *Avadhi Jnâna* is knowledge of the past and the future lives through the psychic power of the soul.

(4) *Manah-paryaya Jnâna* is the knowledge of the ideas and thoughts of others.

(5) *Kevala Jnâna* is omniscience or knowledge unlimited as to space, time or object.

The first three kinds of knowledge when associated with right belief, are called right knowledge and when associated with wrong belief, they are called wrong knowledge. Thus there are eight kinds of knowledge. The living beings have got life, they are not dead—such recognition is done through any of these twelve kinds of conscious attentiveness. These are from the practical point of view. Pure conation and pure knowledge are the two real characteristics of a soul from the real point of view.

III. The soul is non-material from the real point of view, because it has not got colour, smell, taste and touch, the attributes of matter; but from the practical point of view, it appears as material in mundane life, because it is wholly obscured by the dirt of karmic matter. The worldly conditions and all impurities are due to the karmic effects. This impure condition is coming on from eternity, though new karmic matter is mixed and old one is shed off at every instant.

IV. *Doer* :—From the practical stand-point, it is said to be the doer of its impure thought-activities, delusion, love and hatred etc., which are really due to the operation of the material karmas bound previously. It is also called the doer of karmic bondage which is really effected owing to soul vibrations and passions. It is also called the doer of houses, pots, cloths, etc., as they are caused through the activities of its body, mind and speech. From the real point of view, the soul is the doer of its own pure thought-activities.

V. *Enjoyer*—From the practical point of view, it is the enjoyer of pleasure and pain caused by the effect of the past karmas. Really, it is the enjoyer of its own real bliss.

VI. *Has the size according to the body*—From the real point of view, it has innumerable spacial units equal to this universe, *i.e.*, it is as wide as the universe; but from the practical point of view, it contracts and expands according to the body it occupies owing to the effect of karmas; thus it has the size of the body it occupies. There are some special causes, when this mundane soul, while living in the body expands and goes to some distance like the electric current and then again contracts to the size of its original body. Its real size is not material, but it is a non-material conscious one.

VII. *It wanders in the world*:—This soul owing to the effects of its meritorious and demeritorious karmas wanders in the world in the four conditions of life, celestial, hellish, sub-human and human. Beings from one-sensed to five-sensed animals are all sub-human.

The Jain Literature has divided the mundane souls into two kinds also. (1) *Immobiles*—all one-sensed beings such as earth, water, fire, air and vegetable-bodied. (2) ***Mobiles***—All the others form the two-sensed to the five-sensed beings."

VIII. *It can be liberated.* When through self-concentration, all the karmic matter is shed off and all the causes of inflow of new matter are removed, then the soul becomes liberated and attains *Nirvâna.*

IX. *It has the nature of going upward.* From the real point of view, the nature of the soul is to go upward, like the flame of fire. When it is freed from karmas, it goes upward to the top of the universe. But when it is in bondage with the karmas, it goes after death from one incarnation to another instantly in straight directions, *i.e.*, east, west, south, north, upwards and downwards but not in cross lines. If the place of re-birth is in a crooked place, the soul will take turnings through straight directions and reach there. The readers will have some idea of the mundane souls from the above description.

*Panchâstikâya* by Sri Kunda Kunda Acharya says the same :—

**जीवोत्ति हवदि चेदा उपओगविसेसिदो पहु कत्ता ।**
**भोत्ता य देहमत्तो ण हि मुत्तो कम्मसंजुत्तो ॥ २७ ॥**

*Jivôtti havadi chédâ upavôga visêsidô pahu katta,*
*Bhôtta ya déhamattô nahi muttô kammasanjutto* 27.

"The soul is (1) living (2) realizer (3) has conscious attentiveness (4) lord of its destiny, responsible for its good or bad conditions (5) doer (6) enjoyer (7) having size according to the body it occupies (8) non-material (9) and is associated with karmas."

If we compare the actions of the five *Skandhas* of the Buddhists with the mundane condition of the soul in karmic bondage, its sensual and impure knowledge, feeling of pleasure and pain etc., we will come to the conclusion that Jainism and Buddhism are the same in this respect. The pure soul of Jainism agrees with the *Nirvâna* of the Buddhists. Although in the Buddhist literature, it is not clearly stated that any soul is coming on along with the five compound things, body, feeling, sensation, mentation, and (impure) consciousness, yet on deep consideration it will be noted that the positive thing which remains after the destruction of the five *skandhas* is *Nirvâna i.e.*, the pure soul. It means that what was hidden under the effects of the five *skandhas* has now appeared in its pure nature. The soul retains its pure nature of greatest peace and bliss for ever.

If *Nirvâna* is not annihilation, but a positive condition of existence, it must be taken to be nothing else but the pure soul as described in Jainism.

## CHAPTER III.

### THE PATH OF NIRVANA OR LIBERATION.

From the last two chapters, it will be evident to the readers that the nature of *Nirvâna*—the soul as is known from the Buddhist scripture is the same as described in the Jain literature. Now it is to be seen whether the path of *Nirvâna* as given in the Buddhist literature agrees with that of Jain literature or not.

*The path of Nirvâna in Buddhism.*

(1) Majjhim Nikâya Samme ditthi suttam (9).

**अयमेव आरियो अत्थंगिको मग्गो आसव निरोधगामिनि पटिपदा सेय्यथिदंः सम्मादिट्ठि, सम्मासंकप्पो, सम्मावाचा, सम्माकम्मंतो, सम्मा आजीवो, सम्मा वायामो, सम्मासति, सम्मा समाधि.**

I. "*Ayameva ariyo aṭṭhangiko maggo âsava nirôdhagâmini patipada—, seyyathidam: samma ditthi, samma sumkappo, samma vâchâ, samma kammanto. samma ajivo, samma vâyâmô, samma sati, samma samâdhi.*"

"Aryas! it is the eight-fold path which causes prevention of the *Âsavas*; it is this:—right view, right intention, right speech, right action, right livelihood, right effort, right mindfulness, right concentration."

Further this Sutta describes that in order to acquire right view, one should know the following things · -

**रतो खो आवसो आरिय सावको अकुसलं पजानाति अकुसल मूलं च पजानाति, कुसलं च पजानाति, कुसल मूलं च पजानाति कतमं अकुसलं, (१) पाणातिपातो, (२) अदिन्नादानं· (३) कामेसु मिच्छाचारो, (४) मुसावादो, (५) पिसुणावाचा (६) फरुसावाचा, (७) संकप्पलापो, (८) अभिज्झा, (९) व्यापादो, (१०) मिच्छादिट्ठि. कतमं अकुसल मूलं, (१) लोभो, (२) दोसो, (३) मोहो.**

" *Yato kho âvaso ariya savako akusalam pajanâti akusala mulam cha pajanâti, kusalam cha pajanâti, kusala mulam cha pajanâti...katamam akusalam:* (1) *paṇâ tipato* (2) *adinnâdânam* (3) *kâmesu michcha charo* (4) *musâvâdo* (5) *pisu ṇa vâchâ* (6) *pharusâ vâcha* (7) *sanphappa tapo* (8) *abhijjha* (9) *vyâpâdo* (10) *michchha diṭṭhi. Katamam akusala mulam,* (1) *lobho* (2) *doso* (3) *moho.*

" The Ariya *sravaka* knows what is harmful, what is the root of harmfulness, what is useful, what is the root of usefulness. The harmful are (ten) :—(1) injury to living beings (2) taking what is not given (3) wrong engagement in sexual gratification (4)· falsehood (5) back-biting (6) harsh speech (7) chatter (8) greed (9) enmity (10) wrong view. Their causes are temptation, hatred and delusion."

Their opposites are useful and the root of usefulness).

**आहारं पजानाति, आहारसमुदयंच पजानाति आहार निरोधंच पजानाति आहार निरोधपटिपदंच पजानातिः आहार चत्तारो कवलिकारो आहारो ओलरिकोवा सुखुमोवा फस्सो दुतियो मनो संचेतना ततियो विज्ञानं चतुत्थो तण्हसमुदयो आहार समुदयो तण्हनिरोधो आहार निरोधो अत्थंगिको मग्गो आहार निरोधगामिनि पटिपदा.**

*Āhâram pajânâti, âhâra samudayancha pajânâti, âhâranirodhancha pajânâti, âhârâ-nirodha paṭi. padancha pajânâti. âhâra chattaro :—Kavalikâro âhâro olarikova sukhumo va, phasso dutiyo, mano sanchetana tatiyo, vijnanam chatuttho, tanha samudayo âhâra samudayo, taṇha nirôdho âhâra nirôdho, atthangiko maggo âhâra nirôdha gâmini pati padâ.*"

"(A right believer) knows the nutriment, the cause of nutriment, the checking of nutriment, the means of checking nutriment. Nutriments are four :—Mouthful eating gross or fine, contact is the second, volition is the third, (impure) consciousness is the fourth. Rise of desire is the cause of nutriment, prevention of desire is prevention of nutriment, the means of prevention of nutriment is the eight-fold path (described above)."

*Note.* Āhâra is translated as nutriment by some, we may translate it as taking in or grasping.

*Note.* It is evident from the above description that when desire arises, the four kinds of taking in are possible *i.e.*, (1) taking in gross or subtle matter which is nutritious to the body, having contact with sense-objects for enjoyment, thought with regard to sense-enjoyment, and consciousness with regard to that enjoyment. When desire will be checked, there will be neither taking food, nor any enjoyment of senses, neither mental thought-activity pertaining to it, nor the consciousness regarding it. Cessation of desire is possible by following the eight-fold path of liberation.

**दुक्खंच पजानाति, दुक्खस्स समुदयंच पजानाति दुक्खनिरोधंच पजानाति दुक्ख निरोधगामिनी पटिपदं च पजानाति... कतमं दुक्खं (१) जातिपि दुक्खं (२) जरापि दुक्खं (३) व्याधिपि दुक्खं (४) मरणंपि दुक्खं (५) सोकपरिदेव दुक्खदोमनस्सुपायासा (६) यं च इच्छाति तं न लभतितंपि दुक्खं (७) पंच उपादान खंधा दुक्खं कतमं दुक्खसमुदयोः याइयं तण्हा पोनार्भविका नंदिराग सहमता तत्र तत्राभिनंदिनी सेय्यथिदं (१) कामतण्हा (२) भवतण्हा (३) विभवतण्हा । कतमो दुक्ख निरोधो :— योतस्सा एव तण्हाय असेस विराग निरोधो चागो पटिनिस्संगो मुक्ति अनालयो कतमदुक्ख निरोधगामिनी पटिपदा अट्ठंगिको मग्गो.**

"*Dûkkhamcha pajãnâti ; dukkhassa samuaayan cha pajânâti ; dukkha-nirodhancha pajânâti, dukkha-nirodha-gâmini-patipadancha pajânáti ;...Katuman dukkham* (1) *Jatipi dukkham,* (2) *Jarâpi dukkham,* (3) *vyâdhipi dukkham* (4) *maranampi dukkham* (5) *sôkapari deva-dukkha domanassupayasa* (6) *yam cha ichchhati tum na labhatitampi dukkham* (7) *pancha upadana khandha dukkham ; Katamam dukkha-samudayo :—ya iyam tanha ponârbhavika nandiraga sahagata, tatra tatrabhi nandinî ; seyyathidam :*—(1) *Kâma tanhâ* (2) *bhava tanhâ* (3) *vibhava tanhâ.*

*Katamo dukkha nirodha :—Yo tassa eva tanhâya asêsa virâga nirôdhô chago, pati-nissango mukti, anâlayô, ; katama dukkha-nirôdha-gâmini patipada-atthangiko maggo.*"

" (A right believer) knows the pain, the cause of the pain, the prevention of the pain, and the way to prevent the pain. What are the pains ? The pains are (1) birth (2) old-age (3) disease (4) death (5) sorrow, weeping, misery, sadness of mind, confusion (6) not to get the desired object (7) the five root-spheres of body, feeling, sensation, mentation, and consciousness.

The causes of the pain are desire to take re-birth, desire to have pleasure and welcoming the pleasures, just as (1) desire for sense-enjoyments (2) desire to have re-birth (3) desire to have riches or to be destroyed. The prevention of pain is to have total non-attachment with that desire, to check it, to give it up, to throw it off, to be liberated from it, not to be absorbed in it. The means for the prevention of pain is to follow the eight-fold path of liberation."

*Note.* In the Hindi Buddha Charya Page 124 Maha satipatthana sutta Dig. N. 2. 22 the description of the five spheres is given thus :—To have organs of touch, taste, smell, sight, and hearing is body-sphere or *rupa upâdâna* ; feeling of pleasure and pain on knowing the sense-object is feeling-sphere or *vedana upâdâna* ; to know sense-object is sensation-sphere or *sanjnâ upâdâna ;* having continual mental notions is mentation-sphere or *sanskara upâdâna* ; to sustain its knowledge is consciousness-sphere or *vijnâna upâdâna.*

**जरामरणंचपजानाति, जरामरण समुदयंच पजानाति, जरामरण निरोधंच पजानाति जरामरण निरोधगामिनी पटिपदंच पजानाति कतमं जरामरणं या तसं सत्तानं तंहि तंहि सत्तनिकाये जराजिरणता खंदिच्चं पालिच्चं बलितचता आयुनो संहानि इंदियानं परिपाको–अयं वुच्चतेजरा–यं तेसं तेसं सत्तानं तम्हा तम्हा सत्तानिकाया चुति चवनता भेदा अंतरधानं मच्चु मरणं कालकिरिया खंधानं भेदो कलेवरस्स. निक्खेपो इदं वुच्चतेमरणं। जाति समुदया जरामरण समुदयो जाति निरोधा जरामरण निरोधो. अयमेव अट्ठंगिको मग्गो जरामरण निरोध गामिनी पटिपदा.**

"*Jarâ marṇancha pajânâti, jara marana samudayancha pajânâti, jarâ marana nirodhamcha pajânâti jarâ marana nirodha-gâmini pati-padancha pajâ-nâti-Katamam jarâ maraṇam. Yâ tesam sattânam tamhi tamhi satta-nikâya jarâ jîraṇata, khandîchcham, pâlichcham balitta-chatâ, â yuno san-hâ-ni, indiyâ-nam paripâko, ayam vuchchata jarâ yam tesam tesam sattanam tamha tamha sattanikâyâ chuti chavanatâ bhedâ antaradhânam, machchu, maraṇam, kâla kiriyâ, khandhânam bhedo, kalevarassa nikkhepo idam vuchchate maranam. Jati samudayâ jarâ-marana samudayo jâti nirodhâ jarâ marana nirodho, ayameva atthangiko maggo jarâ marana nirodha gâmini pati padâ.*"

"(A right believer) knows old age and death, cause of old age and death, prevention of old age and death, means of prevention of old age and death. What are old age and death? While living in their own bodies, to have by those living beings oldness, infirmity, decay, white hair, wrinkles in body, ripening of sense-organs, approaching to destruction of age is called old age. To be thrown off the living beings from their respective bodies, to be separated from them, their vanishing away, dying, ending life-time, dissolution of the spheres, freedom from body is death.

Birth is the cause of old age and death. Prevention of birth is the prevention of old age and death. The means of prevention of old age and death is the afore-said eight-fold path of liberation."

(5) **जातिंच पजानाति जातिसमुदायंच पजानाति जाति निरोधंच पजानाति जातिनिरोध गामिनी पटिपदंच पजानाति— या तेसं तेसं सत्तानं तम्हि तम्हि सत्तनिकाये जाति संजाति ओक्कंति अभिनिब्बत्ति खधानं पाटभावो आयतनानां पटिलाभो अयं वुच्चते जाति भवसमुदया जातिसमुदयो भवनिरोधा जाति-निरोधो अयमेव अट्ठंगिको मग्गो जातिनिरोध गामिनी पटिपदा.**

"*Jâtincha pajânâti, jâti samudâyancha pajânâti-jati nirodhancha pajânâti, jâti-nirodha-gâmini-patipadam cha pajânâti.*

*Ya tesam tesam sattânam tamhi tamhi sattanikaye jati sanjati ; Okkanti, abhinivvatti, khandhânam pâtabhâvo, âyatânâm pati lâbho, ayam vuchchate jati, bhavo-samudayâ jati samudayo, bhava nirodhâ jati nirodho-ayameva atthangiko maggo jâti nirodha gâmini pati padâ*

" (A right believer) knows the birth, the cause of birth, prevention of birth, the means of prevention of birth. To take birth of the living beings in their own respective bodies, to grow, to rise, to appear in spheres, to have sense-organs is birth.

Becoming or condition of existence is the cause of birth, prevention of condition of existence is the prevention of birth. The means of its prevention is the eightfold path of liberation."

(6) **भवंच पजानाति, भवसमुदयंच पजानाति भवनिरोधंच पजानाति भवनिरोधगामिनी पाटिपदंच पजानाति तया इमे भवा काम भवो रूपभवो अरूपभवो उपादानसमुदया भवसमुदयो उपादान निरोधा भवनिरोधो अयमेव अट्ठंगिको मग्गो भवनिरोधगामिनी पाटिपदा.**

*Bhavancha pajânâti, bhava-samudayancha pajânâti, bhava-nirodhancha pajânâti, bhava-nirôdha gâmini pati padamcha pajânâti, tayâ ime bhavâh-kâma bhavo, rûpa bhavo, arûpa bhavo, upâdâna samudayâ bhava-samudayo, upâdâna-nirodhâ bhava nirodho, ayameva atthangiko maggo bhava-nirodha-gâmini pati padâ."*

(A right believer) knows the condition of existence, cause of condition of existence, prevention of condition of existence, the means of prevention of condition of existence. There are three kinds of conditions of existence: (1) sexual enjoyment–condition of existence (all the conditions of sub-human, human, hellish and celestial till the state they have got sexual desire). (2) body–condition of existence (The sixteen *Brahma lokas*, where there are bodies but no sexual desire). (3) bodiless–condition of existence (they are four where there is no gross body).

Grasping is the condition of existence; prevention of grasping is the prevention of condition of existence. The means of prevention of condition of existence is the afore-said eight-fold path of liberation.

(7) **उपादानंच पजानाति उपादानसमुदयंच पजानाति उपादान निरोधंच पजानाति उपादाननिरोध गामिनी पटिपदंच-पजानाति उपादानं चत्तारोः (१) काम (२) दिट्ठि (३) सीलब्बत (४) अत्तबात तण्हा समुदया उपादानसुमुदयो तण्हा निरोधा उपाधाननिरोधो अयमेव अट्ठंगिको मग्गो उपादान निरोधगा-मिनी पटिपदं.**

"*Upâdânancha pajânâti, upâdâna samudayancha pajânâti, upâdâna nirodhancha pajânâti, upâdâna-nirodha gâmini paṭi padamcha pajânâti. upâdânam chattâro: (1) Kâma (2) diṭṭhi (3) sîlabbâta (4) atta bâta. Tanha samudayâ upâdâna samudayo; Taṇhâ nirodha upâdâna nirodho, ayameva aṭṭhangiko maggo upâdâna nirodha gâmini paṭi padam.*"

"(A right-believer) knows the grasping, the cause of grasping, the prevention of grasping, the means of prevention of grasping. Graspings are four: (1) grasping of sense-desires (2) grasping of speculative opinion (3) grasping in rules and rituals (4) grasping in theory of the self. (wrong view of the self taking the non-self to be the self).

Desire is the cause of grasping. Cessation of desire is the prevention of grasping. The means of the prevention of grasping is the eight-fold path of liberation."

(8) **तण्हंच पजानाति तण्हासमुदयंच पजानाति तण्हा निरोधंच पजानाति तण्हा निरोध गामिनी पटिपदंच पजानाति छय इमे तण्हा (१) रूप (२) सद्द (३) गंध (४) रस (५) फोत्थ (६) धम्मा वेदना समुदया तण्हा समुदया वेदनानिरोधा तण्हा निरोधो अयमेव अट्ठंगिको मग्गो तण्हानिरोधगामिनी पटिपदा.**

*Taṇham cha pajânâti ; taṇha samudâyancha pajânâti tanha nirôdhancha pajânâti, tanha nirodha gâmini paṭi padaṃcha pajânâti, chhaya ime tanha* (1) ***rûpa*** (2) ***sadda*** (3) ***gandha*** (4) ***rasa*** (5) ***phoṭṭha*** (6) ***dhamma vedanâ-samudayâ taṇha samudayo, vedana-nirodhā taṇha-nirodho, ayameva atthangiko maggo tanha nirodha gâmini paṭi padâ.***"

"(A right-believer) knows the desire, the cause of desire, the cessation of desire, the means of cessation of desire. There are six kinds of desires:—(1) of seeing colours or forms (2) of hearing sounds (3) of smelling

(4) of tasting (5) of touching (6) of mental states Rising of feeling is the cause of desire; cessation of feeling is the cessation of desire; the means of the cessation of desire is the eight-fold path of liberation."

(9) **वेदनंच पजानाति वेदनासमुदयंच पजानाति वेदाना निरोधंच पजानाति वेदनानिरोधगामिनी पटिपदंच पजानाति छ इमे वेदनाकाया (१) चक्खु संफस्सजा बेदना (२) सोत संफ-स्सजा (३) घाण संफस्सजा (४) जिहवा संफस्सजा (५) काय संफस्सजा (६) मनो संफस्सजा फस्स समुदया वेदना समुदयो फस्स निरोधा वेदना निरोधो अयमेव अट्ठंगिको मग्गो वेदना-निरोध गामिनी पटिपदा.**

"*Vedanancha pajânạti, vedanâ samudayancha pajânâti; vedanâ nirodhancha pajânâti; vedana nirodha-gâmini pati padancha pajânâti: chhaya ime vedanâ kâyâ* (1) ***chakkhu samphassajâ vedana*** (2) *sota samphassaja* (3) ***ghâṇa samphassaja*** (4) ***Jihvâ samphassaja*** (5) ***Kâya samphassajâ*** (6) ***mano-samphassajâ. Phassa samudaya vedanâ samudayo, phassa nirodhâ vedanâ nirodho, ayameva atthingiko maggo vedanâ nirodha gâmini paṭi pada.***"

"(A right believer) knows the feeling, the cause of the feeling, the cessation of the feeling and the means of the cessation of the feeling. These six are the feeling-spheres:—(1) feeling due to contact with eye (2) due to contact with ear (3) due to contact with nose (4) due to contact with the tongue (5) due to contact with the body (6) due to contact with the mind. Rise of contact is the cause of feeling; prevention of contact is the cessation of feeling, the eight-fold path is the means of the cessation of feeling."

(10) **फस्संच पजानाति फस्ससमुदयंच पजानाति फस्सनिरोधंच पजानाति फस्सनिरोधगामिनी पटिपदंच पजानाति छय इमे पस्सकाया (१) चक्खु संफस्सो (२) सोत संफस्सो (३) घानं संफस्सो (४) जिह्वा संफस्सो (५) काय संफस्सो (६) मनो संफस्सो सलायतन समुदया फस्स समुदयो सलायतन तिरोधो फस्स निरोधो अयमेव अट्ठंगिको मग्गो फस्सनिरोधगामिनी पटिपदा.**

"*Phassancha pajânâti phassa samudâyâncha pajânati; phassa nirodhancha pajânâti, phassa nirodha-gâmini paṭi padân cha pajânâti chhaya ime phassa-kâyâ* :—(1) *chakku samphassô* (2) *sota samphasso* (3) *ghâna samphassô* (4) *jihva samphassô* (5) *kâya samphasso* (6) *mano samphasso satâ yatana samudayâ phassa samudayo, salâyatana nirodho, phassa nirodho, ayameva atthangiko maggo phassa-nirôdha-gâmini paṭi padâ.*"

"(A right-believer) knows the contact, the cause of the contact, the prevention of the contact, and the means of the prevention of the contact. These six are the contact spheres :—(1) contact of eye (2) of ear (3) of nose (4) of tongue (5) of body and (6) of the mind. Rise of six organs is the cause of contact; prevention of six organs is the prevention of the contact, this eight-fold path is the means of the prevention of the contact."

(11) **सतायतनच्चं पजानाति सतायतन समुदयंच पजा-नाति सतायतन निरोधंच्च पजानाति सतायतन निरोधगामिनी पटिपदंच्च पजानाति छय इमे आयतनानि (१) चख्खु (२) सोत (३) धान (४) जिह्वा (५) काय (६) मनो. नामरूप समुदया सतायतने समुदयोः नामरूप निरोधा सतायतन निरोधो अय-मेव अट्ठंगिको मग्गो सतायतन निरोध गामिनी पटिपदा.**

*Satâyatanancha pajânâti, satâyatana samudayan, cha pajânâti, satâyatana nirodhancha pajânâti, satâ yatana-nirodha-gâmini pati padamcha pajânâti ; chhaya ime âyatanâni* :—(1) *chakkhu* (2) *sota* (3) *ghâna* (4) *jihvâ* (5) *kâya* (6) *mano. Nâmarûpa samudayâ satâyatana samudayo Nama rupa* " *nirodha satâyatana-nirodho-ayameva atthangiko maggo satâyatana-nirodha-gâmini pati pada* ".

" (A right believer) knows the six organs, cause of the six organs, cessation of six organs, means of cessation of six organs.

These six organs are :—(1) eye (2) ear (3) nose (4) tongue (5) body (6) mind. Rise of mental and material body is the cause of six organs. The cessation of mental and material body is the prevention of six organs, this eight-fold path is the means of the prevention of six organs."

*Note.—The Doctrine of the Buddha* by George Grimm says, " By *rupa* he means body consisting of inorganic matter and by *nâma* the faculty of sensation, perception, of thought, of contact, of attention and so on. The meaning of *nâma rupa* is that of a body capable of life. *Nâma rupa* is six-sense-machine. *Nama kaya*—mental body. *Rupa kaya*—material body."

(12) **नामरूपंच पजानाति नामरूप समुदयंच पजानाति नामरूप निरोधंच पजानाति नामरूप निरोधगामिनी पटिपदंच पजानाति वेदना, संज्ञा, चेतना, फस्सो मनसिकरो इदं वुच्चतेनाम चत्तारि महा भूतानि चतुनंच महा भूतानि उपादाय रूपं बिज्ञान सुमुदया नामरूप समुदयो विज्ञान निरोधा नामरूप निरोधो अयमेव अट्ठंगिको मग्गो नामरूप निरोध गामिनी पटिपदा.**

"*Nâma rupancha pajânâti, nâma rupa-samudayancha pajânâti, nâma rupa nirodhancha pajâ nâti, nama rupa nirodha-gâmini paṭi padancha pajâ nâti, vedanâ, sanjnâ, chetanâ, phasso, manasi-kâro, idum vuchchate nâma ; chattari mahâ bhutani, chatunnam cha maha bhutani upâdâya rûpam, vijnâna samudayâ nâmarûpa samudayo, vijnâna nirodhâ nâma rûpa nirodho, ayameva aṭṭhangiko maggo nâma rûpo nirodha gâmini paṭi pada.*"

"(A right believer) knows the *nâma rupa*, the cause of *nâma rupa*, the cessation of *nâma rupa*, the means of cessation of *nâma rupa*. Feeling, perception, thought, contact, mind-notions are called *nâma*. The four great elements are earth, water, fire and air. The body is due to these four elements. The rise of consciousness is the cause of *nâma rupa*. The cessation of consciousness is the cessation of *Nâma rupa.* This eight-fold path is the means of the cessation of *nâma rupa.*

*Note.*—Here the *nâma* of the Buddhist philosophy includes all the worldly conscious thought-activities and impure knowledge. *Nâma rupa* means a group of all the worldly conditions. According to the Jain literature also all the impure modifications of body and consciousness of the soul are what is called the world. The destruction of all this world is *Nirvana* just as destruction of *Nâma rupa* is *Nirvâna* in the Buddhist philosophy. Both the Jain and the Buddhist philosophies are agreed upon this point with difference only in name.

**विज्ञानंच पजानाति विज्ञान समुदयंच पजानाति विज्ञान-निरोधंच पज्ञानाति विज्ञान निरोधगामिनि पटिपदंच पजानाति छयइमे विज्ञान काया (१) चक्खु विज्ञानं (२) सोत विज्ञानं (३) धान विज्ञानं (४) जिहवा विज्ञानं (५) काय विज्ञानं (६) मनो यिज्ञानं संखारसमुदया विज्ञान समुदया संखार निरोधा विज्ञान निरोधो अयमेव अट्ठंगीको मग्गो विज्ञान निरोध गामिनि पटिपदा.**

"*Vijṇânancha pajânâti vijṇâna samudayancha pajânâti, vijṇâna nirodhamcha pajânâti, vijnana-nirodha-gamini pati padancha pajânâti; chhaya ime vijṇâna kâyâ (1) chakkhu vijnânam (2) sota vijṇânam (3) ghâna vijṇânam (4) jihva vijṇânam (5) kâyâ vijṇânam (6) mano vijṇânam Sankara samudaya vijnâna samudayo, sankara nirodho, vijnâna-nirodho ayameva atthangiko maggo vijnana nirodha-gamini pati pada.*"

(A right believer) knows the (impure) consciousness, the cause of the consciousness, the cessation of the consciousness, the means of the cessation of the consciousness. These six are the spheres of consciousness: (1) consciousness due to eye (2) to ear (3) to nose (4) to tongue (5) to body and (6) to mind. Rise of mentations is the cause of consciousness, cessation of mentations is the cessation of consciousness. The eight-fold way is the means of cessation of consciousness.

*Note.*—Here *sankhâra* is translated as mentations, while Woodward in his book "Some Sayings of the Buddha" translates sankhâra as activities which make karmas. It appears that this *sankhâra* or *sanskara* is the link of acquisition of (impure) consciousness in the fresh body. This *sanskhara* may be taken to be the group of past karmas.

**संखारंच पजानाति संखारसमुदयंच पजानाति संखार निरोधंच पजानाति संखार निरोध गामिनी पटिपदंच पजानाति तयो इमे संखार (१) काय संखार (२) वाचि संखार (३) चित्त संखार अविज्जसमुदया संखार समुदयो अविज्जनिरोध संखार निरोधो अयमेव अट्ठंगीको मग्गो संखारनिरोध गामिनी पटिपदा.**

(14) "*Sankhârancha pajânâti, sankhâra-samudayancha pajânâti, sankhâra-nirodhancha pajânâti,*

*sankhara-nirodha-gâmini pati padan cha pajâ nâti, tayo ime sankhârâ :—(1) Kâya sankhâro (2) vachi sankhâro (3) chitta sankharo Avijjâ samudaya sankhârâ-samudayo, avijja-nirodha sankharâ-nirodho, ayameva atthangiko maggo sankhara-nirodha-gâmini pati-padâ.*"

"(A right believer) knows the *sanskara*, the cause of *sanskara*, the cessation of *sanskara*, the means of the cessation of *sanskara*. These three are the *sanskaras*: (1) body *sanskara* (2) speech sanskara (3) mind sanskara. Rise of ignorance is the cause of *sanskara*. Cessation of ignorance is the cessation of *sanskara*. This eight-fold path is the means of cessation of *sanskara*."

(15) **अविज्जंच्च पजानाति अविज्जसमुदयंच्च पजानाति अविज्जानिरोधंच्च पजानाति आवज्जानिरोधगामिनी पटिपदंच्च पजानाति दुःखे अज्ञानं दुक्खसमुदये अज्ञानं दुक्ख निरोधे अज्ञानं दुःख निरोध गामिनी पटिपदाय अज्ञानं अयं वुच्चते अविज्जा आसव समुदया अविज्जासमुदयो आसव निरोधा अविज्जानिरोधो अयंच्च अट्टंगिको मग्गो अविज्जानिरोधगामिनी पटिपदा.**

"*Avijjancha pajânâti; avijja samudayancha pajânâti, avijja-nirodhancha pajânâti, avijja-nirodha-gâmini pati padancha pajânâti dukkhe ajnanam, dukkha samudaya ajnanam dukkhe-nirodhe-ajnanam, dukkha-nirodha-gamini pati padâya ajnanam ayam vuchchate avijja âsava samudayâ avijja samudayo âsava-nirodha avijja-nirodho, ayam cha atthangiko maggo avijja-nirodhe gamini pati pada.*"

(A right believer) knows the ignorance, the cause of ignorance, the cessation of ignorance, the means of the cessation of ignorance, 'not knowing what is pain, what is the cause of pain, what is the cessation of pain, what is the means of cessation of pain is ignorance. Rise of *āsavas* (impure thoughts) is the cause of ignorance, cessation of *āsava* is the cessation of ignorance. This eight-fold path is the means of the cessation of ignorance.

(16) **आसवंच पजानाति आसव समुदयंच पजानाति आसव निरोधंच पजानाति आसवनिरोधगामिनी पटिपदंच पजानाति तयो इमे आसवोः—कामासवो, भवासवो अविज्जासवो अविज्जासमुदया आसवसमुदयो अविज्जानिरोधा आसवानिरोधो अयं अट्ठंगिको मग्गो आसवनिरोध गामिनी पटिपदा......एवं आसव निरोधगामिनी पटिपदंच पजानाति सो सब्बसो रागानुसयं पहाय पटिधानुसयं पटिविनोदेत्वा अस्मीति दिट्ठि मानानुसयं सम्मूहनित्वा अविज्जं पहाय विज्जं उप्पादेत्वा दिट्ठेव धम्मे दुक्खस्स अंतकरो होति एत्तावता आरियसवको सम्मादिट्ठिहोति उजुगताऽस्स दिट्ठि अवेचप्पसादेन समन्नागतो आगतो इमं सद्धम्मं ति ।**

"*Āsavancha pajânâti, âsava-samudayancha pajâ nâti, âsavanirodhancha pajânâti; âsava-nirodha-gamini pati padancha pajânâti Tayo ime âsavâ:—Kâmasavo, bhavâsavo, avijjâsavo, avijja samudayâ âsava samu-*

*dayo ; avijjâ nirodha-asava-nirodho, ayameva atthangiko maggo âsava nirodha-gâmini pati padâ.........Evam âsava-nirodha-gâmini patipadam pajânati, so savvaso râgânusayam pahâya patighânusayam pati vino detvâ asmiti ditthi mânânusayam sammu hanitwa avijjam pahâya, vijjam uppadetwâ dittheva dhamme dukkhassa antakaro hoti-ettâvatâ ariya sâvako samma-ditthi hoti ujagatâ ssa ditthi avechap pasâdena saman-nâgato, âgato imam saddhammam ti.*"

"(A right believer) knows the *âsavas*, the cause of the *âsavas*, the cessation of the *âsavas*, the means of the cessation of the *âsavas*. There are three *âsavas* :— sense desire. desire of birth, entanglement in ignorance. Rise of ignorance is the cause of *âsavas*. Cessation of ignorance is the cessation of *âsavas*. This eight-fold path is the means of the cessation of the *âsavas*. Thus he, who knows the path of the cessation of the *âsavas*, having removed the dirt of attachment, has destroyed the dirt of hatred, having removed this pride of "I am" (such and such), having cut off ignorance, having acquired knowledge, ends the miseries even in this very life. Thus an Ârya *srâvaka* is a right believer, and his view becomes right, he maintains firm belief, and he knows this *True Dharma* (the Path of Liberation)."

*Note.*—This samma ditthi sutta describes the means of checking the following things :—(we may count the thirteen things from reverse side)—(1) *âsavas* (2) ignorance (3) *sanskâra* of mind, body and speech

(4) six spheres of consciousness (5) *nâma rupa*, (6) six sense-organs (7) six sense-contacts (8) six sense-feelings (9) desire for six sensual objects (10) four graspings (11) condition of existence (12) birth (13) old age and death. These thirteen things are in succession the cause of the following.

In this sutta, firstly (ten) 10 harmful and 10 useful natures, then four kinds of nutriment have been said. Desire has been said to be the cause of four kinds of nutriment. Then seven kinds of pain have been said and there cause is assigned to three kinds of desire. A right believer should know all these rightly.

It should also be considered here that *âsavas* have been said to be the cause of the remaining twelve things said above in succession and those *âsavas* are three: (1) desire for senses, desire for birth, and entanglement in ignorance. Again ignorance alone is said to be the cause of these three kinds of *âsavas*. It therefore shows that ignorance is the cause of *âsavas* and *âsavas* are the causes of ignorance.

Not to know pain, cause of pain, cessation of pain and means of cessation of pain is ignorance. Pains are seven in number: (1) birth (2) oldness (3) desease (4) death (5) sorrow, weeping etc. (6) not to have the desired things and (7) five root-spheres of body, feeling, sensation, mentation and consciousness.

The cause of these pains has been said to be ***desire.*** That desire is of three kinds: desire for sense-enjoyments, desire for birth, and desire for riches or for not taking birth. If desire is destroyed, all pains are ended.

The purport of all this above description is this that ignorance is the root-cause of constant wanderings in the world. The means of removing ignorance and with it, all its family is to follow the ***eight-fold path.***

The Buddhist literature is full of references to this Path.

*Buddha Charya Hindi* page 126 Maha suti patthana sutta of D. N. 2 : 22.

From the above Hindi description this 8 fold path is described below:—

" (1) *Samyak dristi*—To know rightly and with full belief—the pain, its cause, its prevention and means of its prevention.

(2) *Samyak sankalpa*—firm determination of being rid of ***karmas***, of being free from enmity, of following non-injury.

(3) *Samyak Vachana*—to give up falsehood, back-biting, harsh speech and chattering.

(4) *Samyak Karmânta*—to save himself from injury to living beings, from taking anything not given, from wrong sexual enjoyment.

(5) *Samyak Ājiva*—to have right livelihood and to relinquish unjust one.

(6) *Samyak Vyayâma*—to strongly resolve, try, labour, and control for not having harmful thought-activities which have not yet arisen, to resolve etc. to give up the harmful thought-activities already arisen, to resolve etc. to have useful thought-activities which have not arisen, and to resolve and labour for maintaining the useful thought-activities which have already arisen, and to improve them, meditate upon them, and to lead them to perfection.

(7) *Samyak Smriti*—remembrance of the impurity etc. of the body and not to have grief or greed for it. In the same way having recollection of truth of feelings, mind-notions and other conditions.

(8) *Samyak Samâdhi*—Here the Monk, having freed himself from sense-desires and harmful thought-activities meditates upon the first kind of concentration which is full of love and happiness having been produced by right argument, right thinking and self-discrimination, (2) then he, on getting subsidence of argument and thinking, acquires the second kind of concentration full of love and happiness caused by internal peace, steadiness of mind, freedom from intellect and thinking and self-absorption, (3) then he, on being non-attached to any sort of love, and on having recollection of truth and being experienced, acquires the third kind of concentration in which happiness is realized. Such a monk is called non-attached, full of recollection and walker in happiness by the learned, (4) and then at last

he, on giving up pleasure and pain, on removal of good and bad mentality, acquires the fourth concentration which is without pain, without pleasure, full of purity of recollection of non-attachment or *equanimity*."

It is necessary to know more about the 7th path *Samyak Smriti*, therefore it is described as below :—

Majjhim Nikâya tenth sutta Satipatthâna. Its purport is here given :

**भगवा एतदवोचः—एकायनो अयं मग्गो सत्तानं विसुद्धिया सोकपरिदवानं समातिक्कमाय दुक्खदोमनस्सानं अत्थ गमाय ञायस्स अधिगमाय निब्बानस्स सक्खिकिरियाय यदिदं चत्तारो सति पट्ठाना कतमे चत्तारो इध भिक्खवे (१) काये कायानुपस्सी विहरति आतापी संपजानो सतिमा विनेय्यलोके अभिज्झादोमण्स्सं ; (२) वेदनासु वेदनानुपस्सी विहरति. आतापी (३) चित्ते चित्तानुपस्सी विहरति आतापी (४) धम्मेसु धम्मानुपस्सी विहरति आतापी.**

"*Bhagavâ etadavocha :—Ekâyano ayam maggo, sattánam visuddhiyâ soka paridavânam samati kkamâya, dukkha domanassânam attha gamâya, jhayassa adhigamâya, nibbanassa* saksi*kiriyaya, yadidam chattaro satipatthana-Katame chattaro :—idha bhikkhave (1) Kâye Kayanu-passi viharati, âtâpi, sampajâno, satimâ, vineyya loke abhijjha do-manassam; (2) Vedanâsu vedananupassi viharati âtâpi......(3) chitte chittanupassi viharati âtâpi.........; (4) dhammesu dhammanupassi viharati âtâpi.........*"

*Bhagavan* said thus :—This is the one path for the purification of the beings, for removal of sorrow, weeping etc., for casting away pain and mental griefs, for knowing the truth, for realizing *Nirvana*,—and that is the four kinds of steadfastness in recollections :—What are the four ?—The monk roams seeing his body as body only, knowing feelings as feelings only, seeing mind as mind only, knowing different conditions as conditions only. He must be active, conscious, full of recollection, removing greed and mental bad thought-activities. The mode of recollection of these four has been given in the sutta in detail, here its translation in short is given :—

I. Meditation upon the body :

(1) The monk, having entered into a forest and sitting in a posture (Palyankâṣana) attends to his mouth; when breathing strong or mild, he may know it such and think that this body has nature of the rise and decay, one should have no attachment with it. There is nothing in this body which is liable of being adopted.

(2) When walking, standing, sitting, sleeping, or in any kind of movement of body, the monk should always be careful.

(3) When going near or far, seeing here and there, spreading arms and legs, wearing clothes, taking four kinds of food as eatable, drinkable, tastable, and lickable, casting away refuse, sleeping, awaking, speaking and in

silence etc. activities, the monks should be aware of all these and be careful in them.

(4) Then the monk may meditate that this body from head to foot, from foot to head is altogether full of filth, bones, blood, flesh, fat, perspiration, spitting, filth of nose, impurities etc.; just as a soak is full of different kinds of corn-seeds, a clever man knows them separately as pulse, rice, wheat etc., so he may know the nature of every part of the body separately.

(5) Then he meditates that this body is made up of the elements earth, water, fire and air.

(6) Then he thinks that this body is sure to be destroyed once and to become a dead body.

(7) Then he considers that this body when dead is liable of being eaten by eagles, crows etc.

(8) Then he meditates that the body when dead will be broken into parts of head, legs, arms etc. separately.

Then he thinks that this body will once be grounded and mixed into ashes.

Thus he becomes unattached with the body.

II. Meditation upon feelings :—

The monk knows, when he is feeling pleasure or pain and when there is neither pleasure nor pain. He properly ascertains the nature of the world pleasure and pain, strong and mild and also knows their internal and external features and their causes—knowing thus disinterestedly, he does not believe them to be useful.

III. *Meditation upon mind.*

The monk knows the attached mind as the attached one and non-attached mind as non-attached one, the mind with hate as one with hate and mind without hate as one without hate, the deluded mind as one with delusion, the delusionless mind as one without delusion; the steady mind as the steady and unsteady mind as unsteady; the mind in grandeur as in grandeur and the mind without grandeur as without grandeur. In the same way he recognises the charitable mind, uncharitable mind, peaceful mind, non-peaceful mind, passionless mind, passionful mind,—whatever be the nature of mind, he knows its internal and external features—knowing thus the nature of the thing, he does not identify any one with himself and does not grasp any one in this universe.

IV. *Meditation upon the nature of conditions.*

1. Meditation upon the five impurities (Nivarana):—(1) Sensual desire (2) enmity (3) dullness (4) restlessness and grief (5) doubt. Concerning these five, the monk meditates if they are found in him or not. If they are found, he knows such; if they are not found, he knows such; if they are not in him, he recognises how they can be produced; and if they are in him, he knows how to get rid of them. He also knows the way how not to let them again re-appear on their once disappearance. He is properly aware with the internal'

and external features of these five impurities. He knows the way how they arise and how they are destroyed.

2. Meditation upon five root spheres.

(*Upadana skhandha*).

The monk recognizes the nature, the cause of arising, and the cause of destruction with regard to body, feeling, sensation, mentation and consciousness. He knows their internal and external feature.

3. *Meditation upon the six internal and external sense-organs* (*âyatana*).

The monk recognizes the eye, the object known through the eye, and the impurity of attachment produced in connection with these two; he also knows how the attachment can arise and how to destroy it if it has arisen, also knows the way how it may not again rise after its destruction once. In the same way, he recognizes all about ear, nose, tongue, body and mind.

4. *Meditation upon seven modes of attaining true knowledge* (*Bodhi anga*).

The monk recognizes if he has within himself the recollection of true knowledge; if he has it, he knows such; if he has it not, he knows such. He also knows how to produce it if it is not in him, and how to keep it firmly if it has arisen in him, and how to advance it to its completion. In the same way he meditates upon the other six modes (1) thought of *Dharma* or piety (2) energy (3) love (4) peacefulness (5) equanimity or concentration (6) non-attachment.

5. *Meditation on four Arya truths.*

The monk rightly knows the nature of pain, its cause, cessation of pain and the *means* of cessation of pain.

As to the 8th path *Samyak Samadhi* four kinds of concentration have been mentioned. But there are other concentrations also after them. For them see *Majjhim Nikaya* 8th *sallekhana sutta*.

The other improved concentrations according to Sallekhana sutta are the following :—

(1) *Ākâsa-ânantya-âyatana*, to have concentration on pure infinite space.

(2) *Vijhâna-ânantya-âyatana*—to have concentration on infinite consciousness.

(3) *Ākinchanya âyatana*—to have concentration that nothing belongs to me.

(4) *Naiva Sanjnâ nâ sanjnâ âyatana* to concentrate that there is neither name nor any nameless, neither any sensation nor any non-sensation. This last concentration leads to *Nirvâna*, it appears.

As has been said above, the root cause of worldly wanderings is *ignorance*. We may give some more quotations from the Buddhist works to show the ***path of Nirvâna.***

(4) "The doctrine of the Buddha" by George Grimm, page 287-288. Ignorance is the basis of the whole chain of suffering. Ignorance is the deep night where-in we here so long are circling round (sutta nipâta on P. 730).

If ignorance is abolished, thirst and together with it all causuality is up-rooted for ever, those who have vanquished delusion, and broken through the dense darkness, will wander no more. Causuality exists no more for them (Itivuttaka 114). In dependence on ignorance *avidya*, arises organic process of senses; in dependence on them, arises consciousness *vijnâna*; in dependence on *vijnâna* arises corporeal organization *Nâmarupa*, in dependence on *Nâmarupa* arises six organs of sense *Sata âyatana*, then contact *phasa*, then sensation *Vedana*, then thirst *trisna*, then grasping *upadana*, then becomig *bhava*, then birth *jati*, then old age, death, sorrow, lamentation, pain, grief, despair (Udan I 37).

*Note.*—The eight-fold path described above has its root beginning with *Samyak-darsana*, right view.

The correct view is the very first element of the path constructed by the Buddha for the annihilation of suffering. He himself calls it ditthi or right view.

The same book shows the necessity of right concentration p. 394, Contemplating and contemplating we will purify our deeds; contemplating and contemplating we will purify our thoughts. Thus Rahula, you ought to exercise yourself (M. I. P. 420).

(5) Sacred Books of the East (1881) Vol. X, *Translation of Dhammapada.*

The path of Nirvâna is said in Chapter XX. Page 273. The best of way is the eight-fold; the best of truths, the four words (pain, its origin, its destruction, its way); the best of virtues passionlessness; the best of me–he who has eyes to see.

Page 276, You yourself make an effort. The Tathagatas are only preachers. The thoughtful who enter the way are freed from the bondage of *Mara.*

Page 277. All created things perish; he who knows and sees this, becomes passive in pain; this is the way of purity.

Page 308. He alone who, without ceasing practices the duty of sitting alone, and sleeping alone, subdues himself, will rejoice in the destruction of all desires alone, as if living in a forest.

(6) *Sutta Nipâta* translated by V. Fausböll (1881).

I. *Kâsi bharadvâja Sutta.*

(2) Bhagwan said:—

"Faith is the seed, penance the rain, understanding my yoke and plough, modesty the pole of the plough, mind the tie, thoughtfulness my ploughshare and goad.

(3) I am guarded in respect of the body, I am guarded in respect of speech, temperate in food ; I make truth to cut away (weeds), tenderness is my deliverance.

(4) Exertion is my beast of burden, carrying (me) to *nibbana*, he goes without turning back to the place, where having gone, one does not grieve.

(5) So the ploughing is ploughed, it bears the fruit of immortality, having ploughed this ploughing one is freed from pain."

II. Kulavagga (1) Uttham Sutta 4/333. Indolence (*Pamâda*) is defilement, continued indolence is defilement, by earnestness (*appamâda*) and knowledge let one pull out his arrow.

(6) Garâ sutta (attha vagga IV).

9/812. As a drop of water does not stick to a lotus, so the muni does not cling to anything, namely to what is seen, heard or thought.

The Pali words are :—

**ऊदविंदु यथापि पोक्खरें पदमे यथापि न लिप्पाति एवं मुनीनोपलिप्पाति यत इदं दिट्ठसुतं मुतेसु वा.**

*Uda vindu yathâpi pokkhare-padme yâthâpi na lippati,*

*Evam muni nopalippati yata idam dittha sutam mutesu vâ.*

III. Tuvaluka sutta.

2/916. Let him completely cut off the root of what is called *Papancha* (delusion), thinking "I am wisdom " so said Bhagawata—'all the desires that arise inwardly, let him learn to subdue them, always being thoughtful.'

6/920. As in the depth of the sea, no wave is born, (but as it) remains still, so let the Bikkhu be still, without desire, let him not desire anything whatever.

V. Parayan vagga (4) Pannava manava pukkha.

6/1047. Having considered everything in the world, O Pannava, so said Bhaghavata,—he who is not defeated anywhere in the world, who is calm without the smoke of passions, free from woe, free from desire, he crosses over birth and old age.

(14) Udaya manava pukkha.

3/1106. The deliverance by knowledge, which is purified by equanimity and thoughtfulness and preceded by reasoning or *Dhamma*, I will tell thee the splitting of *ignorance.*

Its Pali text is:—

**उपेक्खासति संसुद्धं धम्म तक्कपुरेजवां अण्णा विमोक्खं प्राब्रूमि अविज्जाय पभेदनं.**

***Upekkha sati sansudham, Dhamma takka pure javam, aṇṇâ vimokkham prabru mi, avijjâya pabhedanam.***

(15) Altadanda sutta (atthakavagga).

20/984. " The muni does not reckon himself amongst the plain, nor amongst the low, nor amongst the distinguished; being calm and freed from avarice, he does not grasp after, nor reject anything."

(7) " Path of Purity " Visuddhi Magga by Buddha Ghosh.

P. 63. " Whence can there be true happiness to him of broken virtue, who does not forsake sensual pleasures, yielding sharper pain than to embrace a mass of living fire."

P. 161. " Where darkness exists, there is no lamp-light, so the concentration does not arise in the presence of sensual desires."

P. 494. " Monks, I do not perceive any one state which is so great an offence as wrong view. Wrong views are supreme offences."

(8) " Manuscript remains of Buddhist literature in E. Turkestan " by A. F. Rudolf—Heornele (1916).

4. Vinaya text :—

**सन्निषितव्यं संप्रजानेन गंतव्यं संप्रजानेन स्थातव्यं संप्रजानेन निषितव्यं संप्रजानेन भोक्तव्यं उपस्थिति स्मृतिना अविक्षिप्त चित्तेन प्रासादिकेन ईर्यापथ सम्पन्नेन सुसंवृत्तेन युगांतर प्रेक्षिना सगौरवेण.**

*" Sannisitavyam samprajâ nena gantavyam samprajâ nena sthâ tavyam samprajâ nena nisitavyam samprajâ nena bhaktavyam upasthiti smriti nâ aviksipta chittena prasâ dikena îryûpatha-sampannena susam vrittena yugantara-preksina sa gouravena."*

"One should sit, go, stand and eat after right understanding, keeping recollection, with steadfast mind, being glad, with control, should walk, seeing earth 4 cubits forward, with thoughtfulness."

(7) *Suvarnâprabha Stotra.*

अयश्चकायो यथा शून्य ग्राम षद्ग्राम चौरोपम इन्द्रियाणी ।
तान्येवग्रामे निवसंति सर्वे नते विजानन्ति परस्परेण ॥
चक्षिवन्द्रियं रूपगतेषु धावति श्रोत्रेन्द्रियं शब्दविचारणं ।
घ्राणोन्द्रयं गंधविचित्रहारि जिह्वेन्द्रियं नित्यरसेषु धावते ॥
कायेन्द्रियं स्पर्श गतेषु धावति मनेन्द्रियं धर्मविचारणेन ।
षडिन्द्रियाणीति परस्परेण स्वकं स्वकं विषयमनातिक्रांता ॥
चित्तं हि मायोपम चंचलंच षडिन्द्रियं विषय विचारणं च ।
यथैव नरो धावति शून्य ग्रामे षड्ग्राम चौरैः समाश्रितश्च ॥
चित्तं यथा षड् विषयाहितंच प्रजानते इंन्द्रियगोचरंच ।
रूपश्चशब्दश्च तथैव गंधो रसश्च स्पर्शस्तथा धर्मगोचरं ॥
चित्तंहिसर्वत्रषडिन्द्रियेषु शकुनिरिव चलमिन्द्रिय संप्रविष्टं ।
यंन्त्रंच यंन्त्रेन्द्रिय संस्कृतंच नचेन्द्रियं कुर्वतु ज्ञानमात्मकम् ॥

*Ayaścha Kâyo yathâ śunya grâmah, ṣadgrâma chauropama indriyani,*

*Tanyeva grâma nivasanti sarve, na te Vijâ nanti parasparena* 4.

*Chaksvendriyam rûpa gatesu dhavati, srotrindriyam śabda vicharanena*

*Ghrânendriyam gande vichittra hâri, jivhendriyam nittya rasesu dhâvate* 5.

*Kayendriyam sparsa gateṣu dhâvati, manendriyam dharma vichâranena,*

*Sadendriyaniti parasparena svakam svakam visaya manâ ti krântâh* 6.

*Chittam hi mâyopuma chanchlancha ṣadendriyam viṣaya vicharṇam cha,*

*Yathaiva naro dhâvati sunya grâme, ṣad grâma chaurebhi samâ sritâncha* 7.

*Chittam yathâ ṣad visaya hitancha prajânate indriya gocha rancha,*

*Rupescha sabdascha tathaiva gandho rasascha sparsa statha dharma gocharam* 8.

*Chittam hi sarvatra ṣadendriyesu sakunireva chala mindriya sampravistham,*

*Yantram cha yantrindriya sanskrittan cha na chendriyam kurvatu jnana matmakam,* 9.

"This body is like a lonely village, the six sense organs are like the village thieves. These senses reside in this village of body, but they do not know each other. The organ of eye runs to see the colour, ear knows sounds, nose knows many kinds of smell, the tongue goes to know different tastes, the body-sense runs to the objects of touch and mind-sense engages in thought of conditions: these six sense-organs do not go against their own respective objects. This mind is feeling like deceit, is entangled in the objects of six senses, as a man goes in a lonely village and is captured by the six village thieves. This mind knows the objects of six senses. This flies to them like a bird. Mind is a machine, which is engaged by the senses. You should not let it go to the senses but engage it in the self-knowledge."

(8) *Ratna rasi sutra.*

**समाधिः आर्याणां ध्वजा, प्रज्ञा .आर्याणां ध्वजा, विमुक्ति आर्याणां ध्वजा, विमुक्ति ज्ञानदर्शनं आर्याणां ध्वजा.**

***Samâdhih âryânam dhvajâ, prajnâ âryanâm dhvajâ, vimuktih âryânâm dhvajâ, vimukti jnâna-darsanam âryanâm dhvajâ.***

"Concentration is the flag of the *Aryas*, self-discrimination is the flag of the *Aryâs*, deliverence is the flag of the *Aryâs*, perception and knowledge of deliverance is the flag of the *Aryâs*."

*Sacred Books of the Buddhists Vol. III by T. W. Rhys Davids* (1910) *Dig. Nik. II. Maha sudassan suttanta.*

P. 194. How transient are all compound things;
Growth is their nature and decay;
They are produced they are dissolved again.
To bring them into full subjection that is *bliss.*

## PATH OF LIBERATION IN THE JAIN SCRIPTURES.

As the eight-fold path has been said to be the means of liberation in the Buddhist scriptures, so the three-fold path has been said to be the means of *Nirvâna* in the Jaina Scriptures.

This three-fold path is contained in the eight-fold path and *vice versa*. This three-fold path is called *Ratnatrya Dharma* or the Truth of the three gems. It is a combination of *Samyakdarsana*, right view or belief, *Samyak jnâna*, right knowledge, *Samyakchâritra*, right conduct.

The Jain Saint Kunda Kunda Acharya says in *Samayasâra* :—

**दंसण णाण चरित्ताणी सेविदव्वाणी साहुणा णिच्चं ।**
**ताणि पुणज्ञाणतिण्णिवि अप्पाणंचेव णिच्छयदो ॥**

*Damsaṇa ṇâṇa charittâni, sevi davvâni sahuṇa ṇichcham,*
*Taṇi puṇa jâṇa tiṇṇivi appânam cheva ṇichchhayado* 19.

"A monk must always follow right belief, right knowledge and right conduct; from the real stand-point, know these three to be the self only."

Jain philosophy, when it describes a thing from the practical point of view, analyses it into kinds and divisions; but when it describes a thing from the real stand-point, it thinks of it as an indivisible whole.

Therefore from the practical stand-point, the path is three-fold, but from the real stand-point, it is the self only.

When one's own self is believed in and known as it is in its own essence and is realized as such—then pure concentration of one's own self appears. It is the real three-fold path or the self itself.

Sri Umaswami says in his *Tattvartha sutra :*

सम्यग्दर्शनज्ञानचारित्राणि मोक्षमार्गः.

*Samayag darsana jnâna châritrâni môkṣa mârgah I.*

" Combination of right belief, right knowledge and right conduct is the way to liberation."

This three-fold path has been described in all the Jain Sacred Books.

Out of the eight-fold path of the Buddhist philosophy, *Samyakdriṣti* or right view and *Samyak-sankalpa* or right determination are included in *Samyag-darsana* or right view and *Samyag jnâna* or right knowledge of the Jain philosophy; while *Samyak vachan*, right speech, *Samayak Karmânte*, right action, *Samyak âjiva* right livelihood, *Samyak vyayâma* right effort, *Samyak smriti* right mindfulness, *Samyak samâdhi* right concentration, these six are included in *Samyak châritra* right conduct of the Jain philosophy. This fact will be known clearly from the description given further.

I. *Samayak darsana* or *Samyak-dristi* Right belief or Right view.

The Jain scriptures describe right belief with knowledge as *Samyak darsana.* From the practical point of view, it is necessary to have firm belief in the seven principles. Umaswami says in *Tattvârtha sutra* :—

**तत्वार्थश्रद्धानं सम्यग्दर्शनम् ॥ २ ॥ जीवाजीवास्रवबन्ध-संवरनिर्जरामोक्षास्तत्वम् ॥ ४ ॥**

*Tattvârtha sraddhanam samyag darsanam* I. 2.
*Jivajivasravabandha sanvara nirjara mokṣastattvam* I. 4.

" Belief in the seven principles as they are, is called right belief. The principles are *Jiva* soul, *Ajiva* non-soul, *Asrava* inflow, *Bandha* bondage, *Samvara* checking, *nirjara* shedding, *Moksa* liberation."

All the modifications and objects of this universe come under the first two principles, soul, and non-soul. *Nâma rupa* of the Buddhist philosophy is included in these two principles. Feeling, perception, mentation, consciousness are found in the impure soul, while body is included in non-soul. Just as in the Buddhist philosophy, the knowledge and belief in the pain, its cause, its cessation and the way of its cessation is Right View; so also in the Jain Philosophy pain and its cause are described by the two principles *Āsrava* inflow and *bandha* bondage, while the cessation of pain is the *Moksa* or liberation and the means of cessation is included in *Samvara*, checking and *Nirjara*, shedding.

It will be noted that in the Jain Scriptures, these principles are described according to the root-meaning of their words as per Sanskrit composition, *e.g.*, Āsrava means "Asravati yat"—that which comes is ***âsrava***. "Yena asravati tat"—that through which comes is *âsrava*.

Karmic molecules, which are very fine particles of matter and which cannot be perceived by any of the five senses, do come near the soul by attraction; their coming is ***âsrava***.

The good and bad activities of mind, body and speech are the causes for the inflow of karmic matter, therefore they are also called *Āsrava*. Inflow of karmic matter is called ***dravya âsarva*** material inflow or objective inflow while its cause is called ***bhâva âsarva*** or subjective inflow. Likewise the fine karmic matter bound with the mundane soul is called ***Dravya bandha***, material bondage or objective bondage.

The thought-activity causing this material bondage is called *bhâva bandha* subjective bondage. Karmic matter which is prevented from inflow is called ***dravya samvara*** or material checking or objective checking, while the thought-activity which checks the inflow is called *bhâva samvara*, subjective checking. Karmic matter which is shed off is called ***dravya nirjara*** material shedding or objective shedding, while the thought-activity which causes shedding is called ***bhâva nirjara*** or subjective shedding. Total freedom of soul from karmic matter is called *Dravya moksa* material liberation or objective liberation ; while pure thought-activity which removes all the karmic molecules is called *bhava mokśa* or subjective liberation.

The Buddhist literature has clearly described the subjective inflow, bondage, checking, shedding and liberation, while the objective inflow, etc. have been dealt with in a vague manner. It appears that the ordinary public will not understand easily the details of the material inflow etc. and perhaps this consideration has prevented them from being clearly and explicitly dealt with.

The Jain philosophy has described the subjective inflow and subjective bondage, *i.e.*, causes of inflow of karmic matter and their bondage as follows :—

**मिथ्यादर्शनाविरतिप्रमादकषाययोगा बन्धहेतवः ॥**

*Mitthyâ darsanâvirati pramâda-kaṣaya yoga bandha hetawah* 1/8.

The causes of bondage (and inflow) are (1) *Mitthya-darsana* or *Mitthva drista,* i.e., wrong belief in the true principles (2) *avirti* not to restrain from *himsa* injury, *Asattya* falsehood, *steya* stealing, *abrahma* unchastity, *parigraha* thirst for worldly possessions (3) *prâmada* carelessness or indifference to useful thoughts leading to *Nirvâna,* (4) *Kaṣaya* passions, *i.e.*, anger, pride, deceit and greed (5) *yoga* activities of mind, body and speech. These five are both the subjective inflow and subjective bondage.

The Jain saint Nâgasêna says as follows in his *Tattvânusâsana* about wrong belief and bondage:

तापत्रयोपतप्तेभ्यो भव्येभ्यः शिवशर्मणे ।
तत्त्वं हेयमुपादेयमिति द्वेधाभ्यधादसौ ॥ ३ ॥
बंधो निबंधनं चास्य हेयमित्युपदर्शितं ।
हेयं स्याद्दुःखसुखयोर्यस्माद्बीजमिदं द्वयं ॥ ४ ॥
मोक्षस्तत्कारणं चैतदुपादेयमुदाहृतं ।
उपादेयं सुखं यस्मादस्मादाविर्भविष्यति ॥ ५ ॥
तत्र बंधः सहेतु भ्यो यः संश्लेषः परस्परं ।
जीवकर्मप्रदेशानां स प्रसिद्धश्चतुर्विधः ॥ ६ ॥
बंधस्य कार्यः संसारः सर्वदुःखप्रदोंगिनां ।
द्रव्यक्षेत्रादिभेदेन स चानेकविधः स्मृतः ॥ ७ ॥
स्युर्मिथ्यादर्शनज्ञानचारित्राणि समासतः ।
बंधस्य हेतवोऽन्यस्तु त्रयाणामेव विस्तरः ॥ ८ ॥
अन्यथावस्थितेष्वर्थेष्वन्यथैव रुचिर्नृणां ।
दृष्टिमोहोदयान्मोहो मिथ्यादर्शनमुच्यते ॥ ९ ॥
ज्ञानावृत्युदयादर्थेष्वन्यथाधिगमो भ्रमः ।
अज्ञानं संशयश्चेति मिथ्याज्ञानमिह त्रिधा ॥ १० ॥
वृत्तिमोहोदयाज्जन्तोः कषायवशवर्त्तिनः ।
योगप्रवृत्तिरशुभा मिथ्याचारित्रमूचिरे ॥ ११ ॥
बंधहेतुषु सर्वेषु मोहश्च प्राक् प्रकीर्तितः ।
मिथ्याज्ञानं तु तस्यैव सचिवत्वमशिश्रियन् ॥ १२ ॥
ममाहंकारनामानौ सेनान्यौ तौ च तत्सुतौ ।
यदायत्तः सुदुर्भेदो मोहव्यूहः प्रवर्त्तते ॥ १३ ॥
शश्वदनात्मीयषु स्वतनुप्रमुखेषु कर्मजनितेषु ।
आत्मीयाभिनिवेशो ममकारो मम यथा देहः ॥ १४ ॥

ये कर्मकृता भावाः परमार्थनयेन चात्मनो भिन्नाः ।
तत्रात्माभिनिवेशोऽहंकारोऽहं यथा नृपतिः ॥ १५ ॥
मिथ्याज्ञानान्वितान्मोहात्ममाहंकारसंभवः ।
इमकाभ्यां तु जीवस्य रागो द्वेषस्तु जायते ॥ १६ ॥
ताभ्यां पुनः कषायाः स्युर्नो कषायाश्च तन्मयाः ।
तेभ्यो योगाः प्रवर्तन्ते ततः प्राणिवधादयः ॥ १७ ॥
तेभ्यः कर्माणि बध्यन्ते ततः सुगतिदुर्गती ।
तत्र कायाः प्रजायन्ते सहजानीन्द्रियाणिच ॥ १८ ॥
तदर्थानिन्द्रियैर्गृह्णन् मुह्यति द्वेष्टि रज्यते ।
ततो बंधो भ्रमत्येवं मोहव्यूहगतः पुमान् ॥ १९ ॥

*Tâpa trayôpa taptêbhyô bhavyêbhyah sivasarmane,*
*Tattvam hêya mupâdeyamiti dvêdhâbhyadhâdasau 3.*
*Bandhô nibhandhanam châsya heyamityupadarsitam,*
*Heyam syaddukkha sukhayor yasmâbhijamidam dvayam, 4.*
*Moksastatkâranam chaitadupâdêya-mudâhritam,*
*Upâdêyam sukham yasmâdasmâdâvir bhavisyati, 5.*
*Tatra bandhah sahêtubhyo yah sanslêsahparasparam,*
*Jîvakarmapradêsânam sa prasiddhaschaturvidhah 6.*
*Bandhasya kâryah samsârah sarva dukkha pradônginâm,*
*Dravya kshêtrâdi bhêdêna sa chânêkavidhah smritah 7.*
*Syurmitthyâdarsana jnânachâritrâni samâsatah,*
*Bandhasya hêtavo anyastu trayânâmêva vistarah 8.*
*Anyathâ vasthitesvarthesvanyathaiva ruchirnrinâm,*
*Dristi mahôdayân môhô mitthyâdarsanamuchyate 9.*

*Jnanavrityudayâ darthê ṣvanyathâdhigamô bhramah,*
*Ajnânam samsayaschêti mitthyâjnâna mihatridha 10.*
*Vritti môhôdayâjjantôh kaṣâyavasavartinah,*
*Yôgapravrittirasubhâ mitthyâchâritra mûchire 11.*
*Bandha hêtuṣu sarvêṣu mohascha prâk prakîrtitah,*
*Mitthyâjnanam tu tasyaiva sachivatva masisriyan 12*
*Mam ihankâran îma nau senânyau tau cha tatsutau,*
*Yadâyattah sudurbhêdô môhavyûhah pravartate 13.*
*Sasva danâtmîyêsu svutanupramkhêsu karma janitêsu,*
*Ātmiyâbhini vêso mama kâro mama yathâ dêhah 14.*
*Ye karma krita bhâvah paramârtanayêna châtmano-bhinnah,*
*Tatrâtmâbhinivêso ahankâroaham yathâ nri patih 15.*
*Mithyâjnânânvritânmôhân mamâhankârsambhava,*
*Imakâbhyâm tu jîvasya râgôdvesastu jâyte 16.*
*Tâbhyâm punah kasâyah syurno-kasayâsch tan mayah*
*Tebhyô yôgah pravartante tatah prâni vadhâdya 17*
*Tebhya karmâni badhyante tatah sugati durgatî ;*
*Tatra kâyâh prajâyantê sahajânindriyâni cha 18.*
*Tadarthâ nindriyairgrahnan muhyati dvesti rajyate,*
*Tatô bandhô bhramatyevam môhavyuhagatah pumân 19.*

" The principles have been said to be of two kinds adoptable and the other avoidable, so that the deserving souls, who are suffering by the heat of birth, old age and death, might attain the bliss of *Nirvâna*, 3.

Bondage with its cause is avoidable, because it is the seed of producing worldly pleasure and pain which are themselves avoidable. 4.

Liberation with its cause is adoptable, because it is the seed producing Spiritual Bliss which is adoptable, 5.

Intermingling of soul and karmic matter owing to its causes is bondage which is of four kinds:—Class-bondage, duration-bondage, fruition-bondage, quantity-bondage. 6.

The fruition of bondage is wandering in this world of many kinds such as material, spacial, etc. causing suffering to the worldly souls. 7.

The root causes of bondage are three, wrong belief, wrong knowledge, and wrong conduct, all else is its detail. 8.

Wrong belief is not to believe in the principles as they are, on account of the operation of right-belief-deluding karma. 9.

Wrong knowledge is to know the substances wrongly or doubtfully or not to care for knowing them on account of the operation of knowledge obscuring karma. 10.

Activities of mind, body and speech caused by passions like anger etc., on account of the operation of right-conduct-deluding karmas are said to be wrong conduct. 11.

Among the causes of bondage, wrong belief is the prominent cause; wrong knowledge is a minister to the king Wrong Belief or Delusion, 12.

'I am this', 'it is mine' these two are the sons as well as commanders-in-chief of the king Delusion; under their control the army of Delusion acts. 13.

That which is always other than the self just as body and other conditions is due to karmas. To identify oneself with them as "it is mine" is just as to believe that body is mine. 14.

To identify oneself with the impure thought-activities due to the operation of karmas which do not really belong to self as 'I am this' 'I am the King, (is wrong). 15.

'I am this' 'it is mine' these two thoughts arise on account of wrong belief with wrong knowledge. Attachment and hatred are due to these two. 16.

Attachment and hatred bring forth passions like anger etc. Affected by these passions, mind, body and speech, act, and through their actions the sins of injury to living beings etc. are caused. 17.

Through these sins, bondage of karmas occurs; on account of the operation of these karmas, good or bad conditions of existence appear, where the beings have fresh outer bodies and with them, sense organs. 18,

There the beings grasp the objects of senses and thereby produce delusion, attachment and hatred. whereby again bondage of karmas occurs; thus the mundane soul wanders with the army of delusion in this world, 19.

*Note.*—From the above description the nature of delusion or wrong-belief is clearly evident. It shows that to identify the self, which is really *Nirvâna* in essence, with any worldly condition is delusion.

This wrong belief is of the subjective inflow or *Asrava* or subjective bondage or *bandha.* Right belief removes the wrong belief.

The Jain Saint Amritachandra says thus about right belief in Tattvârthasâra.

पश्यति स्वस्वरूपं यो जानाति चरत्यपि ।
दर्शनज्ञानचारित्र त्रयमात्मैव स स्मृतः ॥

*Paśyati svasvârûpam yo jânâti charatyapi*
*Darśana jṇâna châritra trayamâtmaiva sasmṛitah.*

" Belief in one's own real self is right belief, knowledge of it is right knowledge, realization of the same is right conduct. Really this self is itself right belief, right knowledge and right conduct."

*Right belief* is to believe in the self as it is in its essence, while *wrong belief* is to identify oneself with all the other conditions and thoughts foreign to this real self.

Checking of the subjective inflow and bondage and of *Vowlessness* is caused by practising the full vows of non-injury, truth, non-stealing, chastity and non-possession. Checking of subjective inflow and bondage, and of carelessness is caused by acting carefully, that is by observing the five kinds of carefulness, *i.e., Samiti.*

(1) *Iryâ samiti*—carefully walking after seeing the way four cubits forward in the day-light.

(2) *Bhâsha samiti*—carefully speaking sweet and non-injurious words.

(3) *Eshanâ samiti*—carefully eating pure food given by a layman out of the food prepared for his family only. A Monk will not arrange for his food himself, nor order any one for it.

(4) *Ādâna-niksêpana samiti*—carefully taking and putting things so as not to cause injury to any life.

(5) *Pratishthapanâ samiti*—throwing out bodily filth so carefully as not to injure any life.

Checking of the subjective inflow and bondage of passions is caused by following the ten rules of piety or *Dasa Dharma*, by contemplating *twelve meditations*, or *dvâdasa bhâvana*, by conquering twenty-two kinds of sufferings or *dvâvinsati parîshaha jaya* and by following five kinds of *right conduct* or *pancha châritra*.

The Ten rules of piety are :—*Uttama Kshamâ* or highest forgiveness, control over anger.

(2) *Uttama mârdava* or highest humility, control over pride.

(3) *Uttama ârjava* or highest straight-forwardness, control over deceit.

(4) *Uttama saucha* or highest contentment or purity, control over greed.

(5) *Uttama sattya* or highest truth, refrain from false-hood.

(6) *Uttama samyama* or highest self-control, restraint of senses and compassionate dealing.

(7) *Uttama tapa* or highest austerities, control of desire and self-meditation.

(8) *Uttama tyâga*, or highest charity, to bestow alms of food, medicine, knowledge and fearlessness to the deserving.

(9) *Uttama âkinchanya* or highest non-attachment, not to regard any non-self to be one's own self.

(10) *Uttama Brahmacharya*—highest chastity, refraining from thoughts of sexual enjoyment.

The Twelve meditations are :—

(1) *Anitya* or *transitoriness*—All created things and modifications are destructible such as riches, family, body, pleasure, pain, impure thoughts etc.

(2) *Asarana* or *unprotectiveness*, no one can protect us from death and karmic effects.

(3) *Sansâra* or *worldly wandering*, all the four conditions of existence, hellish, celestial, sub-human, and human are full of sufferings and are therefore to be avoided.

(4) *Ēkatva* or *solitariness*. The self is alone responsible for its actions; alone it is born, alone it dies, alone it has to suffer. Its nature is free from all non-self.

(5) *Anyatva* or *otherness*. All the good or bad karmas, body, different objects, conditions and non-self thoughts are other than one's own self.

(6) ***Asuchitva*** or ***Impurity.*** Body and its contents are impure; one should not be deluded by this impure body.

(7) ***Asrava*** or ***inflow.*** Wrong belief etc., are the causes of inflow of good and bad karmas.

(8) ***Samvara*** or ***checking.*** Right belief etc., are the causes of checking the karmic inflow.

(9) ***Nirjara*** or ***shedding.*** Right self-concentration, equanimity. and non-attachment are the causes of shedding karmas.

(10) ***Loka*** or ***universe.*** Universe is uncreated, eternal, full of self and non-self substances. It is changing on account of conditions, but indestructible on account of the root substances.

(11) ***Bodhi durlabha.*** Difficulty of obtaining knowledge. It is very difficult to understand the true path and also to follow it. When once it is known, it should be pursued carefully and wisely.

(12) ***Dharma*** or the ***True Path.*** True path is right belief, right knowledge and right conduct. This is the means of liberation and perfect bliss.

***Conquering of Twenty-two Sufferings :—***

The sufferings are: (1) Hunger (2) thirst (3) cold (4) heat (5) biting of mosquitoes, etc. (6) nakedness (7) dislike (8) woman (9) walking (10) sitting (11) sleeping (12) abuse (13) beating (14) asking alms (15) Failure to get alms (16) disease (17) contact with prickly shrubs (18) dirt (19) honour or dishonour

(20) conceit of knowledge (21) ignorance (22) slack belief.

*Five Kinds of Right Conduct* :—

(1) *Sâmâyika*—equanimity or self-concentration.

(2) *Chêdôpasthâpanâ*—Recovery of equanimity after a fall from it.

(3) *Parihâra Visuddhi*—Pure and absolute non-injury.

(4) *Sukshma sâmparâya*—Slightest passion.

(5) *Yathâkhyâta*—Ideal and passionless conduct.

Checking of the subjective inflow and bondage of of mind, body and speech activities is said to be ***Gupti*** or restraint of mind, body and speech by engaging oneself in self-contemplation.

All the kinds of subjective inflow or *Bhâva asrava*, mentioned in the Jaina scriptures, if compared with the *àsravas* dealt with in the Buddhist literature will be found to agree with one another.

See *Majjhim nikâya savvâsava sutta the second.*

Some purport of the above is given below :—

**कतमे धम्मा मनसिकरनीया :—यस्स धम्मस्स मनसिकरोतो अनुप्पन्नो वा कामासवो न उप्पज्ज्ञति उप्पन्नो वा कामासवो पहीयति अनुप्पन्नो वा भवासवो न उप्पज्ज्ञति उप्पन्नो वा भवासवो पहीयति अनप्पन्नो वा अविज्ज्ञासवो न उप्पज्ज्ञति उप्पन्नो वा अविज्ज्ञासवो पहीयति इमे धम्मा मनसिकरनीया.**

*Katame, dhammâ manasi karaniyâ :—*
*Yassa dhammassa manasi karoto anuppanno*
*Vâ kâmâsavo na uppajjati uppanno vâ*

*Kamâ savo pahiyati, anuppanno vâ bhavâ savo*
*Na uppajjati, uppanno va bhavâ savo pahiyâti,*
*Anuppanno vâ avijjâsavo na uppajjati*
*Uppanno vâ avijjâsavo pahiyati, ime dhammá manasi karniyâ.*"

" What thoughts should be kept in mind ? :—

That thought which prevents rising of sensual desire already not arisen, and that which destroys sensual desire if arisen ; that thought which prevents rising of desire of existence already not arisen and that which destroys desire of existence if arisen : that thought which prevents rising of ignorance already not arisen and that which destroys ignorance if risen should be kept in mind."

अहोस्मि अहं अतीतं अद्धानं...भविस्सामि अहं अनायत अद्धानं...पच्चुप्पन्नं अद्धांन अहं अस्मि तस्स एवं मनसिकरोतो छण्णं दिट्ठीनं अण्णतरा दिट्ठि उप्पज्जति (१) अत्थिमेअत्ता (२) नत्थिमे अत्ता (३) अत्तना अत्तानं संजानामि (४) अत्तना अनत्तानं संजानामि (५) अनत्तना अत्तानं संजानामि (६) यो मे अत्ता...कम्मानं विपाकं पाटेसंवेदेति सो अयं अत्ता निच्चो... धुवो सस्सतोअविपरिणामधम्मो......इति दिट्ठिगतं दिट्ठिगहनं दिट्ठिकंतारं दिट्ठिविसुकं दिट्ठिविकंदितं दिट्ठिसंयाजनं दिट्ठिसंयाजन संयुत्तो......न परिमुच्चति जातिया जरामरणेन सोकेहि परिदेवेहि दुक्खेहि दोमनस्सेहि उपायासेहि...सो इदं दुक्खंति योनिसो मनासिकरोति अयं दुःखसमुदयोति...अयं दुःखनिरोधोति अयं दुःखनिरोधो गामिनि पटिपदा तस्स एवम् मानसि

**करोतोतीनि संयोजनानि पहीयनंति (१) सक्कायदिट्ठि (२) विचिकिच्छा (३) सीलब्बत परामासो.**

"*Ahosim aham atitam addhâ nam......bhâvissâmi aham anâyâ tam addhânam pachchappannam add hânam aham asmi—tassa evam manasi karoto-chhaṇṇam diṭṭhinam aṇṇatarâ diṭṭhi uppajjati.*

(1) *atthi me atta.*

(2) *natthi me atta......*

(3) *attanâ attânam sanjânâmi.*

(4) *attanâ anattânam sanjanâmi.*

(5) *anattana attânam sanjanâmi......*

(6) *Yo me atta...Kammânam vipâkam patisamvedeti, so ayam atta nichcho dhuvo sassato avi-parinama dhammo. Iti diṭṭhi gatam diṭṭhi gahanam ditthi kantâram, ditthi visukam ditthi vikanditum, ditthi sanyojanam ditthi sanyojana samyutto...na pari muchchati Jâtiyâ, jarâ marnena sakehi pari-devehi dukkehi domanassehi-upâ-yâsehi......so idam dukkhanti, yoniso manasi karoti, ayam dukkha-samudayoti......ayam dukkha nirodhoti,—ayam dukkha-nirodha gâmini-pati pada, tassa evam manasi karoto tini sanyojana ni pahiyanti.* (1) *sakkâya ditthi* (2) *vichi kichchâ* (3) *Silabbata parâ mâ so.*"

"I was in past time," "I will be in future time," "I am in the present time":—On creating such notions in the mind, he will have one of the six (wrong) views (1) my soul is (2) my soul is not (3) 'I know soul by soul' (4) 'I know non-soul by soul (5) I know soul by non-soul." (6) 'This my soul which experiences the ripening of karmas is eternal, indestructible and unshakeable and has the nature of unchangeability.'

Thus arises the net of (wrong) belief, jungle of belief, the thorn of belief, the cloud of belief, the bondage of belief. On account of this bondage of (wrong) belief the soul is not saved from birth, old age, death sorrow, weeping, pain, grief and miseries. He who actually understands "this is pain," this is the cause of pain; this is the cessation of pain; this is cause of its cessation, removes three kinds of dirts (1) identifies himself with body (2) doubt engages in vows and rituals only. Thus the *asrava* of wrong belief should be removed by right belief.

*Note.*—Really *Nirvana* or the pure soul is realizable only; it cannot be grasped rightly through mind. Whatever notions an ignorant soul forms in his mind about the soul are not the real facts, about the soul, but they are quite against the reality of the soul. In the above statement of the Majjhima nikaya six kinds of wrong beliefs about the soul are described (1) my soul is—here the real soul is identified with the impure conditions of the soul due to ripening of karmas—therefore it is a wrong view. (2) My soul is not—here total non-existence of soul is maintained. (3) I know soul by soul—here also the thinker's mind grasps the impure condition of the soul to be the real soul. He does not take the pure and unthinkable soul into his mind;

therefore it is also a wrong view. (4) I know non-soul by the soul. Here he understands that, he acting through mind and senses and thereby knowing others, is the real soul. This is also a wrong view. He does not consider the pure soul which does not require help of senses and mind, but which can know all himself and others independently. (5) I know soul by non-soul this is also a wrong view. He understands that mind and senses which are not the soul, can know the soul. (6) My soul which experiences the ripening of karmas is eternal and unchangeable. This is also the wrong view, because that impure soul which experiences fruits of karmas is not eternal but is changeable. Here also the pure soul of *Nirvana* has not been taken into consideration. These six kinds of wrong beliefs maintain something else than the real pure soul. Whoever believes in the *Nirvana* or the realizable pure soul, he removes all these wrong views. Then he does not identify his pure soul with the five spheres, body, feeling, perception, mentation and (impure) consciousness. All his doubts are removed, although he follows practical rules of conduct, he believes them to be rejectable. He maintains that only pure concentration or *Samâdhi* is adoptable. This is the *right view* or *right belief* or *Samyak darsana*.

In fact such is the statement of the Jain Saints also about right belief or *Samyak darsana*.

The Jain Saint Kunda Kunda Acharya says in Samayasâra :—

जीवस्स णत्थि रागो णविदोसो णेव विज्जदे मोहो
णोपच्चया णकम्मं णोकम्मं चाविसे णत्थि
णेवयजीवट्ठाणा णगुणट्ठाणाय अत्थिजीवस्स
जेणदु एदे सव्वे पुग्गलदव्वस्स परिणामा.

*Jîvassa ṇatthi râgo ṇavi doso ṇeva vijjade môho,*
*No pachchayâ na kammam no kammam châvi se ṇatthi* 56
*Nevaya jiva tthâṇâ ṇa guna tthâṇâ ya atti jîvassa,*
*Jeṇadu ede savve puggala davvassa pari ṇâmâ* 60

In the pure soul, there is neither affection nor hatred nor delusion, neither causes of *asrava,* nor karmas, nor quasi-karmas even. 56.

Neither there are soul classes nor spiritual stages in the soul, because all these are the modifications of matter only, (because they appear in soul in connection with matter).

*Samayasâra Kalasa* says the same :—

वर्णाद्यावा रागमोहादयोवा भिन्नाभावा सर्वएवास्य पुंसः।
तेनैवान्तस्तत्वत पश्यतोऽमीनोदृष्टाः स्युर्दृष्टिमेकं परंस्यात् ॥

*Varṇâdyâ vâ râga mohâdayo va chinnâ bhâvah sarva evâsya punsah.*
*Tenaivântastattvalâh pasyto mî-no dṛiṣtâh syurdṛiṣtâ mekam param syât 5/2.*

All these colours etc. or affection and delusion etc. modifications are other than the pure soul; therefore while realizing within the self, these are not realized, only the highest one is realizable.

*Note.*—This pure and highest one is nothing but the nature of *Nirvana.* Thus the subective inflow of wrong belief is removed by right view or right belief. Jainism and Budbhism are one in this point.

**कतमे आसवा संवरा पहातव्वाः—भिक्खु पटिसंखा योनिसो चक्खुंदिय संवर संजुतो विहरति—सोतेंदिय संवर संजुतो विहरति......धानेंदिय संवर संजुतो विहरति...... जिह्वेंद्रियसंवरसंजुतो विहरति......कायेंदिय संवर संजुतो विहरति......मनेंद्रिय संवर संजुतो विहरति अस्स विहरतो उप्पज्जेय्यं आसवा विघात परिलाहानहोंति.**

" *Katame âsavâ samvarâ pahâtavva :—Bhikkhu patisankhâ yoniso châkkhun-diya samvara sanjutto viharati, Sotendiya samvara sanjutto viharatti, Ghanendiya samvara sanjutto viharati, Jihvendiya samvara sanjutto viharati, Kayendiya samvara sanjutto viharati, Manendiya samvara sunjutto viharati, Assa viharato-uppajjeyyum âsavâ, Vigatta pari lâhe na honti.*"

" What asavas should be removed by restraint—*Samvara* :—

The Saint, knowing the senses and mind separate from his self through self-discrimination, walks under restraint of eye-sense, ear-sense, nose-sense, tongue-sense, body sense and mind sense. Thus the destructive rise of âsâvâs is restrained."

*Note.*—In the Jain scripture vowlessness is said to be the second cause of subjective inflow and its checking *i.e.*, by following five vows of non-injury, etc. Here in the above statement restraint of five senses and mind is said to check vowlessness. So it is quite right, because restraint of these six senses leads to non-commission of the five sins *viz.*, injury etc., due to lust and sense-gratification and thus the five vows of non-injury, etc. are actually observed. He who has full control over his senses, mind, and thought will never injure any one, nor speak untruth, not steal anything, not act unchastefully, nor have attachment for possessions. The same idea has been expressed by the Jain Saint Sri Umaswami in his *Tattwartha Sutra*, 6th Chapter :—

**इन्द्रियकषायाव्रतक्रियाः पञ्चचतुः पञ्चपञ्चविंशतिसंख्याः पूर्वस्य भेदाः.**

*Indriya kaṣâyâ vrata kriyâ pancha chatuh pancha pancha vinsatisankhya pûrvasya bhedah*, vi, 5.

" Five senses, four passions, five kinds of vowlessness and twenty-five kinds of activity are the kinds of worldly '*asrava*'."

*Note.*—Here five senses have been said to be the main causes of anger, vowlessness, etc. When senses are controlled, every other sin is restrained.

**कतमे आसवा पटिसेवनापहातब्बाः—भिक्खुपटिसंखायोनिसो चीवरं पटिसेवते यावदेव सीलस्स......उण्हस्स......**

दसमंकस वातातप सिरिं सप संफस्सानं पटिघाताय, याव-देवह्रीकोपीन पटिच्छाद नत्थं—पिंडपातं पटिसेवति नवदवाय नमदाय न मंडनाय न विभूसनाय यावदेव इमस्स कायस्स थितिया यापनाय विहिंसूपरितया ब्रह्मचर्य्यानुग्गहायः—इतिं-पुराणंच वेदनं पटिहंखाभि नवंचवेदनंन उप्पादेस्सामि, यात्राम भविस्साते अनवज्जता च फासुविहारोचाति...सेनासनं पटिसे-वति यावदेव सीतस्स पटिघाताय......गिलानपरिच्चय भेषज्ज परिक्खारं पटि सेवति......अस्स भिक्खवे अपाटिसेवतो उप्प-ज्जेय्युं आसवा विघात परिलाहा पटिसेवतो एवं सते आसवा विघातपरिलाहा नहोंति इमे आसवापटिसेवना पहातव्वा.

"*Katame âsavâ pate sevanâ pahâtavva :—Bhikkhu pati sankhâ yoniso chivaram pati sevate yâ vadeva sitassa—...Unhassa...dansa makasa vâ tâ tapa sirim sapa samphassanam pati ghâtâya, yâvadeva hri kopin patichcha-danattham,......pindapâtam patisevati na va davâya na madâya na manda-naya na vibhusanaya yâwadeva imassakâyassa thitiya yâpanâya, vihinsa-paritâya brahmacharyâ muggahâya. Iti puranam cha vidanam patihankhaminavam cha vedanam uppades-sami, yâtrâ me bhavissati anavajjata cha phasuviharo chati,...senasanam pati sevati yâvadeva sîtassa pati-ghâtayâ...gilâna parichchâya bhe-sajja parikkharam patisevate...assa bhikkhave apati sevato uppajjeyam âsavâ vighâtâ paritaha, potisevato evam sa te âsvâ vighata-paritâha na honti-ime âsavâ patisevana paha-tavva.*"

"What *Asavas* are restrained by careful dealing (note :—*pati sevana* appears to be the equivalent of *samiti* in Jainism).

The Monk, knowing himself separate through self-discrimination, uses clothes to keep off cold, heat, mosquito-biting, air, sun-shine, serpents, etc. and for shame; takes alms not for sport, nor for pride nor for glory, but for keeping the body, to be saved from injury and to follow chastity; so that old troubles may be removed and new ones may not arise and that my journey of life may go on defectless, and I may walk easily. He uses seats and beds for the removal of cold, etc., takes medicine for the removal of diseases—all these functions are done with carefulness; then those harmful *âsavâs* which would have been caused by carelessness would not happen.

**"कतमे आसवा अधिवासना पहातव्वा :—भिक्कु पटिसंखायोनिसो खमोहोति सीतस्स उण्हस्स जिघच्छाय पिपासाय दंसमकसवातातप सिरिंसप संफस्सनानं दुरुत्तानं दुरागतानं बचनपथानं उप्पन्नानं सारीरिकानं वेदनानं दुःखानं तिप्पानं खरानं कटुकानं असातानं अमनापानं पाणहराणं अधिवासक जातिकोहोति अस्स भिक्कवे अनधिवासयतो...... नहोंति......इमे आसवा अधिवासना पहातव्वा."**

"*Katame âsavâ adhi vâ sanâ pahâ-tavva. Bhikkhu paṭi sankhá yoniso khamo hoti sitassa unhassa, Jighachchâya pipâsâya dansa makasa vâtâ-tapa sirim sapa samphassânanam duruttânam durâgatânam*

***vachana pathânam uppannânam sâriri kânam vedanânam dukkhânam tippânam khrânam katukânam asâtânam amanâpânam pâna-horânam adhivâsaka jâtiko hoti, assa bhikkhave anadhi vâ sayato...no honti...ime âsavâ adhi vâsanâ pahâtavva."***

" What *âsavâs* are removed by calm suffering :—

The Bhikkhu, full of self-discrimination, calmly suffers cold, heat, hunger, thirst, mosquito-biting, wind, sun-shine, touch of serpents, etc., hearing abusive words, bodily troubles, hard pains, unbearable to mind and other deadly matters ; then he removes all those harmful *âsavâs* which would have been caused by his not calmly suffering them ; thus *âsavâs* should be removed by calm suffering.

*Note* :—The Conquering of 22 sufferings described in Jainism for the restraint of inflow includes what is described above.

**" कतमे आसवा परिवज्जनापहातव्वा :—भिक्कु पटिसंखा योनिसो चंडं हत्थिं, चंडं अस्सं, चंनं गौणं, चंडं कुक्कुरं, अहिं, खाणुं, कटकाधानं, सोब्भं, पपातं, चंदनिकं, ओलिगल्लं, (परिवज्जेति) यथारूपे अनासने निसन्नं यथारूपे अगोचरे चरंतं यथारूपे पापके मित्ते भजंतं विञ्ञू स ब्रह्मचारी पापकेसु थानेसु ओकप्पेयुं सोतं च अनासनं तं च अगोचरं ते पापकेमित्ते...... परिवज्जेति—अस्स भिक्खवे अपरिवज्जयतो उप्पज्जेय्युं आसवा विघाता परिलाहा परिवज्जयतो ते आसवा......नहोंति—इमे आसवा परिवज्जनापहातव्वा."**

" *Katame âsavâ pari vajjana pahâ-tavvâ :—Bhikkhu paṭi sankhâ yoniso chanḍam hatthim, chanḍamassam, chanḍam gouṇam, chanḍam kukkuram, ahim, khânum, khanṭaka dhânam, sobbham, papâtam, chandanikam, oligallam, (pari vajjeti) yathâ rûpa anâ sane nisaṇnam yathâ rupa agochare charantam yatha rûpe pâpake mitte bhajantam vijna sa brahmachâri pâpakesa thânesu okappeyum so tan cha anâsanam tan cha agocharam ti pâpake mitte . . .parivajjetî - assa bhikkhave apari vajjayato uppajjeyyam âsavâ vighata pari-taha parivajjayato te âsavâ . . . na honti - ime âsavâ parivajjana pahâ tavva.*"

What *asavas* should be removed by avoiding :—

The Monk, full of self-discrimination, carefully walks avoiding the fearful elephant, rude horse, striking bullock, wrathful dog, serpent, column, thorny place hill, spring, pond and place of refuse. He avoids those unfit seats, and those sinful freindships on account of which the learned, chasteful monk may be liable to commit sin. Thus those harmful *asavas* which would have been caused by non-avoiding them are not caused. Thus Asavas should be removed by avoidance.

*Note.*—This is included in the five kinds of carefulness (*Samiti*) of the Jains stated before to avoid the inflow due to carelessness.

" कतमे आसवा विनोदनापहातव्वा :—भिक्कु पटिसंखायो-निसो - उप्पन्नं कामवितक्कं - व्यापादवितक्कं - विहिंसावितक्कं-

पापके अकुसले धम्मे नाधिवासेति पजाहति विनोदेति ब्यंति-करोति, अनभावं गमेति – अस्स भिक्खवे अविनोदयतो उप्पज्जेय्युं आसवा विघातपरिलाहा विनोदयतो ते- नहोंति - इमे आसवा विनोदेवपहातब्वा."

"*Katame âsavâ vinô danâ pahâ tavvâ :—Bhikkhu pati sankhâ yoniso-uppannam kâma vitakkam-vyâpâda vitakkam vihâmsâ vitakkam-papake akusale dhamme nâdhi vâ seti pajahati, vinodete ; vyanti karoti, ana-bhävam gameti-assa bhikkhave avinodayato uppajjeyyum âsavâ vighâtâ paritaha vinodayato te-na honti-ime âsavâ vinodeva paha tavva.*"

What *asavas* should be removed by destruction :—

The Monk, full of self-discrimination, does not grasp the arising thought of sensual desire of anger, of injury and other harmful thoughts, gives them up, destroys them, ends them, and clears them off. Thus three harmful *asavas* which would have been caused by not destroying them do not occur by their destruction. Thus *asavas* should be removed by destruction.

*Note.*—According to Jainism, the ten rules of piety of highest forgiveness etc. described before include the above.

"कतमे आसवा भावना पहातब्वा :—भिक्खु पटिसंखायो-निसो (१) सति संबोज्झंगं भावेति (२) धम्म विचय संबोज्झंगं भावेति (३) वीर्य संबोज्झंगं भावेति (४) पीति संबोज्झंगं भावेति (५) पस्सद्धि संबोज्झंगं भावेति (६) समाधि संबोज्झंगं भावेति (७) उपेखा संबोज्झंगं भावेति. विवेकनिस्सितं विरागनिस्सितं

**निरोधनिस्सितं, वोस्सग्गपरिणामं—अस्स भिक्कवे अभावयतो उप्पज्जेय्युं आसवा विघातपरिलाहा भावयतो न होंति इमें आसवा भावनापहातव्वा.**"

"*Katame âsâva bhâvanâ panâ tâvvâ :—Bhikkhu pati sankhâ yonîso* (1) *sati sambojjhangam bhâveti* (2) *dhamma vichaya sambojjhangam bhâ veti* (3) ***virya sambojjhangam bhâveti*** (4) ***piti sambojjhangam bhâveti,*** (5) ***passaddhi sambojjhangam bhâveti*** (6) ***samâdhi sambojjhangam bhâveti, upekhâ sambojjhangam bhâveti, viveka nissitam viraga nissitam nirodha nissitam vassagga parinamim-assa bhikkave abhâ vayato uppajjeyyum âsavâ vighâtô paritaha bhâvayato-na honti-Ime âsavâ bhavana pahâ tavvâ.***"

"What *asavas* should be removed by meditation :—

The Monk meditates upon (1) the recollection of true knowledge (2) upon thoughts of *Dharma* or piety (3) upon energy (4) upon love (5) upon peacefulness (6) upon equanimity or concentration (7) and upon non-attachment-with discrimination, with, passionlessness, with restraint and with determination of renunciation. Then those harmful *asâvâs* which would have been caused by their non-meditation do not happen by their meditation. Thus *asavas* should be removed by meditation.

*Note.*—The twelve meditations already described according to the Jain Scriptures for restraint of inflow of passions do very correctly include the above stated seven meditations

The Buddhist *Asrava Suttra* of Majjhim Nikaya correctly agrees with the subjective inflow and the subjective checking of karmas described in the Jain Scriptures.

The Jain philosophy mentions *self-concentration* as the means for the shedding of karmic dirt. This self-realization purifies the soul, and thereby the soul attains *Nirvâna.*

The Jain Saint *Sri Umaswami* says in the *Tattvârtha sutra* :—

**तपसा निर्जरा च** IX 3.

**अनशनावमोदर्यवृत्तिपरिसंख्यानरसपरित्यागविविक्तश - य्यासन कायक्लेशा बाह्यं तपः** IX 19.

**प्रायश्चित्त विनयवैयावृत्त्यस्वाध्यायव्युत्सर्गध्यानान्युत्तरम्** IX 20.

**उत्तमसंहननस्यैकाग्रचिन्तानिरोधो ध्यानमान्तर्मुहूर्त्तात्** IX 27.

**आर्तरौद्रधर्म्यशुक्लानि** IX 28.

**परे मोक्षहेतु** IX 29.

**आज्ञापायविपाकसंस्थानविचयाय धर्म्यम्** IX 36.

**पृथक्त्वेकत्ववितर्कसूक्ष्मक्रियाप्रतिपातिव्युपरतक्रियानिव - र्तीनि** IX 39.

*Tapasâ nirjarâ cha.* IX. 3.

*Anasanâ-va môdarya vritti parisankhyâna rasa parityâga vivikta sayyâsana kâya klesa bâhyam tapah IX. 19.*

*Prāyaschitta vinaya vaiyyâ vritya svâdhyaya vyutsarga dhyânanyuttram IX. 20.*

*Uttama sanhananasyaikagrachintanirôdha dhyâna mantar mahurtât.* IX, 27.

*Ârta raudra dharmya suklani, IX. 28.*

*Parê môksa hêtu, IX. 29.*

*Ajnapâya vipâka sansthâna vicha-yâya dharmyam, IX. 36.*

*Prithaktvaikatva vitarka suksmakriya pratipâti vyupurata kriya nivartini, IX. 39.*

Translation and purport :—

The Shedding of karmas is caused by austerities. They are of two kinds; external and internal. The external austerities are of six kinds :—

(1) *Anasana*—fasting. Not taking any of the four kinds of food *e.g.* eatable, drinkable, lickable and tastable, for promoting self-control, for destroying lust and for attaining self-concentration.

(2) *Avamôdarya*—Taking less than what is required for the appetite, for awakening in control, subsidence of defects, contentment, easy engagement in reading and meditation.

(3) *Vritti pari sankhyâna*—to have a sacred pledge in mind before going for alms such as to go till so many homes, etc. If the pledge is not fulfilled and if alms are not procured then to have satisfaction and to subdue desires.

(4) *Rasa parityâga*—to give up one or more of the six kinds of rasas *e.g.*, ghee, curd, milk, sugar, salt and oil, for the control of senses and for easy engagement in reading and meditation.

(5) *Vivikta sayyâ sana*—to sleep and to sit in a lonely place for the observance of chastity and for the attainment of deep meditation and deep knowledge.

(6) *Kâyaklesa*—Mortification of the body so long as the mind is not disturbed. To practise austerities in forest, on mountains and on the shore of a sea or the bank of a river etc. for advancing in self-concentration and spiritual bliss. Others may know that the monks are suffering hardships, but they may not feel any kind of uneasiness. These six external austerities ars practised by a monk according to his own might, so that he may not feel any pain but feel internal happiness and love. It is said in "Tattvartha sutra" *Saktitastapah* 24/6. "*Aniguhita viryasya margavirodhi kâya klesa stapah*—i.e., this *kâyaklesa tapa* should be followed according to one's own power which may not be inconsistent with the real path of liberation.

The six internal austerities are :—

(1) *Prâyaschitta*—Expiation—to remove one's transgressions in vows on adopting punishment through the teacher.

(2) *Vinaya*—Reverence—for the right belief, right knowledge and right conduct and for the worthy followers.

(3) *Vaiyya vritya*—Service—serving the distressed, fatigued and sick saints.

(4) *Svâdhyâya*—Reading holy scriptures.

(5) *Vyutsarga*—Giving up attachment to body etc.

(6) *Dhyana*—Concentration.

Concentration is of four kinds :—

(1) *Arta dhyana*—painful concentration as feeling sorrow etc. (2) *Raudra Dhyana*—wicked concentration—to have pleasure in teasing others. (3) *Dharma dhyana*—right concentration. (4) *Sukla dhyana*—Pure concentration. Right concentration is of four kinds :—

(1) *Ajna vichaya*—to meditate upon the right principles according to the scriptures.

(2) *Ajna vichaya*—to meditate on how to remove one's affection and hatred and karmas and how to remove wrong belief and knowledge of others.

(3) *Vipaka vichaya*—to meditate upon the causes of pleasure and pain, the ripening of karmas.

(4) *Sansthana vichaya*—to meditate upon the nature of the universe and upon the pure soul itself.

*Pure concentration*—is of four kinds :—

(1) *Prithaktva vitarka vichara.* Absorption in meditation of the Self, but unconsciously allowing its different attributes to replace one another.

(2) *Ekatva vitarka avichara*—Absorption in one aspect of the Self, without changing the particular aspect concentrated upon.

(3) *Suksma kriya-pratipati*—The very fine vibratory movements in the Soul, even when it is deeply absorbed in itself, in a Kevali.

(4) *Vyupurata kriya nivarti*—Total absorption of the self in itself, steady and undisturbably fixed without any motion or vibration whatsoever.

In Jainism, practical right belief has been said to be firm belief in the seven principles, of which subjective inflow, subjective bondage, subjective checking and subjective shedding have been described above.

Self-concentration or perfect equanimity or *Samyak Samâdhi* is the subjective shedding which removes karmic dirts. Subjective liberation or *Nirvana* is the same thing and has been described in the first chapter. *Nâma rûpa* of the Buddhists is included in the two principles soul and non-soul. Some more details of these two principles may be useful to the readers :—

*The soul principle*—

The natute of the soul from both the practical and real points of view have been described in the second chapter. All the conditions pertaining to the worldly souls are included in *Nâma rûpa* of the Buddhists, while the pure soul *i.e.*, (worldly soul minus worldly conditions and matter) is what is *Nirvana* of the Buddhists and the Jains.

*Non-soul principle :*—

There is no consciousness in it. It is of five kinds. They are the five root-substances :

(1) *Pudgala*—matter. That in which atoms may have union and disunion is called *Pudgala*. Its special natures are touch, taste, smell and colour. Indivisible matter is particle and different kinds gross and fine molecules are formed by their different numerical union. The four elements of earth, water, fire and air are formed from matter. Karmic molecules which inflow towards the mundane soul and are bound with it are fine material molecules invisible to the senses. Sound, bondage, fine things, gross things, material figures, pieces, darkness, shades, light and sun-shine etc. are all the modifications of matter.

*Tattvârthasâra* says:—

**भेदादिभ्यो निमित्तेभ्यः पूरणाद्गलनादपि ।**
**पुद्गलानां स्वभावज्ञा कथ्यंते पुद्गलाइति ॥**

*Bhedâdi bhyo nimittebhyah Purṇadgalanadapi*
*Pudgalânâm svabhâvajnaih kathyante pudgalâ iti*
*55/3.*

Pudgalas are so called, because they unite and disunite, owing to breaking and mingling, on account of external causes.

(2) *Dharma sti kâya*—medium of motion. It is one immaterial substance all pervading in the universe which is a very essential auxiliary cause for the motion of souls and matter. It does not induce them to move.

(3) *Adharmâsti kâya*—medium of rest. It is one immaterial substance all pervading in the universe which is a very essential auxiliary cause for the resting of souls and matter. It does not induce them to rest.

(4) *Ākâsa.* Space—It is infinite, is the greatest of all substances in dimension, immaterial, one whole substance—which has the capacity of giving space to all the other substances.

(5) *Kala*—Time. Time-atoms called *kalanu* are separate existing on each of the spacial points of the universe. As the spacial units of the universe are innumerable so the Time-atoms are also innumerable in number. Their function is to be the auxiliary cause of the modification of all the substances.

*Note.*—As far as I have read the Buddhist literature, I have not found such divisions of the substances in it. The Buddhist books say that Goutama did not describe 'what is in the universe.'

According to Jainism right belief and right knowledge of the seven principles, soul, non-soul, inflow, bondage, checking, shedding and liberation are practical right belief and right knowledge, while firm belief in the pure nature of one's own self is the real right belief and right knowledge.

Let us describe *Right Conduct ;* Dravya Samgraha, a Jain work says :—

**असुहादो विणिवित्ती सुहे पवित्ती य जाण चारित्तं ।**
**वदसमिदिगुत्तिरूवं ववहारणया दु जिणभणियं ॥ ४५ ॥**

*Asuhâdo viṇvittî suhe pavittê ya Jâṇa chârittaṃ,*
*Vadasamidiguttirûvam vavahâraṇayâ du Jiṇabha-*
*ṇiyaṃ.*

Giving up bad engagement and following good engagements should be known to be conduct; (five) vows, (five) carefulness and (three) restraints have been said to be practical conduct by the Jina.

Five *Mahâvrata* or great vows are non-injury, truth, non-stealing, chastity and non-possession.

Five *Samiti* or carefulness are carefulness in walking, speaking, eating, handling and casting refuse.

Three Gupti or restraints are control over mind, body and speech.

These thirteen kinds of conduct are for the monks from the practical point of view.

Dravya-Samgraha says:—

**बहिरब्भंतरकिरियारोहो भवकारणप्पणासट्ठं ।**
**णाणिस्स जं जिणुत्तं तं परमं सम्मचारित्तम् ॥ ४६ ॥**

*Bahirabhantarakiriyâroho bhava-kâraṇappaṇâ satthaṃ,*
*Nâṇissa Jaṃ Jiṇuttaṃ taṃ paramaṃ samma-chârittam.*

Cessation of external and internal activity for the destruction of causes of the worldly existence by a right knower has been said to be the real right conduct by the Jina.

Self realization or self-absorption is surely the real right conduct.

*Note.*—The readers must note that the Buddhist books describe the eight-fold path of liberation which agrees with the three-fold path of liberation described in the Jain books.

*Samyak dristi*—right view and *Samyak sankalpa*—right determination, are included in the *Samyag darsan*—right belief and *Samyag jnana* right knowledge of the Jains; while the remaining six i.e., *Samyak vachana*—right speech, *Samyak karmante*—right action, *Samyak-ajiva*—right livelihood, *Samyak-vyayama*—right effort, *Samyak smriti*—right recollection and *Samyak samadhi*—right concentration are included in *Samyak charitra*—right conduct of the Jains.

Just as self-concentration has been prominently said to be the means of deliverance in the Buddhist Books, so also it has been said in the Jain books. Let us give some passages from the Jain books.

(1) Dravya Samgraha of Sri Nemichandra :—

**दुविहंपि मोक्खहेउं झाणे पाऊणदि जं मुणी णियमा ।**
**तम्हा पयत्तचित्ता जूयं झाणं समब्भसह ॥ ४७ ॥**

***Duvihaṃpi mokkha heuṃ jhâṇe, pâûṇadi Jaṃ muṇi ṇiyamâ,***

***Taṃha payattachittâ jûyam jhâṇam samavbhasaha,***

" Because a Saint while absorbed in self-concentration gets both the causes of liberation, (practical and real), therefore (all of) you practise self-concentration with careful mind."

(2) *Samayasâra Kalasa says* :

एकोमोक्षपथो य एषनियतो दृग्ज्ञप्ति वृत्यात्मक ।
स्तत्रैव स्थितिमेति यस्तमनिषां ध्यायेच्च तं चेतति ॥
तस्मिन्नेवनिरंतरं विहरति द्रव्यान्तराण्यस्पृशन् ।
साऽवश्यं समयस्य सार मचिरान्नित्योदयं विन्दति ॥

*Eko mokṣa patho ya eṣa niyato*
*drig Jṇapti vrittyâtmakas*
*Tattraiva sthiti meti yastanisum*
*dyâyechcha tam chetati,*
*Tasmin neva nirantaram viharati,*
*dravân tar âṇyaspṛiś an,*
*So vaśyam samayasya sára machirân*
*nittyodayam vindati, 47/10.*

"The path of Liberation is one which is a combination of real right belief, right knowledge and right conduct. He, who not having connection with all the other substances day and night stays in it, meditates upon it, relises it and always walks in that same only, necessarily and at once experiences the essence of soul shining for ever."

(3) *Samâdhi sataka* says :—

इतिदं भावेयन्नित्यमवाचा गोचरंपदं ।
स्वत एव तदाप्नोति यतो ना वर्ततेपुन ॥ ९९ ॥

*Itidam bhâveyen nittyamavacha gocharam padam,*
*Svata eva tadâpnoti yato nâ vartate punah* 99.

" Thus meditate upon this eternal and inexpressible path, by which only one can reach that from which there is no return."

(4) *Istopadêsa* says :—

आत्मानुष्ठाननिष्ठस्य व्यवहारबहिः स्थितेः ।
जायते परमानन्दः कश्चिद्योगेन योगिनः॥ ४७ ॥

*Ātmânusthâna nisthasya vyvahâra bahih sthiteh,*
*Jâyate parmânandah kaśchidyaogena yoginah.* 47

"On being fixed in real self-conduct and remaining outside the practical one a kind of highest bliss is experienced by a meditator by force of concentration."

आनंदो निर्दहत्युद्धं कर्मेन्धन मनाग्तं ।
न चासौ खिद्यते योगी बहिर्दुःखे स्वचेतनः ॥ ४८ ॥

*Ānando nirdahatyuddham karmêndhana manâratam,*
*Na chasau khidyate yogî bahir dukkhe ṣva chetanah.* 48

"This bliss continuously burns groups of karmic fuels; the meditator at that time does not feel pain being inattentive to external miseries."

(5) *Tattvânusâsana* says :—

स च मुक्तिहेतु निद्धोध्यानेयस्मादवाप्यते द्विविधोपि ।
तस्मादभ्यसन्तु ध्यानं सुधियः सदाप्युपास्यालस्यं ॥ ३३ ॥
एकाग्र निरोधो यः परिस्पंदेन वर्जितः ।
तद्ध्यानं निर्जराहेतुः संवरस्य च कारणं ॥ ५६ ॥
स्वात्मानं स्वात्मनि स्वेन ध्यायेत्स्वस्मै स्वतोयतः ।
षट्कारक मयस्तस्माद् ध्यानमात्मैव निश्चयात् ॥ ७३ ॥
संगत्यागः कषायाणां निग्रहो व्रत धारणं ।
मनोऽक्षाणां जयश्चेति सामग्री ध्यान साधने ॥ ७५ ॥
स्वाध्यायात् ध्यानं मध्यास्तां ध्यानात् स्वाध्याय माननेत् ।
ध्यानस्वाध्यायसंपत्त्या परमात्मा प्रकासते ॥ ८१ ॥

दिधासुः स्वं परं ज्ञात्वा श्रद्धाय च यथास्थितं ।
विहायान्यदनार्थित्वात् स्वयं वावैतु पश्यतु ॥ १४३ ॥
कर्मजेभ्यो समस्तेभ्यो भावेभ्यो बिन्न मन्वहं ।
ज्ञ स्वभाव मुदासीनं पस्येदात्मानमात्मना ॥ १६४ ॥
समाधिस्थेन यद्यात्मा बोधात्मानानुभूयते ।
तदा न तस्य तद्ध्यानं मुर्छावान् मोह एव सः ॥ १६९ ॥
यथा यथा समाध्याता लप्स्यते स्वात्मनिस्थितिं ।
समाधि प्रत्ययाश्चास्य स्फुटिस्यंति तथा तथा ॥ १७९ ॥
ध्यान्स्य च पुनर्मुख्यो हेतु रेतच्चतुष्टयम् ।
गुरूपदेशः श्रद्धानं सदाभ्यासः स्थिरं मनाः ॥ २१८ ॥

*Sacha mukti hetu riddho dyane yasmâda-vâpyate dvividhopi*
*Tasmâdabhyasantu dhyânam sudhiyah sadâpyupâsyâlasyam* 33

*Ekâgra nirodho yah parispandena varjitah*
*Taddhyânam nirjarâ hetuh samvarasyu cha kâranam* 56

*Svâtmânam svâtmani svena dhyâyetsvasmai svato yatah*
*Satkâraka mayastasmâd dhyâna-mâtmaiva niśchayât* 73

*Sangatyâgah kasâyânâm nigraho vrata dhâranam*
*Mano ksânâm Jayaścheti sâmagri dhyâna sâdhane* 75

*Svâdhyâyât dhyâna madhyastam dhyânât svâdhyâya mananet*
*Dhyânasvâdhyâya sampattva paramâtma prakâsate* 81

*Didhâ suh svam param jnâtva śriddhâya cha yathâ-sthitam,*
*Vihâyû nyadanarthi tvât svameva-vaitu paśyatu* 143
*Karmajibhyo samastebhyo bhavebhyo bhinna manva ham*
*Jṇa svabhâva mudâ śinam pasyedâtma namâtmanâ* 164
*Samadhis thena yadyâtmâ bodhâ tma nânubhuyate*
*Tadâ na tasya taddhyanam murchhâvan moha eva sah* 169
*Yatha yatha samâdhyâtâ lapsyate svatmani sthitim,*
*Samâdhi pratyayâschâsya sphutisyanti tatha tatha* 179
*Dhyanasya cha punar mukhyo hetu retachch atusṭayam,*
*Gurupadesah śriddanam sadu bhya-sah sthiram manah* 218

" Because both kinds of practical and real paths of liberation can be attained in self-concentration, therefore the wise after giving up slothfulness, should always practise concentration."

" Attention to one special object (soul) without wavering is concentration. It is the cause of checking karmas and shedding them also."

" Becauce the soul concentrates upon itself, in itself, through itself, for itself and from itself, therefore the soul itself present in the six cases is concentration, from the real point of view."

" Renunciation of property, control of passions, practising of vows and conquering of mind and senses are the materials for the practice of concentration."

" Practise concentration from scriptural reading, and come to scriptural reading from concentration—thus by the gift of concentration and reading the pure soul is enlightened."

" He, who wants concentration, should know and believe the self and the non-self as they are and then giving up the non-soul thinking it to be useless, should perceive and know the self only."

" He should always see the self through the self, as distinct from all the thought-activities arising by karmas, having knowledge as nature and indifferent to others."

" As far as the concentrating person attains steadiness in his own self, so far the glories of concentration would be realised."

" Again there are four special causes of concentration :—(1) Instruction from a Teacher (2) conviction (3) continual practice (4) and steady mind."

(6) *Vairagya mâla* by Chandra.

विरम विरम बाह्यादि पदार्थे रम रम मोक्षपदे च हितार्थे ।
कुरु कुरु निजकार्यं च वितंद्रः भव भव केवल बोध यतीन्द्रः ॥६८॥
मुंच मुंच विषयामिष रोगं लुंप लुंप निजतृष्णारोगं ।
रुंध रुंध मानस मातंगं धर धर जीव बिमलतर योगं ॥ ६९ ॥
चिंतय निज देहस्थं सिद्धं आलोचय कायस्थं बुद्धं ।
स्मर पिंडस्थं परम विसुद्धं कल केवल केलीशिव लब्धं ॥ ७० ॥

*Virama Virama bâhyâdi padârthe, rama rama*
*moksapade cha hitârthe,*
*Kuru Kuru nija Kâryam cha vitandrah bhava*
*bhava kevala bodha yatindrah.* 68
*Munche Munche visayâmisa rogam lumpa lumpa*
*nija trisnâ rogam,*
*Rundha rundha mânasa mâtangam, dhara dhara*
*jiva vimala tara yogam* 69
*Chintaya nija dehastham siddham Alochaya*
*kâyastham buddham*
*Smara pindstham parama vissuddham kala kevala*
*keli śiva labdham* 70

"Be unattached to all the foreign objects. Be absorbed in the useful path of liberation, do the duty of the self carefully, and become the lord of saints, gifted with perfect knowledge." 68

"Give up the desire of sensual enjoyment like flesh, remove the disease of desire, control the mind-elephant and adopt the pure concentration, O Soul!" 69.

"Meditate upon the perfect soul living in your body; think of the enlightened one staying in your body, remember the purest one in the body and take ease in the independent amuser who has attained the Bliss."

(7) *Tattva sâra* by Devasena says :—

**तम्हा अब्भसउ सदा मुत्तूणां रायदोस वा मोहो ।**
**झायउ णिय अप्पाणं जइ इच्छइ सासयं सुक्खं ॥ १६ ॥**
**णाणमयं णियतच्चं मिल्लिय सव्वेवि परगया भावा ।**

तं छंडिय भावेज्जो सुद्धसहावं णियप्पाणं ॥ ४३ ॥
जो अप्पाणं झायदि संवेयण चेयणाइ उवजुत्तं ।
सो हवइ वीयरायो णिम्मल रयणप्प ओ साहू ॥ ४४ ॥

*Tamha abbhasau sadâ muttunam raidosa vâ moho*
*Jhâyan ṇiya appâṇam Jai ichchai sâsayum sukkham.* 16
*Nâna mayam ṇiya tachcham milliya savvevi pargayâ bhâvâ*
*Tam chhandiyo bhâvejjo suddha-sahâvam niyappâ-nam* 43
*Joappânam jhâyadi samveyana cheyanâi uvajuttam*
*So havai viya râyo nimmala rayaṇappa o Sâhu* 44

"If you desire eternal bliss, then giving up affection, hatred and delusion, always practise your own self. 16

"Excepting one's own nature which is full of enlightenment all the other conditions are non-self; leaving them, one should meditate on the pure nature of one's own self." 43

"The monk, who being attentive to self-realization meditates upon the self, becomes free from attachment, pure, and lord of the three gems—right belief, right knowledge and right conduct. 44

(8) *Yogasâra* by Yogindra says :—

सुद्ध सचेयण बुद्ध जिणु केवल णाण सहाउ ।
सो अप्पा अणुदिण मुणहु जइ चाहउ सिवलाहु ॥ २६ ॥
जेहउ जज्जर णरयघरु तेहउ बुज्झि सरीर ।

अप्पा भावहु णिम्मलहु लहु पावइ भवतीर ॥ ५० ॥
अप्प सरुवइ जो रमइ छंडवि सहु ववहारु ।
सो सम्मादिट्ठी दवइ लहु पावइ भवपारु ॥ ८८ ॥

*Suddu sacheyana buddhu Jinu, Kevala nâṇa sahâu,*
*So appâ aṇudiṇa muṇahu Jai châhau siva lâhu* 36
*Je hau Jajjara ṇaraya gharu tehau bujjhi sarîra,*
*Appâ bhâvahu ṇimmalahu lahu pâvai bhavu tîra* 50
*Appa saruvai yo ramai chhandavi sahu Vavahâru,*
*So sammâditthi havai lahu pâvai bhava pâru* 88

" If you wish to attain *Nirvana,* then day and night meditate upon the self which is pure, conscious, enlightened, victorious, and has all—knowledge." 36.

" Know this body to be filthy like a home of hell. Meditate upon the pure soul, then you will soon attain liberation." 50

" He, who giving up all engagements, finds peace in the nature of the self, is the right believer able to cross the Ocean of *Samsâra* very soon."

(9) *Brihat samâyika pâtha* by Amitgati says :—

शूरोहं शुभधीरहं पटुरहं सर्वाधिक श्रीरहं
मान्योहं गुणबानहं विभुरहं पुंसामह मग्रणी ।
इत्त्यात्मन्नपहाय दुष्कृत्करीं त्वं सर्वथा कल्पनां
शश्वद्ध्याय तदात्म तत्त्व ममलं नैः श्रेयसी श्रीर्यतः ॥ ६२ ॥

*Surôham subhadhiraham paturahâm sarvâdhika sri raham*

*Mânyoham guṇavânaham Vibhu-raham punsâ maha magraṇi*
*Ityatmannapahâya duskrit karim tvam sarvathâ kalpanâm*
*Saśavad dhyayâ tadâtma tattva mamalam naih śreyasi śrir yatah.* 62

"I am brave, wise, clever, having highest property, honourable, lord, qualified, the first of all men—all these harmful notions, O Soul, you should give up and always meditate upon that pure self, by which the Goddess of *Nirvâna* can be acquired."

(10) *Sâra Samuchchaya* by Kulabhadra says :—

भवभोगशरीरेषु भावनीयः सदा बुधैः
निर्वेदः परयाबुद्ध्या कर्माराति जिघृक्षुभिः ॥ १२७ ॥
यायन्न मृत्यु बज्रेण देहशैलो निपात्यते
नियुज्यतां मनस्तावत् कर्माराति परीक्षये ॥ १२८ ॥
त्यज कामार्थयोः संगं धर्मध्यानं सदा भज ।
छिंद्धिस्नेहमयान् पासान् मानुष्यं प्राप्य दुर्लभं ॥ १२९ ॥

*Bhavabhoga śariresu bhâvaniyah sadâ budhaih*
*Nirvedah parayâ buddhyâ Karmârâti Jighri Kṣubhih.* 127
*Yâvanna mrityu bajrena dehasailo nipâtyate.*
*Niyujyatam manas tâvat karmârâti pariksaye* 128
*Tyaja kâmârthayoh samgam dharmadhyânam sadâ bhaja*
*Chhindhi snehamayânpâsân mânusyam prâpya durlabham* 129

"The wise, wishing to destroy the enemies of karmas, should always contemplate non-attachment with the world, enjoyments and body through high discrimination." 127

"As long as this hill of body is not broken by the adamantine death so long fix the mind on the destruction of karmic enemies." 128

"Give up the company of enjoyment and property, break the net of affection and always adopt the right concentration, when you have acquired a human birth difficult to be had." 129

(11) *Sadbhôdha chandrôdaya* by Padmanandi says :—

**कर्मभिन्नमनिसं स्वतोऽखिलं पश्यतो विशद बोध चक्षुषा ।**
**तत्कृतेपि परमात्मवेदिनो योगिनो न सुखदुःख कल्पना ॥ २१ ॥**

*Karma bhinna manisam svato-khilam pasyato viśada bodho chakṣuṣa*

*Tatkritepi parmâtma vedino yogino na sukha dukkha kalpanâ.* 21

"The monk who realizes himself always distinct from karmas through the eye of pure discrimination, does not attend to pleasure and pain, although they arise through karmas, because he is attentive to the realization of pure soul."

**बोधरूप मखिलै रूपाधिभिर्वार्जितं किमपि यत्तदेव नः ।**
**नान्यदल्पमपि तत्त्वमीदृशं मोक्षहेतु रितियोगानिश्चयः ॥ २५ ॥**

*Bodarûpa makhilai rupâdhi-bhir varjitam kimapi yattadeva nah,*

*Nânyodalpa mapi tattva midrasam moksa hetu riti yoganischayah.* 25

"That principle, which has the nature of knowledge and is free from all defects, only belongs to us; there is no other principle like it which is the cause of *Nirvâna;* such is the belief of the Monks."

**आत्मबोध शुचि तीर्थमद्भुतं स्नानमत्र कुरुतोत्तमं बुधाः ।**
**यन्नयात्यपर तीर्थकोटिभिः क्षालयत्यपि मलं तदंतरं ॥ २८ ॥**

*Âtmabôdha suchi tirtha mad-bhutam snâna matra kuru tottamam budhâh,*

*Yanna yâtyapara tirth koti bhih ksâlsyatyapi malam tadantaram.* 28

"Self-knowledge is a marvellous river, O wise men, perform the best bath here; that internal dirt, which cannot be washed by millions of rivers, can be washed by it."

(12) *Ekatva adhikâra* by the same author, says :—

**संयोगेन यदायातं मत्तस्तत्सकलं परं ।**
**तत्परित्यागयोगेन मुक्तोऽहमिति मे मतिः ॥ २७ ॥**

*Samyogena yadâyâtam mattastat-sakalam param,*
*Tat parityâga yôgena mukto hamiti me matih* 27

"In connection of which I have been coming on, that whole is apart from me; by its relinquishing I am liberated—this is my view."

तदेव महतीविद्या स्फुरन्मंत्रस्तदेवहि ।
औषधं तदपि श्रेष्ठं जन्मव्याधि विनाशकम् ॥ ४९ ॥
अक्षयस्याक्षयानन्द महाफल भराश्रियः ।
तदेवैकं परंबीजं निःश्रेयसलसत्तरोः ॥ ५० ॥

*Tadeva mahati Vidyâ sphuran mantrastadeva hi,*
*Ausadham tadapi śresth.ım janma-vyâdhi vinâ*
*sakam.* 49
*Aksayasyâ ksayâ nanda mahâ phala-bhara śri yah*
*Tadevaikam param bijam nihsre-yasa lasattaroh* 50

"That (self-realization) only is the greatest learning, that is the shining charm, that is the best medicine for the destruction of the disease of worldly existence."

"That only is the best seed for the tree of the eternal *Nirvâna* which supplies the greatest fruit of indestructible bliss."

साम्यं स्वास्थ्यं समाधिश्च योगश्चेतो निरोधनं ।
शुद्धोपयोग इत्त्येते भवन्त्येकार्थवाचकाः ॥ ६४ ॥
साम्यमेकं परंकार्यं साम्यं तत्त्वं परं स्मृतम् ।
साम्यं सर्वोपदेशानामुपदेशो विमुक्तये ॥ ६६ ॥
साम्यं सद्बोध निर्माणं शाश्वदानन्द मंदिरं ।
साम्यं शुद्धात्मनोरूपं द्वारं मोक्षैक सद्मनः ॥ ६७ ॥

*Sâmyam svâsthyam samâdhischo yogas cheto*
*nirodhanam,*
*Suddhopayoga ittyete bhavantye kârtha vâchakâh* 64
*Sâmyamekam param kâryam sâmyam tattvam*
*param smritam,*
*Sâmyam sarvopadesânâmupa-deśo vimuktaye* 66

*Ṣâmyam sadbodha nirmânam śâsvadâ nanda mandiram,*
*Sâmyam suddhâtmano rupam dvâram mokṣaika sadmanạh.* 67

" Equanimity, self-absorption, concentration, meditation, control of mind, pure conscious attentiveness—all these are synonyms."

" Equanimity is the only action, it has been said to be the best principle; equanimity is the best of the teachings for *Nirvana*."

" Equanimity produces right knowledge, it is the home of eternal bliss. Equanimity is the nature of the pure soul, it is the door to the castle of *Nirvâna*."

Ignorance (avidya) and desire (trisna) have been said to be the root causes of pain in the Buddhist literature; the same has been said in the Jain Scriptures also.

---

## JAIN VERSES ON IGNORANCE AND DESIRE.

(1) *Svayambhu stôtra* by Sri Samantabhadra.

**आयत्यां च तदात्त्वे च दुःखयोनिर्निरूत्तरा ।**
**तृष्णा नदीत्वयोत्तीर्णा विद्यानावा विविक्तया ॥ ९२ ॥**

*Āyattyâm cha tadâttve cha dukkha yonir niruttarâ,*
*Tṛiṣṇa nadi tvayottirṇâ vidyâ nâvâ viviktayâ.* 92

" You have crossed over the river of desire which s the incomparable cause of miseries here and herefter with the help of the boat of unattachment."

शतह्रदोन्मेष चलंहि सौख्यं तृष्णामयाप्यायन मात्वहेतुः ।
तृष्णाभिबृद्धिश्च तपत्यजश्रं तापस्तदायासयतीत्यवादिः ॥ १३॥

*Sa ta hṛidon meṣa chalam hi saukhyam trisnâ mayâpyâyan mâtra hetuh*

*Trisnâbhibriddhischa tapatyajasram tapastadâyâsaya titya vâdih. 13.*

" This sensual pleasure is fleeting like lightening, and is only the cause of increasing the disease of desire; the increase of desire always burns, which is miserable; thus you have said."

(2) *Samâdhisataka* by Pujyapada.

अविद्या संज्ञितस्तस्मात्संस्कारो जायते दृढः ।
येन लोकोऽगमेव स्वं पुनरप्यभि मन्यते ॥ १२ ॥

*Avidyâ sanjṇitas tasmâtsanskâro jâyate dradhah,*
*Yena lokongameva svam punarapyabhi manyate 12*

"Through the continuous ignorance, firm engraving is produced, on account of which this human being again and again maintains his body to be the self."

तद्ब्रूयात्तत्परान् पृच्छेत्तदिच्छेत्तत्परोभवेत् ।
येनाविद्यामयं रूपं त्यक्त्वा विद्यामयं ब्रजेत् ॥ ५३ ॥

*Tat bruyât tatparân prich chettadichchhet tatparo bhavet*

*Yenâvidyâ mayam rûpam tyaktva vidyâ mayam brajet. 53*

" Speak that, ask that from the others, have longing for that and be absorbed in that, by which the ignorant nature may be removed and the enlightened nature may be acquired."

(13) *Istopadeśa* by the same author says :—

**मोहेन संवृतं ज्ञानं स्वभावं लभतेनहि ।**
**मत्तःपुमान् पदार्थानां यथामदनकोद्रवैः ॥ ७ ॥**
**रागद्वेषद्वयी दीर्घ नेत्राकर्षणकर्मणा ।**
**अज्ञानात्सुचिरं जीवः संसाराब्धौ भ्रमत्यसौ ॥ ११ ॥**

*Mohena samvritam jṇânam svabhâvam labhate nahi,*
*Mattahpumân padârthânâm yathâ madana kodravaih 7*
*Râga dveṣa dvayi dirgha netrâkâr ṣa ṇa karmaṇâ,*
*Ājṇânât suchiram jivah sansârâbdhau bhramat-yasau. 11*

" Knowledge obscured by delusion does not realize the nature of the self, just as a man having eaten the intoxicating grain *Kondo* does not see the objects rightly."

" This living being, from beginningless time, having attracted karmas through affection and hatred, caused by ignorance is floating in the Ocean of *Samsâra*."

(4) *Samayasâra Kalasa* by Amritachandra says :—

**अज्ञानान्मृगतृष्णिकां जलधियाधावन्ति पातुं मृगा**
**अज्ञानात्तमसि द्रवन्ति भुजगाध्यासेन रज्जौ जनाः ।**
**अज्ञानाच्चविकल्पचक्रकरणाद्वातोत्तरंगाब्धिः व**
**च्छुद्ध ज्ञानमया अपि स्वयं ममी कर्त्रीभवन्त्याकुलाः ॥१३-३॥**

*Ajṇânân mṛiga tṛiṣṇikâm Jala dheya dhâvanti*
*pâtum mṛigâ,*
*Ajnânâttamasi dravanti bhujagâ-dhyasena rajjau*
*Janâh,*
*Ajná nâchcha vikalpa chakra karana dvâtotta-*
*rangabdhi va*
*Chchhuddha Jnânamayâ api svaya mami kartri*
*bhavantyakulah 13/3.*

" Through ignorance, the deer runs to drink mirage, thinking it to be water; through ignorance men run away in the dark mis-taking a rope to be a serpent; as the waves in the sea are tossed by winds, the beings. who are really full of pure knowledge, become doers of actions, through ignorance having been perplexed by different notions."

अज्ञानी प्रकृति स्वभावनिरतो नित्यं भवेद्वेदको
ज्ञानीतुप्रकृति स्वभाव विरती नो जातु चिद्वेदकः ।
इत्येवं नियमं निरूप्य निपुणै रज्ञानिता त्यज्यतां
शुद्धैकात्ममये महस्यचलितै रासेव्यतां ज्ञानिता ॥ ५८-१० ॥

*Ajṇâni prakriti svabhâva nirato nittyam bhaved-*
*vedako,*
*Jṇâni tu prakriti svabhâva virato no Já tu chid-*
*vedakah,*
*Ityevam niyamam nirûpya nipuṇai rajnâ nita*
*tyjyatâm.*
*Suddhai kâtma maye mahasya chalitai râ sevyatam*
*Jṇânita 58/100.*

"The ignorant being addicted to the nature of matter always becomes its enjoyer, the learned being unattached to the nature of matter never becomes its enjoyer; thus knowing the rule, the wise men must give up ignorance and should serve knowledge being steadfast in the light of the pure self." 58/10

**व्यवहार विमूढदृष्टयः परमार्थं कलयान्ति नो जना ।**
**तुषबोधबिमुग्ध बुद्धयः कलयंतीह तुषं न तंडुलं ॥४९-१० ॥**

*Vyavahâra vimûdha dristayah, parmârtham*
*kalayanti no janâh*

*Tuṣa bodha vimugdha buddhayah kalayantih*
*tuṣam no tandulam.* 49/10

"Just as those, who are foolish in understanding husk to be rice, are attentive to husk only, but not to rice; so also those, who are deluded in worldly affairs, never pay attention to the real substance."

(5) *Tattvânusâsanam* by Nâgasena says:—

**यत्तु संसारिकं सौख्यं रागात्मक मशाश्वतं ।**
**स्वपरद्रव्यसंभूतं तृष्णासंतापकारणं ॥ १२४३ ॥**

*Yathu sansârikam saukhyam ragâtmaka masas-*
*vatam*

*Svapara dravya sambhutam triṣnã santâpa*
*kâranam. 1243*

"That which is sensual pleasure produced by the connection of the self with the non-self, is full of lust, is transitory and is the cause of creating desire and pain."

(6) *Tattva-sära* by Devasena says :—

**रूसइ तूसइ निच्चं इंदिय विसयेहि संजवो मूढो ।**
**सकसाओ अण्णाणी णाणी एदो दु विवरीदो ॥ ३५ ॥**

*Rusai tusai nichcham indiya visa yêhi sanjao mûdho,*
*Sakasâo aṇṇâni ṇaṇi eto du vivarido.*

" The deluded one always is either pleased or pained in connection with the sensual objects, and is full of passions and ignorance, while the learned remains free from them."

(7) *Jnâna lochana stotra* by Vâdirâja says :—

**अनाद्यविद्यामय मूर्छितांगं कामोदरक्रोधहुतशतप्तं ।**
**स्याद्वादपीयुष महौषधेन त्रायस्व मां मोह महाहिदाष्टम् ॥ ३१॥**

*Anâdya vidyâ maya murchhi tângam kâmodara krodha hutasa taptam,*
*Syâdvâdapiyûsâ mahouṣadhena trâyasvamâm mohâ mahâ hidasṭam. 31*

" I have been deluded from the beginningless time by ignorance, I am burning with the fire of sensuality and anger, and I am bitten by the great serpent of delusion ; save me by supplying me the great nectar-like medicine of knowledge which is not one-sided."

(8) *Sâra Samuchchaya* by Kulabhadra :—

**तृष्णांधा नैव पश्यंति हितं वा यदि वा हितं ।**
**संतोषांजनमासाद्य पश्यंति सुधियोजनाः ॥ २३९ ॥**
**हृदयं दह्यतेऽत्यर्थं तृष्णाग्नि परितापितं ।**
**न शक्यं शमनंकर्तुं विनासंतोष वारिणा ॥ २४५ ॥**

यैः संतोषामृतंपीतं तृष्णातृद् प्रणाशनं ।
तैश्च निर्वाण सौखस्य कारणं समुपार्जितम् ॥ २४७ ॥

*Trișnándhâ naiva pasyanti hitam vâ yadivâ hitam,*
*Santoșânjana mâsâdya paśyanti sudhiyo janâh,* 239
*Hridayam dahyate tyartham trișn·âgni paritâpitam.*
*Na sakyam śamanam kartum vina-santoșa vârinâ* 245
*Yaih santosâmritam pîtam trisņa trit pranâsanam,*
*Taischa nirvâņa saukhasya kârnam samupârjitam.* 247

"Blinded by desire do not look to their benefit or loss, while the wise men having antimony of contentment look to that."

"This heart is strongly burning with the flame of desire, which cannot be extinguished without the water of contentment."

"They, who have drunk the nectar of contentment, which removes the thirst of desire, have attained the means of enjoying the bliss of Nirvâna."

(9) *Subhașita ratna sandoha* by Amitagati, contains :—

रे जीवत्वं विमुंचक्षणरुचि चपला निन्द्रियार्थोपभोगा
नभिर्दुःखं ननीतः किमिह भववनेऽत्यन्त रौद्रै हतात्मन् ।
तृष्णां चेत्तेन तेभ्यो विरमति विमतेद्यापि पापात्मकेभ्यः
संसारात्यन्त दुःखान्कथमपि न तदा मुग्ध मुक्तिं प्रयासि ॥४१०॥

*Re Jiva tvam vimuncha ksaņa ruchi—chapata-*
*nindriyarthopabhogâ,*
*Nebhirdhukkham na nitâh kimih bhava vane tyanta*
*roudri hatâtman,*

*Trisnân chettena tebhyo viramati, vrimate, dyâpi pâpâtmakebhyah,*
*Sansârâtyanta dukkhân kathamapi na tâda mugdha muktim prayâsi.* 410

" O Soul ! give up these sensual enjoyments which are fleeting like lightening ; O Soul, there is no such pain which has not been suffered by you in this very dangerous forest of Samsara. If you have any desire, O Wisdomless, for these sinful enjoyments, you should give it up even now, otherwise, O Fool, you can never go to Nirvâna being freed from the great miseries of this *Samsara*."

---

## *PRAJNA* OR SELF-DISCRIMINATION.

The Buddhist literature has shown the great necessity for *Prajna* in very strong terms :—

(1) Hindi Buddha Charya page 415 (D.N. 1-10.2) Sangita pariyaya Sutta. There have been described four right spheres :—

*Prajna* (discrimination), *Sila* (practical vows), *Samâdhi* (concentration) and *Vimukti* (liberation). Out of these four, the last is the result while the first three are the means to *Nirvâna,* and they are included in the eight-fold path *Samyak dristi,* etc. During my talks with the learned Buddhist Monks of Ceylon I came to know that *Samyak dristi* and *Samyak sankalpa* are included in *prajna ; Samyak Vachana, Samyak*

*Karmanta*, *Samyakajiva*, *Samyak Vyayama and Samyaksmriti* are included in *Sila;* while *Samyak Samâdhi* is itself *Samâdhi*.

The Jain scriptures also describe the three-fold path which very closely resembles the Buddhist three-fold path. *Samyak darsana* and *Samyak Jnana* of the Jains are included in *Prajna*, because it means right discrimination such as " my self is distinct from non-self and all other substances, and that I am only realizable alone " ; while practical *Samyak-châritra* of the Jains is included in *Sila* and the real *Samyak châritra* is included in *Samâdhi*.

(2) Buddha Charya p. 244 D.N. 1-4 *Sinadanda Suttâ*—

It says: " Self-discrimination is purified by conduct, conduct is purified by self-discrimination. When there is conduct there is discrimination; when there is discrimination, there is conduct; self-discrimination is procured by conduct, while conduct is procured by self-discrimination. Still conduct is said to be the foremost of all the self-discriminations. Self-discrimination is purified by conduct and conduct is purified by self-discrimination."

*Note.* In fact, practical conduct is necessary for right belief and right knowledge, thereby the mind will become mild and self-discrimination will appear, while on procuring self-discrimination, practical conduct will be improved and concentration will arise. Both are the means for concentration.

The Jain scriptures also glorify *prajna* or self-discrimination thus :—

*Samayasâra* says :—

**पण्णाएघित्तव्वो जो चेदा सो अहं तु णिच्छयदो ।**
**अवसेसा जे भावा ते मज्झे परेत्ति णादव्वा ॥ ७१ ॥**

*Paṇṇâe ghittavvo Jo chadâ so aham tu nichchhayado,*
*Avasêsâ Je bhâvâ te majjhe paretti nâ davvâ*

"That conscious being which is to be grasped by self-discrimination is I am myself from the real point of view ; all the other conditions are foreign to me—this should be known."

*Sâra Samuchchaya* says :—

**प्रज्ञांगना सदासेव्या पुरुषेण सुखावहा ।**
**हेयोपादेयतत्वज्ञा या रता सर्व कर्मणी ॥ ७५ ॥**

*Prajnâ ṅganâ sadâ sevya purseṇa sukhâ vahá,*
*Heyôpâdeya tattvajna ya rata sarva karmani.*

"The Maiden of self-discrimination, which is always obedient in knowing the adoptable and the rejectable principle in all the actions and is blissful, should always be served by a man."

## FOUR MEDITATIONS.

The Buddhist literature speaks highly of the four meditations :—*maitre* or friendship, *pramôda* or delight, *kârunya* or compassion, *Upêksa* or *madhyastha* or indifference.

*Buddha Charya* pa. 186 M. N. 2. 1. 2. Mahâ Râhula-vâda sutta (1) Rahula! meditate upon friendship; by such friendly feelings enmity will be destroyed. (2) Rahula! meditate upon compassion; by compassionate feelings, injurious thoughts will be destroyed. (3) Rahula! meditate upon delight, by delightful thoughts you will remove dissatisfaction. (4) Rahula! meditate upon indifference, by which your thought of enmity will be destroyed.

The Jain scriptures also declare that these should be meditated upon by every saint and layman :—

(1) *Tattvârtha sutra* by Umaswami says :—

**मैत्रीप्रमोदकारुण्य माध्यस्थानि च सत्त्वगुणाधिक क्लिश्यमाना विनयेषु ॥ ११-७ ॥**

*Maitri-pramôda kârunyamadyas-thani cha sattva gunâdhika kliśyamânâ vinayeshu. 11/7*

" Friendship towards all the beings, delight towards those great in qualifications, compassion towards the afflicted and indifference towards those who are perversely inclined."

(2) *Samâyika path* by Amitagati says :—

**सत्वेषु मैत्री गुणिषु प्रमोदं क्लिष्टेषु जीवेषु कृपापरत्वं ।**
**माध्यस्थ भावं विपरीतवृत्तौ सदा ममात्मा विदधातु देवः ॥१॥**

***Sattvesu maitri gunisu pramodam, Klitesu Jivesu Kripa parattvam.***

***Mâdhyastha bhâvam viparita vrittau sada mamatme vida dhâtu deva : 1***

"O Lord, let my soul always have friendship towards all the beings, delight towards the qualified, compassion towards the afflicted and indifference towards those perversely inclined."

The above statements will clearly show that the eight-fold path of *Nirvâna* in Buddhism quite agrees with the *three-fold* path of *Nirvâna* in Jainism. Both Jainism and Buddhism believe that one can attain *Nirvâna* by one's own efforts; never can it be given through compassion by any personal God.

Both the religions lay stress on self-discrimination. Both strongly recommend the giving up of affection, hatred, delusion. Both say that Nirvâna is realizable. Both lay stress on the control of the five senses and the mind. Both teach relinquishing injury, false-hood, theft, unchastity and desire.

Both declare that mind, body and speech must be kept free from harmful actions and they should be applied to those useful means which result in procuring *Nirvâna*.

## CHAPTER IV.

### KARMAS AND THEIR FRUITS.

It is evident from the Buddhist literature that every being experiences fruits of his good and bad deeds in the very life or in the future life and that the being takes another birth owing to *Sanskara* or mentation of previous birth ; and that as far as continuation of five spheres of body, feeling, perception, mentation and (impure) consciousness goes on, so long has the being to undergo many births and that when all the *âsavâs* (impure thought-vitalities) will be destroyed, *Nirvâna* will be procured.

Although Buddhist literature does not seem to give clear, direct and detailed description of bondage and fruition of *Karmas*, still there are scattered passages here and there which show that the writers of the Buddhist literature had in their mind the description of karmas according to what the Jain scripture says.

A metaphysician can know it by *devoted* and critical study. Jain authors say that there are fine karmic molecules made up of material particles floating throughout the universe. They are so fine that they cannot be known by our senses. This mundane soul attracts them according to good and bad thought-activities when performing actions through mind, body and speech. This is called *âsravâ* or inflow. Their existence with the soul for some duration is called *Bandha* or bondage.

When these bound karmas are ripened, they give agreeable or disagreeable results. They can be destroyed before their ripening-time by self-concentration. When there is no inflow of karmas through passions, the soul is called *Ksinâsrava* or destroyer of inflow. Thus by checking inflow and by destroying the old accumulated karmas, the soul attains liberation or *môksa* or *Nirvâna*.

*Môksa* has been described in *Tattvârtha sutra* by Umaswami thus:—

**बंधहेत्वभावनिर्जराभ्यां कृत्स्नकर्मविप्रमोक्षो मोक्षः.**

*Bandha hetva bhâva nirjarâbhyâm kṛitsna karma vipra môksô môksah.*

"Liberation (is) the freedom from all karmic matter, owing to the non-existence of the causes of bondage and to the shedding of karmic molecules."

Before describing in detail the karmic philosophy as given in the Jain scriptures, it is advisable to let the readers know those passages in the Buddhist literature which in short give the description of karmas as is given in Jainism.

(1) *Majjhim nikaya* ; *deotia sutta savvâsava.*

" *Âsavâ samvarâ pahâ tavva,*" is a Pali question. Which *âsrava* should be removed by *samvara?* Here both these words are the same as in Jainism. If their liberal meaning is taken into consideration, they would mean that something, which comes, is checked.

" Bhikkhu savvâsava samvara samvuto vihorati." This means that the monk roams while checking all the *âsravas* (i.e., all the karmas which had to come were checked).

(2) Majjhim nikaya bhaya bhairava sutta Chatuttham.

" Yathâ kam mupage satte pajanami " i.e., I know the beings when they are prone to ripening of their karmas.

*Note.* Here the word " kam mupage " shows that karmas are ripened " Michchhâ ditthi kamme samadânâ " (i.e.) having wrong belief karma.

*Note.* This passage refers to a class of karma named *mithyâ-dristi karma* which is bound by a wrong believer.

(3) Digha Nikaya Vol. III—33, Sangita Suttanta.

" Tayo râsi—michchatta—niyato râsi, sammatta niyato râsi, aniyato râsi." Here the word *rasi* means a collection or group,

The passage means " the group of wrong belief only, the group of right belief only, the group of their mixed."

These terms refer to three classes of karmic molecules as described in Jain scriptures:—wrong belief deluding karma is of three kinds, wrong belief karmas, clouded right belief karma and mixed right and wrong belief karma. The word *rasi* refers to group of karmic molecules as said in the Jain scripture.

(4) Buddha Charya page 370 Anguli mala sutta (M. N. 2-4.8.)

" O Brahmana, you are suffering the fruit of that karma (*karma vipaka*) in the very life, which would have to be suffered for many centuries, many millenniums in the hell by you. Then the Saint *Angulimala*, while enjoying the bliss of freedom in self-concentration at a solitary place said the verse which means."

" He at first collects the karmas and then destroys them. He is shining in the universe like the moon within the clouds. His acquired bad karmas are covered with good karmas."

*Note.* Here the words *karma vipaka*, '*arjite*' '*marjit*', the example of cloud and moon show that karmas are something material distinct from the pure soul; which can be ripened, collected and destroyed and they obscure the soul in the same way as the clouds obscure the moon and when they are removed, the moon-like soul is shining forth.

(5) *The Doctrine of the Buddha* by George Grimm (1926.)

*Page 252.* First of all, of course, our present body, like every future one, together with all its sense-organs and mental faculties ; thus what we have called before the six-sense-machine is exclusively a product of our previous action, in-as-much as it has brought about the grasping in the material womb ; This not, ye disciples, your body, nor the body and another, rather must it be regarded as the *deed* of the *past*, the deed that has come to fruition, the deed that is willing actualized. That has become perceptible. (S. N., II p. 64.)

The eye, ye monks, is to be recognized and regarded, as determined through former action, the ear, the nose, the tongue, the body, the mind, ye monks ; to be recognized and regarded as formed and determined through former action (S. N. II. p. 72.)

*P. 256.* These, ye disciples, a man has won insight with the body, has practised himself in virtue, has developed his mind, has awakened knowledge, is broad-minded, magnanimous, dwelling in the immeasurable. In such a man, ye disciples, the same small crime which he has committed ripens even during his life-time.

*Note.* In the above passage, the word *kamma* is translated by *deed* while it really means karmic molecules.

(6) Manuscript Remains of Buddhist literature in Eastern Turkestan by A. F. R. Hoernl (1916).

Sata-panchâ sika stotra by *Matricheta.* Its 73rd

verse has the words "*Raga renam praśam ayati*" means—"subsiding the ashes of affection."

*Note.* Here the word '*raga*' shows that affection producing karma is a material like ash.

Part II *Vajra Chhedika*:

**"प्रज्ञापारमितां एतां संकलितवान् सर्वज्ञः भगवान् तां त्रिशतिकाम् वाचयति प्रकाशयति यः एव वज्र छेदिकाम् नाम सर्वाणि कर्माणि तथा आवर्णस्य पापानि सम्यक् वज्रः यथा तेन वज्रछेदिका नाम."**

"*Prajṇâ pâra mitam etâm sankalita vân—sarvajṇah bhagawân tâm tri satikâm vâchayati prakâsuyati yah eva vajra chhedikâm náma sarvâni karmâni tathâ âvarṇasya pâpâni samyak vajra yuthâ tena vajra chhedikâ nâma.*"

"This *Prajná páramita sutra* has been declared by the omniscient lord. It has three hundred verses. He who reads and expresses it, for him its name is assigned "*vajra chhedika* i.e., it cuts off all the karmas and obscuring demerits like adamant, therefore it is named such."

*Note.* This statement very clearly shows that karma is a material thing which obscures and which can be cut and broken.

*Fage 289.* *Apari mitâyuh sutra.* It has twenty verses.

**"य इदम् अपरिमितायुः सूत्रं लिखिष्यति लिखापियिष्यति तस्य पंचान्तरायाणि कर्मावरणानिपरिक्षयं गच्छंति."**

"*Ya idam apari mitâyuh sûtram likhi syati, likhe payisyati, tasya panchantara yani karma varnani-pariksayam guchchhanti.*"

"He who writes this *apari mitayuh sutram* or makes another write it, his five obstructive karma-obscurings are destroyed."

*Note.*—Here the obscuring of karmas and their destruction is described just like what the Jain scripture says. Jain literature describes *antaraya* karma or obstructive karma to be of five kinds:—*Dânântaraya* (obstructing charity), *Lâbhântaraya* (obstructing gain), *Bhôgântaraya* (obstructing the use of once-enjoyables) *Upa bhôgântaraya* (obstructing the use of many-times-enjoyables), *Viryantaraya* (obstructing power).

They are material molecules, which are collected and destroyed.

(7) "*Some sayings of the Buddha*" by Woodward (1925).'

*Page 196.* Then make thyself an island of defence, strive quick ; be wise : when all thy Taints of dirt and dust are blown away, the saints shall greet thee entering the happy land (Dhammapada)."

*Note.*—Here the words 'taint,' 'dirt' and 'dust' refer to some fine matter which can be blown away.

(8) Sacred books of the East Vol. X 1881 Dhammapada.

Cha. XVIII. Impurity.

*Page 243.* "But there is taint worse than all taints, ignorance is the greatest taint. O mendicants, throw off that taint and become taintless."

*Note.* Here the word 'taint' refers to some material thing which is dirty.

Page 369, Cha. XXV. The Bhiksu.

"O Bhiksu! empty this boat! if emptied, it will go quickly, having cut off passion and hatred, thou wilt go to '*Nirvâna*.'

*Note.* Here the passage shows that the boat is heavy on account of some matter which should be thrown off and the boat should be emptied.

(9) *Sacred books of the Buddhists Vol. III* by T. W. Rhys Davids. Dialogue of the Buddha from Digh Nikaya (1910).

Page 148 Chap. IV. *Mahâparinibbân suttanta.*

"There has heen laid up by *Chunda,* the smith a karma redounding to length of life, redounding to good birth, redounding to good fortune, redounding to good fame, redounding to the inheritance of heaven and of sovereign power."

*Note.*—This statement clearly shows what the Jains say. His deed has collected karmas which would be ripened into all the merits said here.

(10) "*Sansara* or Buddhist philosophy of birth and death" by Bhiksu Narada, published by P. D. M. Perera, Post Master, Talavakele (16-10-1930).

Page 5. Buddha tells us that the coming into being of the linking consciousness (Pati sandhi-vinnana) is dependent upon the passing away of another consciousness in a past birth, and that the process of coming into being and passing away is the result of the powerful force known as *kamma*.

Page 10. The multifarious forms are merely the manifestation of kamma force.

It is common to say after witnessing an out-break of passion or sensuality in a person, whom we deemed characterized by a high moral standard, "How could he have committed such an act, or followed such a conduct ?" It was not the least like what he appeared to others and probably to himself." What did it denote ? It denoted, Buddhists say, part at any rate of what he really was, a hidden but true aspect of his actual self, or in other words his *karmic* tendencies."

Page 15. "By death is here meant, according to the *abhidhamma*, the ceasing of psychic life of one's individual existence, or to express it in the words of a western philosopher, the temporary end of a temporary phenomenon of the so-called being, for, although the organic life has ceased, the force which hither-to actuated it, is not destroyed. As the *kammic* force remains entirely undisturbed by the dis-integration of the fleeting body, the passing away of the present consciousness only conditions a fresh one in another birth."

"The new being which is the present manifestation of the stream of *kamma* energy is not the same as, and has no identity with, the previous one in its line; the agregate that makes up its composition being different from, and having no identity with those that make up the being of its predecessor. And yet it is not an entirely different being, since the same stream of *kamma* energy, though modified per-chance just by having shown itself in that last manifestation, which is now making its presence known in the sense-perceptible world as the new thing" (*na ca so na cha anno*)—(neither the same nor another).

(11) The tract *The Bodhi Satta Ideal* by the same author *Narada Bhiksu.*

Page 18. "No person what-so-ever is exempt from the inexorable law of *Kamma.* It is law in itself. It alone determines the future birth of every individual. A Bodhisatta enjoys the special privilege of not seeking birth in eighteen states, in the course of his wanderings in *Sansara*, as the result of the potential *Kammic* force accumulated by him.

*Note.* The above statements clearly show the same kind of description of karmas as the Jain literature says and the Jains understand.

We give below some description of the karmic philosophy according to the Jain scriptures in short.

## KARMIC PHILOSOPHY OF THE JAINS.

As karmas are attracted and bound, they must be material in nature They are the karmic molecules made up of material particles; they are very fine, not cognizable by the senses. They are floating throughout the whole universe. As their fruition is material therefore they are matter. Just as a person may speak and act like a mad man—a reasonable man will infer from it that he has taken some intoxicating thing, similarly when it is proved that the nature of the real self is what is called *Nirvâna* where there is not any material bondage nor any mentation or *Sanskara*, then whatever conditions of anger, pride, deceit, greed, etc. appear in the mundane life of the self must have been caused in association with something different from the self. That which is associated with the self in mundane existence is that which is called *Karma*.

Anger etc. passions can never be the nature of the real self, because when anger arises, body trembles, eyes become red. Body is matter and some matter has made material effect on it, therefore that which has made the body tremble must be a material thing. It proves that anger is a material poison or dirt. Just as red and green waters show that there is mixture of red and green coloured matter with water, so anger etc. impure thought-activities prove that there is mixture of some dirt with the soul. And that dirt must be opposed to the soul which is really non-material. This is nothing else but *karmic matter*.

There are three acting agents in the mundane soul. They are mind, body and speech. As these three or any of the three are in joint connection everywhere with the soul, so whenever any activity through them happens, there occurs some wavering or vibration in the soul.

At the very time when vibrations occur in the mundane soul, the attractive power called *yoga* inherent in the soul begins to work. Yoga is a force which attracts karmic matter towards the soul and connects the same with it. This force of *yoga* attracts karmic molecules which are mixed with the other previously collected molecules in the *karmic fine* body which is continually coming on with the mundane soul. It should be noted that in this beginningless world phenomena, this mundane soul was never free from this karmic body. It is continually coming on in bondage. Through the fruition of different kinds of karmas in that fine body, there happen birth, death and different kinds of miseries. When any person dies, this karmic body is not left here. It goes with the mundane soul; only outer physicial body is left. The mundane soul going with the karmic body at once takes another birth under the influence of its karmas which are in operation. Old karmic molecules must shed off at the proper time whether they fructify or not from this karmic body and new molecules are added to it, which are attracted by *yoga* power, when any of the three, mind, body and speech is working and causing soul vibrations. This shedding and binding is going on in all the mundane souls at every instant. Vegetable, animal, human and other beings all have to obey this karmic law.

The Jain scripture, therefore, describes this mundane soul as material like, because it is totally obscured by material karmas just as sky is obscured by smoke, sun-light is obscured by clouds or water is made impure by dirt. If once all the karmic molecules are shed off, this soul will at once attain *Nirvâna* and remain non-material, and it is in essence like a sky.

As the nature of pure sky is not affected by matter, so the nature of pure liberated soul cannot be affected by karmas. In the mundane life, this soul is from beginningless time totally obscured by karmic matter. It is why it experiences its fruits good or bad.

Saint Amritachandra says in *Tattvârthasara* :—

यज्जीवः सकषायत्त्वात्कर्मणो योग्य पुद्गलान् ।
आदत्ते सर्वतो योगात् स बन्धः कथितोजिनैः ॥ १३ ॥
न कर्मात्म गुणोऽमूर्तेस्तस्य बंधा प्रसिद्धितः ।
अनुग्रहोपघातौ हि ना मूर्तेः कर्तुमर्हति ॥ १४ ॥
औदारिकादि कार्याणां कारणं कर्म मूर्तिमत् ।
नह्यमूर्तेन मूर्ताना मारम्भः क्वापि दृश्यते ॥ १५ ॥
न च बन्धप्रसिद्धिः स्यान्मूर्तैः कर्मभिरात्मनः ।

अमुर्ते रित्यनेकांतात्तस्य मूर्तित्व सिद्धितः ॥ १६ ॥
अनादि नित्यसम्बन्धात्सह कर्मभिरात्मनः ।
अमूर्तस्यापि सत्यैक्ये मूर्तत्त्व मवसीयते ॥ १७ ॥
बंधंप्रतिभवत्यैक मन्योन्यानुप्रवेशतः ।
युगपद्मानितः स्वर्णरौप्यवज्जीव कर्मणोः ॥ १८ ॥
तथा च मूर्तिमानात्म सुराभि भवदर्शनात् ।
नह्य मूर्तस्य नभसो मदिरा मदकारिणी ॥ १९ ॥

*Yajjivah sakasâyattvât karmano yogya pudgalân*
*Ādatte sarvato yog ât sa bandhah kathito Jinaih* 13
*Na Karmâtma guno murtestasya bandhâ prasiddhitah,*
*Auugrahopaghâtâu hi na murteh Kartu marhate* 14
*Audarikâ dikâryânam Kârnam karma murti mat,*
*Nahyamurten murtâ nâ marambhah kvâpi drśyate* 15
*Nacha bandha prasiddhih syan murtaih karmabhirât-manah,*
*Amurte rittya ne kântâttasya murtitva siddhitah* 16
*Anâdi nittyasambandhât saha karmabhirâtmanah*
*Amurtasyapi satyai Kye murtatva-mavasi yate* 17
*Bandham prati bhavetyai Kyama-nyonya nupravesa tah* 18
*Tathâ cha murti mânâtmâ surabhi-bhava darśanât,*
*Nahya murtâsya nabhaso madira mada Kârini* 19

"Taking in karmic material molecules from all-round through attracting power *yoga* by the passionate soul has been said to be bondage by the Jina 13.

"Karma is not any non-material attribute of the non-material soul because neither the non-material objects can be bound nor can there be destruction or any mutual benefit between non-material ones." 14.

"Mundane souls have got physicial bodies etc. which are material and created; their creating cause must therefore be the material karmas; because creation of material objects is never seen by any non-material thing." 15

"Bondage of this mundane soul by the material karmas is not an unproved fact, although from the real point of view this soul is non-material, yet from the practical standpoint it is like a material thing." 16

"There is beginningless and continual connection of this mundane soul with the karmas, therefore the soul being non-material by nature is seen as material, as it is intermixed with the material karmas." 17

"Just as gold and silver when melted together become one mixture, so also there is mixture of soul and karmas on account of its bondage with karmas." 18

"This mundane soul is material, because its knowledge is seen to be affected on drinking intoxicating liquor; while sky being non-material cannot be affected by it." 19

The mundane soul is from beginningless time continually coming mixed with material karmas. *Yoga* power attracts them and passionate thoughts make them stay for greater or less time.

When karmic bondage occurs, it appears in four kinds, therefore bondage is said to be of four kinds.

*Dravya Sangraha* says :—

**पयडिट्ठिदि अणुभागप्पदेसबेधादु चदु विधोबंधो ।**
**जोगा पयडिप्रदेसा टिदि अणुभागा कसायदो होंति ॥**

*Paya ḍi ṭhidi aṇu bhâga ppadesa-bhedâ du chadu vidho bandho,*
*Jogâ payadi pradesâ ṭhidi aṇu-bhâga kasâ yado honti*

" Bondage is of four kinds, *Prakriti* or class-bondage, *sthiti* or duration bondage, *anubhaga* or fruition bondage, and *pradesa* or molecular bondage ; of these class and molecular bondages are caused by *yoga* or attractive power working and soul vibrations ; and duration and fruition bondages are caused by passions.

When karmic molecules are bound, then they assume different kinds of nature according to different thought-activities of the being, this is called *Prakriti Bandha.*

The number of molecules bound for each class or sub-class bearing different natures is called *pradesa bandha.* The bound up molecules will be exhausted till such a period—this duration is called *sthiti bandha.*

When they will be ripened, their fruition will be mild or strong. This is called *anubhâga bandha.*

*Yoga* or attractive power working under soul vibrations is good or bad according to good or bad activities of the mind, body and speech. According to strong or mild *yoga* power under good and bad activities, greater or less number of karmic molecules having more or less number of classes are attracted and bound. Thus yoga causes two kinds of bondage, class and molecule.

When anger, pride, deceit, or greed etc. passions are strong then all the classes of karmas except age karmas have more duration ; if they are mild, the duration will be for smaller periods. The karmas which are bound are either good or bad.

When passions are strong, there is less fruition in good karmas, while more in bad ones ; but when passions are mild, there is more fruition in good karmas and less in bad ones.

As to age karma, if it is bad age karma of hell, there will be greater duration, if passions are strong ; but lesser, if they are mild ; but for the good age karmas of sub-human, human, celestial, if passions are mild there will be more duration ; if they are strong, duration will be for short period.

***Prakriti or class bondage.***

There are eight classes according to the nature of karmas ; even these eight have got one-hundred and forty-eight sub-classes according to their different varieties of natures. It will be useful to know all of them.

Class I. Sub-classes 5. *Jnâna varaṇa karma.* Knowledge—obscuring karma—It obscures the attribute of knowledge. As knowledge is of five kinds, so their obscuring karmas are also five :—

1. *Mati J.*—sensitive knowledge obscuring.
2. *Sruta J.*—Scriptural knowledge obscuring.
3. *Avadi J.*—Visual knowledge obscuring.
4. *Mana parhyaya J.*–mental knowledge obscuring.
5. *Kevala J.*—Perfect knowledge obscuring.

Class II, Sub-classes 9. *Darsana varana* karma or conation obscuring karma. It is of 9 kinds :

1. *Chaksu* d.—ocular conation obscuring.
2. *Achakṣu* d.—non-ocular conation obscuring.
3. *Avadhi* d.—visual conation obscuring.
4. *Kevala* d.—perfect conation obscuring.
5. *Nidra*—Sleep.
6. *Nidra nidra*—Deep sleep.
7. *Prachala*—Drowsiness.
8. *Prachala prachala*—Heavy drowsiness.
9. *Styanagriddhi*—Somnambulism.

Class III. Sub-classes 2. Vedaniya karma—feeling karma. It is of two kinds:

1. *Sata* v.—pleasure-feeling.
2. *Asata* v.—pain-feeling.

This karma makes the soul feel pleasure or pain.

Class IV. Sub-classes 28. *Mohaniya karma*, deluding karma, it deludes the right belief and conduct—it produces in the soul attachment, affection, hatred, fear etc. It is of two kinds :—

(1) *Darsana mohaniya* or right belief deluding karma.

(2) *Charitra mohaniya* or right conduct deluding karma.

*Darsana mohaniya* is of three kinds :—

(1) *Mityatva* wrong belief.

(2) *Samyaktva* clouded right-belief which produces defect in right-belief.

(3) *Samyaktva—mithyatva* or *misra*—mixed right and wrong belief.

*Note.* These three *rasi* are dealt with in D.N. 3.33 Sangita suttanto *as michhatta niyato rasi ; sammatta niyato rasi ; aniyato rasi.*

*Charitra m.* is of 25 kinds—

(4) to (7) *Anantânubhandhi krodha, mâna, mâya, lôbha,* error-feeding anger, pride, deceit and greed.

(These passions prevent right-belief from appearing).

(8) to (11) *Apratyâkhyâna krodha, mâna, mâya, lôbka,* partial-vow-preventing anger, pride, deceit and greed.

(12) to (15) *Pratyakhyâna krôdha, mâna, mâya, lôbha.* Total—vow preventing anger, pride, deceit and greed.

(16) to (19) *Sanjvalana krôdha, mâna, mâya, lôbha,* perfect-conduct preventing anger, pride, deceit and greed.

(20) to (28) *Hâsya*, risibility ; *Rati*, indulgence ; *arati* dissatisfaction ; *soka*, sorrow ; *bhaya*, fear ; *Jugupsa* disgust ; *Stri veda*, feminine inclination ; *Pum Veda*, masculine inclination ; and *Napunsaka Veda* neuter sex inclination.

Class V. Sub-classes 4. *Ayu karma*, age karma. It is of four kinds : This karma is the cause for keeping the soul imprisoned in any body.

(1) *Naraka*—hellish age.

(2) *Tiryancha*—sub-human age.

(3) *Manusya*—human age.

(4) *Deva*—celestial age.

Class VI. Sub-classes 93. *Nama karmas*, Body-making karmas.

It causes formation of different kinds of bodies. It is of 93 kinds.

(1) to (4) *Gati* condition of existence. It is of four kinds : (1) *Naraka* hellish ; (2) *Tiryancha* sub-human ; (3) *Manusya* human ; (4) *Deva* celestial.

(5) to (9) *Jâti* genus of beings ; it is of 5 kinds (1) *Ekendriya* one-sensed ; (2) *Dvindriya* two sensed ; (3) *Tendriya* three-sensed ; (4) *Choundriya* four-sensed (5) *Panchendriya* five-sensed.

(10) to (14) *Sarira* bodies. They are of five kinds : (1) *Audârika* physical ; (2) *Vaikriyaka* fluid ; (3) *Aharaka* assimilative ; (4) *Taijasa* electric ; (5) *Kârmana* karmic.

(15) to (17) *Angopângo*, limbs and minor limbs.

They are of three kinds pertaining to 3 bodies:

(1) *Audarika* physical. (2) *Vaikriyaka* fluid.
(3) *Āharaka* assimilative.

(18) *Nirmana* formation of limbs etc. in relation to situation, and dimension.

(19) to (23) *Bandhana* Bondage. It is of 5 kinds with relation to 5 bodies, physical, etc. described above.

(24) to (28) *Sanghâta*—interfusion (interfusion of molecules). It is of 5 kinds in relation to 5 kinds of bodies.

(29) to (34) *Sansthana* figure (of the body). It is of six kinds—

(1) *Sama chaturasra* symmetrical. (2) *Nyagrôdha muri mandala*—banyan tree-like (short in lower part, but larger in upper part.) (3) *Svâti*—Tappering like snake-hole, (broad in the lower and short in the upper part). (4) *Kubjaka*—hunch-back. (5) *Vamana*—dwarf. (6) *Hundaka*—unsymmetrical).

(35) to (40) *Samhanana*—Skeleton. It is of six kinds: (1) *Vajra risabha nâracha samhanana* adamantine nerves, joints and bones. (2) *Vajra nâracha s.* adamantine joints and bones. (3) *Nâracha s.* joints and bones. (4) *Ardha nâracha s.* semi joints with bones. (5) *Kîlita s.* Jointed bones. (6) *Asamprapta ṣripatika s.* Loosely jointed bones.

(41) to (48) *Sparsa*—touch. It is of eight kinds:— (1) *Sita*—cold (2) *usna*—hot; (3) *snigdh*—smooth; (4) *rûksa*—rough; (5) *komala*—soft; (6) *kathora*—hard; (7) *laghu*—light; (8) *guru*—heavy.

(49) to (53) *Rasa*—taste. It is of 5 kinds:— (1) *Tikta*—pungent (2) *katuka*—bitter (3) *kàsaya*—astringent (4) *amla*—acid (5) *madhura*—sweet.

(54) and (55) *Gandha* smell. It is of 2 kinds:— (1) *Sughanda*—good smell. (2) *Durgandha*—bad smell.

(56) to (60) *Varna* colour. It is of five kinds:— (1) *Krisna*—black. (2) *Nîla*—blue. (3) *Rakta*—red. (4) *Pîta*—yellow. (5) *Sukla*—white.

(61) to (64) *Ânupurvi* migratory form. It keeps the figure of soul in transmigration according to the body it leaves till it reaches the new body. It is of four kinds with reference to the four conditions of existence such as *Naraka gatyanupurvi*—hellish migratory form (while going to hell).

(65) *Aguru laghu* not-heavy—light (body neither too heavy nor too light).

(66) *Upaghâta* self-destructive (possessing a limb which destroys the self).

(67) *Parghâta*—fatal to others (by which others are injured)

(68) *Atapa* radiant light (which may give heat to others).

(69) *Udyota* cold light.

(70) *Uchchvasa* respiration.

(71) and (72) *Vihayogata* movement. It is of two kinds:—

1. *Subha* graceful. 2. *Asubha* awkward.

(73) *Pratyeka* individual body (a body enjoyable by one being).

(74) *Sadharana*—common body (a body enjoyable by many souls together).

(75) *Trasa* mobile (having bodies from 2 to 5 sensed).

(76) *Sthavara* immobile (having one-sensed bodies).

(77) *Subhaga* auspicious.

(78) *Durbhaga* inauspicious.

(79) *Suswara* sweet-voiced.

(80) *Dusvara* harsh-voiced.

(81) *Subha* beautiful.

(82) *Asubha* ugly.

(83) *Suksma*, fine (uncuttable).

(84) *Badara* gross.

(85) *Paryapta* developable.

(86) *Aparyapta* undevelopable.

(87) *Sthira* steady.

(88) *Asthira* unsteady.

(89) *Adeya* impressive.

(90) *Anâdeya* non-impressive.

(91) *Yasahkirti* fame.

(92) *Ayasah kirti* notoriety.

(93) *Tîrthankara* Great Teacher.

Class VII. Sub-classes 2. *Gotra karma* family determining karma. It is of two kinds :—(1) *Uchcha*—high ; (2) *Nicha*—low.

Class VIII. Sub-classes 5. *Antarâya karma*, Obstructive karma. It is of five kinds :

(1) *Dânântarâya*—charity obstructive.

(2) *Lâbhântarâya*—gain obstructive.

(3) *Bhôgântarâya*—enjoyment obstructive.

(4) *Upabhôgantarâya*—re-enjoyment obstructive.

(5) *Vîryantarâya*—power obstructive.

When karmas are bound, different sub-classes with different natures are determined according to soul vibrations effected by different kinds of passionate thought-activities.

*Pradesa bandha.* The number of karmic molecules of each sub-class and class is determined according to the strong or mild vibrations. Strong vibrations attract greater number of molecules, while mild vibrations less number of molecules.

At a particular instant of karmic bondage, age karma will have the least number, body-making karma will have more than that of age; family determining karma will have equal proportion to body-making karma. Knowledge-obscuring karma will have more than body-making karma. Conation obscuring and obstructive karmas will have their proportion equal to the knowledge obscuring karma. Deluding karma will have more than knowledge obscuring karma ; and the feeling karma will have the maximum number of molecules.

*Sthiti bandha.* Duration period of karmas is of three kinds, maximum, middle and minimum. Middle duration is of many kinds. Let us give below the maximum and minimum durations of the 8 main classes :—

| Name of class. | Maximum. | Minimum. |
|---|---|---|
| I *Knowledge obs.* | 30 Koti x Koti sâgars. | 1 *antar muhurta.* |
| II *Conation obs.* | do. | *do.* |
| III *Feeling.* | do. | 12 *muhurtas.* |
| IV *Deluding.* | 70 do | 1 *antar muhurta.* |
| V *Age.* | 33 sâgars. | *do.* |
| VI *Body-m.* | 20 Koti x Koti sâgars. | 8 *muhurta.* |
| VII *Family d.* | do. | *do.* |
| VIII *Obstructive.* | 30 do. | 1 *antar muhurta.* |

*Note.* *Sagara* = innumerable years ;
*Koti* = 10 millions.
*Muhurta*...48 minutes.
*Antar Muhurta*...within 48 minutes.

***Anubhâga bandha***—Out of the 8 classes the four, knowledge obscuring, conation-obscuring, obstructing and deluding karmas are called ***ghâtîya*** obstructive, because they obscure the nature of the soul. They are bad or demeritorious karmas. When there is a strong passionate thought–activity, the force of fruition will be stronger in them, but if the passions are mild the force of fruition will be weaker. Their forces being taken as stronger, strong, weak and weaker are exemplified by four examples in hardness and softness respectively of stone, bone, wood and creeper.

At the time of ripening the karmas will yield fruits in proportion to their strength and then shed off.

The other four karmas are called ***aghâ-tîya***—non-destructive. Each one of them is of two kinds good and bad. Good age, body making, family and feeling karmas are merits, while bad age, body-making, family and feeling karmas are demerits.

The fruition of these four good karmas is milder, mild, strong, and stronger exemplified by sweetness of molasses, sugar, refined sugar and nectar respectively: while the fruition of the above four bad karmas is also, milder, mild, strong and stronger exemplified by bitterness of a ***neem*** tree leaf, ***kânjira*** fruit, poison and deadly poison respectively.

Thus every mundane soul has four kinds of bondage according to its ***good or bad*** thought-activities.

***How the karmas operate and shed off:***

When the karmic molecules are bound, they take some time to become ripened; till then they remain in existence without operation and shedding. This time of quiescence is one hundred years for a duration of one koti koti sagars. According to this proportion if duration is one koti sagaras or less than that, the period of quiescence will come to one *antar muhurta.* After the proportionate lapse of quiescence time, the molecules begin to operate and shed at every instant till their full duration period is ended. These molecules of a particular group bound at a particular time are distributed for its full duration minus the quiescence time with a proportion of successive less number. The greater number operates before. The least number will operate at the last instant of the duration. Whenever karmic molecules are on the point of operation, they appear in their fruits, if the outward circumstances agree with them if the outward position is not agreeable, they will shed off without giving any result. For example: suppose any one has bound karmic molecules of all the four passions e.g., anger, pride, deceit and greed simultaneously with equal duration for each. They will take equal time for ripening. After their equal period of quiescence they all will begin to shed at every instant, but all the four cannot give results at a time. When there is anger, there is not pride, nor greed nor deceit; only one kind of passion appears at a time in the thought-activity. Suppose there is outward situation of creating anger, then anger karmic molecules will appear in fruit, while the molecules of the other three passions will shed of at that very instant without showing any result. Suppose any good person is attending to reading any pious book peacefully for half an hour; then his thought has good and pious feeling only. It is the result of mild greed. Till half an hour only, greed karma molecules are shedding after giving results, while the molecules of the other three passions shed off during that very half an hour without giving any fruit. Suppose within that half an hour there appears any outward cause of anger, some one may speak abusive words and that very person attending to pious book cannot endure them owing to the weakness of soul power, then anger will appear for some time; then the molecules of greed will shed without showing any fruit.

The Karmic law being such: it is therefore necessary that we should always try to have good circumstances and associations; then we can be saved from suffering fruits of bad karmas. True knowledge and soul-force are the means for effort. This force of effort is soul's own property which has expressed itself on the subsidence of destructive karmas. We may call it soul-will, soul-power, or soul-exertion. A minutest creature of the vegetable kingdom also has got this soul-power. It has some knowledge and soul-force which is not obscured by karmas. Thus every being has got capacity of applying its free will. They, who have got strong operation of deluding karmas are under control of ignorance or *avidya*. But they, who can remove this ignorance, have their pure soul-power more in store. They, who act after full consideration and mindfully, perform thoughtful and useful acts. If they succeed in their efforts, the meritorious karmas have helped them ; if they fail, the demeritorious karmas have made obstruction. As we, ordinary men cannot know what kinds of karmas are in store and when and how they will operate, it is our duty to perform every action with strong and thoughtful soul-power.

It should also be known that we can destroy the existing bound demeritorious karmas by self-concentration and pure thought-activities before their ripening time ; we can diminish their fruition and duration. We can increase the fruition of old good karmas. Our thought-activities can modify the past-bound karmas.

By the operation of age karma a being goes from one condition of existence to another. Karmic body goes along with it.

Those saints, who destroy the causes of inflow of karmas, are called *Ksiṇasrava*. This term is used in many Buddhist works. Vide Buddha Charya page 264 Sandaka sutta M. N. 2.3.6, page 55 Nanda-Rahula-Sanyasa Jataka N. 4 Mahâvagga, Mahâ Khandaka Rahula-Vastu.

How karmas can be checked and destroyed has

been dealt with in the third chapter while describing *Samvara* and *Nirjara*.

Let us show the special thought-activities for the bondage of each of the eight karmas. They are the special causes for the karmic bondage of a special karma.

*I. Causes for the bondage of knowledge and conation obscuring karmas :—*

(1) Displeasure on hearing truth (2) concealment of knowledge, not allowing others to ask him and take his time (3) not to teach others due to malice (4) to make obstructions to the progress of true knowledge (5) to dishonour the learned and the learning (6) to falsify the truth by misleading arguments.

*II. Causes for the bondage of pain-feeling karmas :*

(1) to feel pain or to make others painful.
(2) to be sorry or to make others feel sorry.
(3) to feel remorse or make others remorseful.
(4) to weep or make others weep
(5) to cry in a way to arouse compassion for him in others or to make others cry in such a way.
(6) to beat or to kill, etc.

*III. Causes for the bondage of pleasure-feeling karmas :—*

(1) to have compassion for all the beings (2) to feel great regard for the Vowful (3) to give charity of food,

medicine, knowledge and safety to the deserving pious men with honour and to the distressed through compassion (4) to follow rules of conduct of a saint (5) to follow rules of conduct of a layman (6) to practise meditation (7) to forgive others (8) to feel contentment etc.

*IV. Causes for the bondage of deluding karmas* :—

(1) To find fault with and speek ill of the true worshipful Lord, Teacher and the Truth itself (2) to have strong anger, pride, deceit and greed (3) to have strong laughter, indulgence, dissatisfaction, sorrow, fear and hatred (4) to have strong sex inclination, etc.

*V. Causes for the bondage of hellish age karma* :—

To earn money by unjust and ugly means, to have strong attachment for worldly possessions and not to spend money in charity and good works.

*VI. Causes for the bondage of sub-human age karma* :—

Deceit, *e.g.*, cheating others and preaching false doctrines.

*VII. Causes for the bondage of human-age karma* :—

(1) to deal justly and with contentment, to have little attachment with the worldly possessions, to have natural modest feelings.

*VIII. Causes for the bondage of Celestial-age-karma* :—

(1) to have firm right belief (2) to follow the rules of conduct of a saint (3) to follow the rules of conduct

of a layman (4) to endure hardships with patience (5) to follow austerities without self-knowledge.

*IX. Causes for the bondage of bad-body-making karmas :—*

(1) deceitful engagement of mind, body and speech (2) to quarrel and make disturbance.

*X. Causes for the bondage of good-body-making karmas :—*

(1) Straightforward dealing of mind, body and speech (2) to have love for others and not to quarrel with anybody.

*XI. Causes for the bondage of low-family determining karma :—*

(1) to speak ill of others (2) to boast oneself (3) to conceal others' good qualities (4) to express one's non-existing qualities.

*XII. Causes for the bondage of high-family-determining karma :—*

(1) to speak ill of oneself (2) to praise others' qualities (3) to conceal one's own qualifications (4) to express others' good qualities (5) to be submissive (6) not to feel proud.

*XIII. Causes for the bondage of obstructive karmas:*

(1) To put obstacles to charity (2) to obstruct the gain of others (3) to put obstacles for things being enjoyed by others (4) to obstruct others from enjoying

re-enjoyable things (5) to disturb the zeal of others for good works.

Thus the special thought-activities for the bondage of eight karmas have been described here very briefly. It should also be noted that generally a being binds seven or eight kinds of karmas at a time by its thought-activity; but there occurs difference in fruition bondage of each karma. The special thought activity pertaining to a particular karma will cause more mild or strong fruition in that very karma.

We find in the Buddhist literature also some description of the special thought-activities for the bondage of special karmas.

(1) Manuscript Remains of Buddhist literature in Eastern Turkestan by Hoernle (1916).

Page 48 (10) Suka Sutra of Madhyama Agama.

**"दशधर्मा महाशक्य संवर्तनीयः—कतमेदश-अनिर्व्यूकः, परस्य लाभ सत्कारः, आत्तमनता, परस्यकीर्त्तिः शब्दश्लोकेन आत्तमनता, यात्रा प्रदानं, बोधिचित्तोत्पादः, तथागतबिम्बकरणं, मातृपितृणां प्रत्युद्गमनं, आर्याणां प्रत्युद्गमनं, अल्पशक्यात्. कुशलमूलाद् विच्छंदनं महाशाक्य कुशलमूले समापादनं—इमे दशधर्मा महाशक्य संवर्तनीयः.**

"*Daśa dharmâ mahâ-śa-kya samvartaniyâh-katame dasâ-anirvyukah, parasya lâbha satkârah, âtta manatâ, parasya kirtih sabda slokena âtta-manatâ, yâtrâ pra-dânam, bodhi-chittotpâdah, Tathagata bimba Karṇam, matri pitrinâm pratyanugamanam, âryâ nâm pratyud-*

*gamanam, alpa sakyât Kuśala mulad vichchhandanam mahâsâkya-Kusala mule samâpâdanam-ime dasâ dharmâ mahâ sakya samvartaniyâh.*

There are ten thoughts which procure great power in the future life (1) not to have malice (2) to receive and honour others (3) to have worthy mind, to speak highly of others with good mind (4) to spend money for journey pilgrimage etc. (5) to strive to understand Truth (6) To construct images of Lord Buddha (7) to honour parents (8) to honour and receive the Virtuous men (9) to save one from good action of low degree (10) to induce one for good action of high degree. These ten should be followed for high might.

**" दशाधर्मानिच कुलसंवर्तनीयः—कतमेदश - अमातृज्ञाता, अपितृज्ञाता, अश्रामण्यता, अब्राह्मण्यता, कुले न ज्येष्ठानुपालनम्, आसनादि न प्रत्युत्थानम्, आसने न निमंत्राणं, मात्रापित्रोरश्रूषा, आर्याणां अश्रूषा, नीचकुल जातानां पुद्गलानां अन्तिक परिभवः, इमे दशाधर्मानीच कुलसंवर्तनीयाः. "**

*" Dasa dharmâ nîcha kula samvarta niyâh-katame dasâ-amâtrignatô-apitrignata, aśrâmanyati, abrâhma nyata, kule na Jesthânupâlanam, âsanâdi na pratyutthânam, âsane na nimantrânam, mâtra pitror aśruṣâ. âryâṇâm aśrūṣâ, Nîcha Kula jâtânâm pudgalânâm antike paribhavah, ime daśa dharmâ nîcha kula samvarta niyâh."*

The following ten actions are the causes for the birth in low family :—(1) Dishonour to mother (2) dishonour to father (3) being a monk, not to act as a monk, (4) being a Brahman, not to act as Brahman (5) not to protect the elders in the family (6) not to receive them properly (7) not to give them proper seats (8) not to serve the parents (9) not to serve the monks (10) to disgrace the poor and low people.

" **दशधर्मा उच्चकुल संवर्तनीयाः कतमे दश मातृज्ञाता, पितृज्ञाता, श्रमण्यता, ब्रह्मण्यता, कुले ज्येष्ठानुपालकत्वम्- आसनात् प्रत्युत्थानम्, आसनेनाभिनिमंत्रणं, मातापित्रो शुश्रू, षा, आर्याणां सुश्रूषा, नीचकुल जातानां पुद्गलानां अपरिभवः— इमे दशधर्मा उच्चकुल संवर्तनीयाः.** "

" *Dasa dharmâ uchcha kula samvarta-niyâh-katame dasa mátṛijṇatâ, piṭrijnata, śramanyatê; Brâhmanyat kule Jyesthanupâlakatvam âsanatpratyutthânam, âsane-nâbhi-nimantraṇam, mâtâ pitroh śuśruśâ âryânâm susṛusâ, nicha kula jâtânam pudgalânâm apari bhavah ime dasa dharmâ uchchakula samvartaniyah.*"

The following ten actions are the causes for the birth in a high family. (1) Honour to the mother (2) Honour to the father (3) to observe monk-hood (4) to observe the duties of a Brahmana (5) To protect the elders in the family (6) to receive them and honour them (7) to give them proper seats (8) to serve the parents (9) to serve the monks (10) not to hate those born in a low family.

" **दशधर्मा अल्पभोग संवर्तनीयाः- कतमे दश अदत्ता-दानं; अदत्तादान समादापनं, अदत्तादानस्य च वर्णवादिना,**

**अदत्तादानेन आत्तमनता, मातापितॄणां वृत्त्युच्छेदः, आर्याणां वृत्त्युच्छेदः, परस्य अलाभेन आत्तमनता परस्य लाभेन मात्तमनता, परस्य लाभांतरायो, दुर्भिक्ष याचना च इमे दशधर्मा अल्पभोग संवर्तनीयाः.**"

"*Daśa dharmâ alpa bhôga samvarta-niyâh Katame dasa adatta dânam adattadâna samadâ-panam, adatta dânasya cha varna vâdita, adattadânena atta-manatâ, mâto pitrinâm vrittyuchchhedah, âryânâm vrittyuchchhedah, parasya alâbhena attamanata para-sya labhena natta mânatâ, parasya labhântarâ yo, durbhiksa yâchanâ cha ime dasa dharmâ alpa-bhoga samvartaniyah.*"

The following ten actions cause insufficient enjoyments in the future (1) to take what is not given (2) to accept the things brought by theft (3) to speak good of theft (4) to be pleased with theft (5) to obstruct the livelihood of the parents (6) to obstruct the alms of the monks or the livelihood of good persons (7) to be pleased if one has not gained anything (8) to be displeased on another's gain (9) to obstruct the gain of others (10) to wish for famine.

"**दशधर्मा महाभोग संवर्तनीयाः कतमेदशः—दानं, अदत्तादानवैरमणं, अदत्तादानवैरमणस्य वर्णवादिता, अदत्तादान वैरमणेन आत्तमनता, परस्य अलाभेन अनात्तमनता, परस्यलाभेन आत्तमनता, परस्यलाभोद्योगः, दानस्याभ्यनुमोदनं, दानाधियुक्तानां, पुद्गलानां संप्रहर्षणं, सुभिक्षयाचना च इमे दशधर्मा महायोग संवर्तनीयाः.**"

"*Daśa dharmâ mahâ bhôga samvartaniyah :— Katame daśa :—dânam, adatta dâna-vairamaṇam, adattâ dâna vairamaṇasya varṇa vâdita, adattâ dâna vairamaṇeṇa atta manatâ parasya alâbhena anâttamanata, parasya labhena atta-manata, parasya labhodyogah, dâ nasya bhyanumodanam, dânâdhiyuktânâm, pudgalânâm sampraharsaṇam, subhiksa yâchana cha ime daśa dharmâ mahâ bhoga sumvartani yah.*"

The following ten actions are causes for having many enjoyments in future :—(1) charity (2) to be aloof from theft (3) to praise the person who does not steal (4) to be satisfied by not taking anything without being given (5) to be sorry if one has not gained anything (6) to be pleased on another's gain (7) to try for procuring gain to others (8) to be pleased on knowing others practising charity (9) to induce people for charity (10) to wish for favourable time.

*Note.* All these causes as stated in Buddhist literature are included in the causes of bondage of low and high family karmas and pleasure and pain feeling karmas as given before according to the Jain literature.

There is a great detailed description of bondage; fruition, checking and shedding of the Karmas in the Jain scriptures. The following books should be consulted :—

(1) Tattvârtha Sutra by Umaswami

(2) Tattvârtha Sâra by Amritchandra

(3) Sarvârtha Siddhi by Pujya pada
(4) Râja Vartika by Akalanka
(5) Gommatasâra by Nemichandra
(6) Labdhi Sâra by ,,
(7) Kṣapaṇa Sâra by ,,

English translation of No. 1 & 5 have been published and can be had from (1) "Jain Gazette" Office, 436, Mint Street, Madras, (2) Jain Publishing House, Ajit-ashram, Lucknow, (3) Jain Parishad Publishing House Bijnor.

Hindi translations of the above-said books can be had from the Digambar Jain Book Depot, Chanda Wadi, *Surat.* We have very briefly described the Karmic philosophy here. Whatever we have noted above shows that even the description of the Karmic law according to Jainism and Buddhism is not different. It is possible to have detailed description of Karma philosophy in Buddhist books also. If they could be traced, everything will agree with that of Jainism.

I believe that those who have compiled the old Buddhist literature must have had knowledge of the Karmic philosophy according to Jainism. The present literature, no doubt, does not speak of it so explicitly as the Jain literature does. The educated must study this subject calmly and carefully.

# CHAPTER V.

## AHIMSA.

*Ahimsa* is a famous cult of the Jains. I find that the Buddhist literature also speaks highly of *Ahimsa.* If minutely considered it is not in any way different from what the Jains say. As regards flesh-eating some statements in Buddhist literature appear doubtful. We have to consider whether they are the real sayings of the Buddha or not.

We give below some quotations about Ahimsa from the Buddhist books :—

(1) *Majjhim nikaya sallekha suttam atthaman :—*

"**पाणातिपातिस्स पुरिस पुग्गलस्स पाणातिपातवेरमणी-ह्मेति परिनिव्वानाय.**"

"*Paṇâtipâ tissa purisa puggalassa pâṇâti pata veramani hoti parinivvâ nâya.*"

"He who is addicted to injure the vitalities of living beings, should give up injury—this is for his liberation."

(2) *M. N. Samma ditthi suttam navama.*

"**पाणातिपातो अकुसलं पाणातिपातवेरमणीकुसलं.**"

"*Pâṇâ it pâto akusalam paṇâti pâte-verama ṇi kusalam.*"

"It is harmful to deprive one of vitalities; while it is useful to be aloof from injury."

(3) *Digha nikaya Vol. 3 Singalo vâda Suttante 31*

" पाणातिपातो अदिन्नादानं मुसावादो च वुच्चति परदारागमनंचेव नप्पसंसंति पंडितातिं. "

" *Panâtipâdo adinnâdânam musâvâdo cha vuchchati paradâragamanam cheva nappasansanti panditâti.*"

" The wise men do not praise injury of vitalities, theft, falsehood and intercourse with other women."

(4) *Digha N. Vol. 3 Sangit Suttanta 33*

" दश अकुशलकम्मपत्थ—(१) पाणातिपात (२) अदत्तादान (३) कामेसु मिच्छाचारो (४) मुसावादो (५) पिसूनवाचा (६) पुरुसावाचा (७) सम्फप्पलापा (८) अभिज्झा (९) व्यापादो (१०) मिच्छादिट्ठि. "

" *Dasa akusâla kamma-pattha—(1) pânâti-pâta (2) adattâ dâna (3) Kâmesu michchhâ-châro (4) musâ vâdo (5) pisuna vâchâ (6) phurusâ vâchâ (7) samphap-palâpâ (8) abhijjha (9) Vyâpâdo (10) michchhâ ditthi.*"

" The following ten are the harmful ways of Karmas :—

(1) injury of vitalities (2) theft (3) wrong sexual desire (4) falsehood (5) back-biting (6) harsh speech (7) useless talk (8) greed (9) enmity (10) wrong belief.

(5) *Anguttara nikaya 5-177*

" पंच इमा भिक्खवे बणिज्जा उपासकेन अकरणीयः—कतमे पंचसत्थबणिज्जा, सत्थबणिज्जा, मंसबणिज्जा, मुज्जबणिज्जा, विसबणिज्जा. "

*Pancha ima bhikkave baṇijja upâsakena akaraniyâh-katâ me panch-sattha banijja, satta banijja, mansa banijja, mujja banijja, visa banijja.*"

O Monks! The following five trades should not be followed by a layman :—

(1) trade in arms (2) trade in living creatures (3) *trade in meat* (4) trade in wine (5) trade in poison.

(6) *Buddha Charya.*

Page 100 (1) Mahâ vagga 10. "He, who returns after taking alms from the village, eats and what is left, if he does not wish to eat it, is thrown in such a place where there are no herbs or in water devoid of living beings."

*Note.*—This shows protection of immobile one-sensed beings.

(2) Page 144 Pârâjika I.

"It is the conduct of Buddhist monks that after finishing the rainy season and performing fast on the last day of *asvini* month, they should roam for public good—they finish their tour in nine months. But those monks who have not finished their pledge of *concentration* fast on the last day of *Kartika* month and leave the place on the first date of *marga sirkha* and finish their tour in eight months."

*Note.*—Here not to roam in the rainy season proves the regard for non-injury.

(3) Page 167—Mahâvagga 6 Keniya Jatil.

Goutama Sramana does not eat at night, which is not the proper time for eating.

(4) Page 173–A. N. A. K. 2.4.4.

Chule hatthi padopam sutta.

Lord Buddha keeps himself aloof from destroying the group of seeds and the group of beings, eats only once (in 24 hours), does never eat at night (untimely even after noon); does not put on flower garlands, and scents, does not use besmearing, nor ornaments, neither any decoration.

*Note.*—Here not eating at night shows regard for non-injury.

(5) Page 232–240 D. N. 1–5 Kutadante Sutta; on prohibition of animal sacrifice.

" Brahman! In that *Yagṇa* (sacrificial ceremony) cows were not killed, lambs and goats were not killed, fowls and pigs were not murdered, neither different kinds of creatures were murdered; neither trees were cut for post (Yupa), nor grass was cut which is injury. That ceremony of *Yajna* was performed with *ghee,* oil, butter, curd, sweets and molasses. Brahmana! He, who with cheerful mind follows rules of vows which are (1) to be aloof from injury of vitalities (2) not to take what is not given (3) to be aloof from sexual desire (4) not to speak untruth (5) not to take any intoxicating thing causing carelessness, performs the true *yajna.* Brahmana! This sacrifice is glorious and brings great fruit...

Gotama! I take shelter in Lord Goutama, in the Path of Truth and in the Order of Monks, from to-day kindly accept me your follower with folded hands.

Gotama! I now order for releasing seven hundred bullocks, seven hundred calves, seven hundred goats, seven hundred lambs. I give them safety of life. They now eat green grass, drink cold water, and walk in cold air.

*Note.*—This shows compassionate regard for trees and grass even.

(5) Page 255 M. N. 2–2–10 Kilagiri Sutta. Once Goutama Buddha with a large assembly of the monks went to Kashi. Then the Lord addressed the monks thus:—

"O monks, I tour avoiding eating at night. By not eating at night I experience health, zeal, power, easy walking. Come! monks, you should also eat—avoiding eating at night."

(6) Page 371—Angulimla sutta M. N. 2.4.6.

"He will protect the immobile and mobile creatures, having obtained highest peace."

(7) Page 390—Simdauka Bharadvas Sutta S. N. 7—1—9.

"Throw this remaining estable into the place free from grass or into water free from creature."

(8) Page 464—Samanja phala Sutta D. N. 1–1–2.

The Conduct of monks is described in it. Monk keeps aloof from destruction of seed—groups and groups of creatures, takes food once, does not eat at night, neither eats at untime. He is aloof from destroying groups of seeds and creatures: such as those grown through roots, grown through trunk, grown through fruit, grown through fruit-stem and grown through seeds.

*Note.*—Here the protection of vegetable kingdom is well described.

It agrees with the description given in the Jain Scripture *Gommatasara Jiva Kanda.*

*Chapter on Yoga* :—

**मूलग्ग पोरबीजा कंदातह खंदबीज बीजारुहा ।**
**सम्मुच्छिमाय भणियापत्तेयाणांतकायाय ॥ ८३ ॥**

*Mulagga pora bijâ Kandâ tah Khànda bijâ Bijâ ruhá,*
*Sammuchchhimâya bhaniyâ patteyâ ṇanta Kâyâya 186*

Vegetables are described as follows:—

(1) *Mula Bîja* having root as their seed just as ginger, turmeric.

(2) *Agrabîja* grown through front stem.

(3) *Parba bîja* grown through knot as sugar-cane.

(4) *Kanda bîja* grown through esculent root as garlic.

(5) *Skandha bîja* grown through trunk.

(6) *Bîja bîja* grown through seeds as wheat, and gram.

(7) *Sammurchchana* grown by itself through earth etc. as grass, etc.

(9) "*Some Sayings of the Buddha*" by Woodward.

Page 68. In rainy season recluses tread down the green grass, they crush the living thing that has one sense, they trample to death many a tiny life, I enjoin on you, brethren, that ye observe the retreat during the rains (Vin. Pit. Mahâvagga III. I.)

(10) *Manuscript remains of B. Lit. in Eastern Turkestan*, by Hoernle—*Page 4* Vinaya texts.

"*Samprajânena gantavyam...Īryâ-patha sampannena susamvritten yugantara prekṣiṇâ sa gauravena.*"

"The monk should walk through discrimination, seeing ground four cubits forward with control of mind and with respectability."

(11) "*The Doctrine of the Buddha*" by George Grimm, P. 339. "Inflamed by desire, evil-disposed by hate, confused by delusion, overcome, entirely influenced internally, O Brahmin, we think of hurting ourselves, we think of hurting others, we think of hurting both ourselves and others, and feel mental pain and grief. But if we have abandoned desire, then we do not think any more of hurting ourselves, nor of hurting others, nor of hurting both ourselves and others, and we do not feel mental pain and grief. Thus, O Brahmin, *Nibbâna* is visible and present, inviting to come and see, leading to the goal, intelligible to the wise, each for himself." (M. I. p. 303 A. III p. 55).

Page 434 F. Note. "What is sinful in the taking of food lies in this, that other life is destroyed, and thereby suffering is caused in the world. Since animal life is more highly organized and much more sensible to pain than plant life, the good man will in no case, either directly or indirectly, be the cause of the killing of animals for his food. In consequence of this, he will not eat the flesh of any animal in any case where he has seen or heard or supposes that it has been killed for his sake. "There are three cases, Jivaka, where I say that meat shall not be accepted; Seen, heard and supposed. (M. I. p. 369). For the same reason, no one may offer the Perfected One or his disciples, the flesh of an animal killed for this purpose. "Whoever, Jivaka, takes life for the sake of the Perfected One, incurs five-fold serious guilt. Because he commands: 'Go and fetch that animal!', thereby the first time he incurs serious guilt. Because then the animal, led to him in fear and trembling, experiences pain and torment, he for the second time incurs serious guilt. Because he then says: 'Go and kill this animal,' he for the third time incurs serious guilt. Because the animal then in death, experiences pain and torment, he for the fourth time incurs serious guilt. Because he then gives unfitting refreshment to the Perfected One or the Perfected One's disciple, he for the fifth time incurs serious guilt." (M. I. 369).

469. As a mother protects her only child with her own life, cultivate such boundless love towards all beings. (Metta Sutta S. N.)

(12) *Sutta Nipate Dhammaka Sutta.*

पाणं नहाने न च घातयेय्य न चानुमण्या हनतंपरेसं ।
सव्वेसु भूतेसु निधायदंडं ये थावरा ये च तसंतिलोके ॥

*Pâṇam na hâne na cha ghâtayeyya*
*na chânumanyâ hanatam paresam,*
*Savvesu bhûtesu nidhâya daṇḍam*
*ye thāvarā ye cha tasamti lôke.*

Neither one should injure the creatures, nor induce others to do so, nor should be pleased when others injure them; one should have compassion on all the beings in the universe, whether they may be immobile or mobile.

*Note.* In the Jain literature one-sensed beings are called *sthâvara.* They are earth-bodied, water-bodied, fire-bodied, air-bodied, vegetable-bodied; while beings from the two-sensed to the five-sensed are called *trasa.*

(13) *Majjhim Nikâya Vatthupama Sutta 71.*

**"सेय्यथापि भिक्खवे वत्थं संकिलिट्ठं मलग्गहीतं अच्छं उदके आगम्म परिसुद्धं होति परियोदानं...एवमेव भिक्खवे भिक्खु एवं सीलो एवं धम्मो एवं पञ्ञो सालिनं चेदिपिंडपातं भुंजति विचितकालिकं अनेकसूयं अनेकव्यंजनं नैव ये अस्सतं होति अंतराय."**

***"Seyyathâpi bhikkhave battham sankilittham malagga hîtam achchham udake âgamma pari suddum hoti pariyodânam......evameva bhikkhave bhikkhu evam sîlô evam dhammo evam pajno sâlinam chedi pinda-pâtam***

*bhunjati vichita kâlikam aneka suyam aneka vyanjanam naiva, ye assatam hoti antarâya......"*

"O Monks! Just as a dirty cloth is cleansed by pure water, so eating alm of rice makes him chaste, pious and intelligent; this the monk knows; leaving this, he does not accept many kinds of sauces and sweetmeats—, for they will be obstructing."

(14) Sacred Books of the East Vol. XI (1881) by Max Muller. p. 189. The Tevigga Sutta

Ch. II Kûla sîlam.

"He abstains from destroying life. Full of modesty and pity, he is compassionate and kind to all creatures that have life. He refrains from injuring any herb or any creature. He takes but one meal a day; abstaining from food at night time or at the wrong time."

Page 192 The Magghima Silam.

"He lives on food provided by the faithful, refrains from injuring plants or animals."

(15) Sutta nipâta, translated by Fausböll (1881). Mahâvagga 11 Nâlaka Sutta. p. 128.

27/705. "As I am, so are these, as these are so am I, identifying himself with others, let him not kill nor cause (any one) to kill."

(16) "Path of Purity" by Buddha Ghôsha I & II.

Page 79. "Diseases caused by eating do not harm the monk who at once sitting eats his food."

(17) Sacred Books of the East by Max Muller.
Vol. XLIX Buddhist Mahâyana. Page 121

(65) "To kill a helpless victim through a wish for future reward,—it would be an unseemly action for a merciful-hearted good man, even if the reward of the sacrifice were eternal; but what if, after all, it is subject to decay?"

(67) "Even that happiness which comes to a man, while he stays in this world, through the injury of another, is hateful to the wise compassionate heart; how much more if it be something beyond our sight in another life?"

*Note.* From the statements given above, it will be known that *ahimsa* has been correctly described in the Buddhist Scriptures. We shall see later on that this description quite agrees with what is given in the Jain literature.

## FLESH-EATING.

It appears in the present time that flesh-eating is much prevalent among the Buddhists. If I independently think of its cause, it appears to me that the old Poli books were first compiled in Ceylon in the 1st century, as is written in the introduction to *Buddha Charya*. "In the first century A. D. at Ceylon, Sutra, Vinaya and Abhidhamma, which till that time were learnt by heart only, were at first written. This is the Tripitaka."

I did not find in these Pali books the quotations explicitly prohibiting the taking of flesh.

" The Life of the Buddha " by Edward J. Thomas, 1927.

On page 129 there is the following statement :—

" As meat-eating was made an ethical question, the ritual aspect ceased to have a meaning for the Buddhist. Hence the practice was not in itself condemned, but only in so far as the partaker was in some way contributory to killing or giving pain. This position is stated most clearly in the *Jîvaka Sutta* (M. N. I. 368). Jivaka * told Buddha that he had heard that people killed living things intending them for Buddha, and that he ate the meat prepared on that account. He asked if such persons were truth-speakers and did not accuse the Lord falsely. Buddha replied that it was not true, but that in three cases meat must not be eaten : if it has been seen, heard, or suspected that it was intended for the person. If a monk who practises the brahma-vihara of love accepts an invitation in a village, he does not think, " verily this house-holder is providing me with excellent food ; may he provide me with excellent food in the future." He eats the food without being fettered and infatuated. " What do you think, Jivaka, does the monk at that time think of injury to himself, to others, or to both ?" " Certainly not, Lord." " Does not a

* The famous physician of Bimbisara and Ajatasattu.

monk at that time take blameless food ?" "Even so Lord."

The teaching is the same in the Vinaya, where Buddha is said to have accepted a meal from the Jain general *Siha*, who had provided meat. The report went about that he had killed an ox for Buddha, but the fact was that he had sent for the meat already killed in order to furnish the meal. The Vinaya forbids certain kinds of flesh, human, that of elephants, horses, dogs and certain wild animals. (F. N. Vinaya 1. 218-237 ; *Macchamamsa* is expressly allowed ; This is usually taken to mean 'flesh of fish.'

Pali books state in one or two places that Goutama Buddha ate flesh—Whether this was true or not is to be properly considered.

*Buddha Charya* P. 148 M. N. 8. 1. 2. 2. Siha Sutta.

" It appears that Jain Commander-in-Chief Siha of Vaisali served meat to Goutama Buddha."

*Note.* It seems to me quite impossible that a Jain minister or King could have served Buddha with meat. Neither it seems to be possible that the compassionate Buddha who preached for the protection of immobile and mobile beings would have accepted flesh. Moreover he was so kind that he did not eat even at night and prohibited his disciples from taking food at night.

*Buddha Charya* Page 433. Chulla Vagga 7.

DEVADATTA VIDROHA.

This Sutta tells that Devadatta told Buddha, "He only, who does not accept fish and flesh for the whole life, should be received in the Order"; then Goutama said, "I have ordered for the pure flesh which is not seen, nor heard, nor supposed to be prepared."

*Note.* How far this statement is correct, is to be considered. Buddha Charya P. 535 Mahaparinibbana Sutta D. N. 2; 3.

In this Sutta it is said that in the last part of his life Goutama Buddha had taken *Sûkara maddava* from *Chunda*, the smith. Here this italicised word is translated by some as flesh of pig and by some as soft rice cooked with milk.

So much is the statement about flesh in ***Buddha Charya***.

Sacred Books of the East Vol. III by Rhys Davids D. N P. 11. 1910 at Page 110. At Vesali, he (Buddha) had finished eating the rice.

Page 138. "Now when the Exalted One had eaten the rice prepared by *Chunda*, the worker in metals, there fell upon him a dire sickness, the disease of dysentery and sharp pain came upon him, even unto death."

***Note.*** Here the word ***Sûkara maddava*** is translated as rice. Except the few statements given above, no other statement in the whole Buddhist literature, as far as I have read, has been found to denote that Buddha or his disciple have ever taken flesh or fish or any other creature. While the above passages of the Pali book express doubt about flesh eating, old Sanskrit Buddhist literature expressly prohibits flesh-eating, by any follower of Buddhism.

There is one *Lankavatara Sutra*—published in Sanskrit by Bunyin-Nangio, M.A. (Oxon) D. Litt., Otam University—Kyoto (Japan) in 1922. It is also a very old Sutra. Its first translation in the Chinese language was done by one *Gunabhadra* of Central India in 443 A.D. Its second translation in the Chinese was done by *Bodha ruchi* of India in 513 A. D. Its third translation in the Chinese was done by Siksanand of India in 700 A.D.

The eighth chapter of the book deals specially about flesh-eating.

This is called *Mansa bhakṣana pari varto.* From this chapter, it is fully proved that any follower of Buddhism, whether he may be a monk, or a layman, should never eat any kind of flesh either of fish or of any other animal. We give below some Sanskrit passages with the translation :—

"देशयतु मे भगवांस्तथागतोऽर्हन् सम्यक् संबुद्धो मांस-भक्षणे गुणदोषं येनाहं चान्ये च बोधिसत्वामहासत्वा अनागत प्रत्युत्पन्न काले सत्वानां कुव्याद् सत्वगति वासना वासितानां मांसभोजन गृद्धाणां रसतृष्णा प्रहाणाय धर्मदेशयाम."

*Deśayatu me Bhagavan stathagatorhan samyak-sambuddho mânsa bhakṣaṇe guṇadoṣam yenâham chânyecha bôdhisatvâ mahâsatva anâgata pratyutpanna Kâle sattvânâm Kuvyâda sattva gati Vâsanâ-Vâsitânâm mânsabhojana griddhânâm rasa trisṇâ prahâ ṇâya dharmam deśa yâma."*

" May the Lord *Tathagata, Arhan* rightly enlighten and preach to us the merit and demerit of flesh-eating, so that I and the other followers of Buddhism in the present time and in the future may preach the truth to those who are flesh eaters for the destruction of their desire for flesh."

" भगवांस्तस्यै तदवोचत् अपरिमितै र्महामते कारणै र्मांसं सर्वमभक्ष्यं कृतात्मनो बोधिसत्वस्य तेभ्यस्तूपदेशमात्रं वक्ष्यामि'. "

" *Bhagavânstasyai tâdavochaṭ aparimitair mahâmate Kâranair mânsam sarvamabhakṣyam Kripâtmano bodhisattvasya tebhyastûpadeśa mâtram vaksyami.*"

"The Lord said to him, " O Great wise man! On account of innumerable causes all flesh is to be avoided by the merciful follower of Buddhism! For them I shall preach in brief."

" इह महामते अनेन दीर्घेणाध्वना संसरतां प्राणिनां नास्त्यसौकश्चित्सत्वः सुलभरूपो यो न माताभूत्पिता वा भ्राता वा भगिनी वा पुत्रा वाा दुहिता वा अन्यतरान्यतरो वा स्वजन

**वंधुबंधु भूतो वा तस्यान्य जन्मपरिव्रत्ताश्रयस्य मृग पशुपक्षि योन्यन्तर्भूतस्यवंधोः बंधूभूतस्य वा सर्वभूतात्म भूतायागन्तु कामेन सर्वजन्तु प्राणिभूतसंभूतं मांसं कथामिव भक्षयं स्याद्बुद्ध धर्मकामेन बोधिसत्वेन महासत्वेन.**"

"*Iha mahâ mate anena dirghenâ dhvanâ sansartâm prâninâm nâstyasau Kaśchitsattvah sulabha-rupo yo na mâtâbhûtpitâvâ bhrâta vâ bhagini vâ putro vâ duhitâ vâ anyatarânyataro vâ svajana bandhu bandhūbhūtō vâ tasya-nya janmaparivrittâśrayasya mṛiga pasu pakṣi yonyantarbhûtasya bandhoh bandhu bhūtasya va sarva bhūtâtma bhūtā yâgantu kâmena sarva jantu prani bhūte sambhūtam mânsam kathamiva bhakṣyam syâdbuddha dharma kâmena bodhi-sattvena mahâ sattvena.*"

"O Great wise man! In this beginningless world the living beings having been wandering, there is not a single creature which had not been sometimes mother, father, brother, sister, son, daughter or any other relative. The same adopting many re-births, are born as deer or other animal, bird etc. which are really our relatives. How can a follower of Buddhism, a saint or a disciple, who sees all the creatures as his brethren, cut the flesh of all these creatures ?"

"**श्वखरोष्ट्राश्वबलीबर्दमानुष्य मांसादीनि हि महामते लोकस्याभक्ष्याणि मांसानि तानि च महामते वीथ्यन्तरेष्वौरभ्रिका भक्ष्याणिति कृत्वा मूल्यहितोर्विक्रीयन्ते यतस्ततोपि महामते मांसमभक्ष्यं बोधिसत्वस्य.**"

" *Śva Kharoṣṭra śva balibarḍa mânuṣa mânsâdinihi mahâ mate lokasyâ bhaksyâni mânsani tâni cha mahâ mate bithyan taresvairabhrika bhakṣyániti kṛitvâ mūlyahitor vikri yanti yatastitopi mahâmati mänsa mabhakṣyam bodhisattvasya.*"

" O wise man ! The flesh of dog, ass, camel, horse, bullock and human beings is taken to be un-eatable by the people; but even their flesh calling it to be that of lambs is sold in the streets for money. It is, therefore, not eatable by a follower of Buddhism."

" शुक्रशोणित संभवादपि शूचिकामतामु दाय बोधिसत्वस्य मांसमभक्ष्यं."

" *S'ukraśoṇita sambhavâdapi śuchi-kâmatâ-mupâdâya bodhi sattvasya mânsa mabhaksyam.*"

" As the flesh is formed from the blood and sperm, so it is not eatable by a follower of Buddhism, who wishes to have purity."

" उद्वेजनकरत्वादपि महामते भूतानां मैत्रीमिच्छतो योगिनो मांसं सर्वं मभक्ष्यं बोधिसत्वस्य तद्यथापि महामते डोम्ब चांडाल कैवर्तादीच्छपि शिताशिनः सत्वान् दुरत उव दृष्ट्वा-श्वानः प्रभयंति भयेन मरण प्राप्ताश्चैके भवन्त्यन्यानपि मारयिष्यन्ती एवमेव, महामतेऽन्योऽपि ख भूजल संश्रितान्सूक्ष्मजंतवो ये मांसाशिनो दर्शनाद्दूरादेव पटुना घ्राणोनाघ्राय गन्धं राक्षस्येव मानुषाद्दत मुपसर्पयन्ति मरणादेहाश्चैकेभवति."

" *Udvejana karatvâdapi mahâ mate bhūtânâm maitrimichchha to yogino mânsam sarvamabhakṣyam bodhi sattvasya Tadyathapi mahâmate ḍomba chânḍala-*

*kaivartâ dichchhapi sita sinah sattvân durata eva dristva svânah prabhayanti bhayena marana prâptâs-chaike bhavantyanyânapi mâra yis yantiti evameva, mahâ mate nyopi kha bhujala sansritânsûksma jantavo ye mâsâsino darsanâddurâdeva patunâ ghrâ-nenâghrâya gandham râksyo-syeva mânusâ druta mupa-sarpayanti maranasandehâs chaike bhavanti.*"

"As it is a cause of producing fear, therefore, O wise man! this flesh is not eatable by a Buddhist monk who desires friendship with all the creatures. Just as on the sight of hunters, fishermen and other flesh-eaters from a distance, dogs become fearful, even some die on account of fear ; they understand that they would kill others, similarly the other small animals of sky, land and water having seen the flesh-eaters from a distance and having known their smell by their sharp smelling power flee far away from the man taking him to be a ghost in fear of their death."

"अनार्यजनजुष्टं दुर्गंधमकीर्तिकरत्वादपि महामते आर्य-जन विवर्जितत्वाच्च मांसमभक्ष्यं बोधिसत्वस्य, ऋषि भोजनाहा रोहि महामते आर्यजनो न मांसरुधिराहार इत्यतोऽपि बोधिसत्वस्य मांसमभक्ष्यं."

"*Anârya jana justam durgandha ma-kîrti karatvâ-dapi mahâ mate arya-jana vivarjittvâchcha mânsa mabhaksyam bodhi sattvasya, risi bhoja nâhârohi mahâ mate âryajano, na mansarudhirâhâra ityatopi bodhi-sattvasya mânsamabhaksyam.*"

"Flesh is eatable by savages, is bad smelling and is the cause of ill-fame, and is to be prohibited by gentlemen; therefore, O wise man! this flesh is not eatable by a follower of Buddhism. O wise man! a gentleman eats only that food which is eatable by the saints but never eats flesh and blood; therefore a follower of Buddhism must never eat flesh."

**"बहुजनचित्तानुरक्षणतयाऽपवादपरिहारं चेच्छतः शासनस्य महामते मांसमभक्ष्यं कृपात्मनो बोधिसत्वस्य, तद्यथा महामते भवन्तिलोकेशासनापवाद वक्तारः किंचित्तेषां श्रामण्यं कुतो वा ब्राह्मण्यं यन्नामैते पूर्वर्षिभोजनान्यपास्य क्रव्यादा इवामिषाहाराः परिपूर्णकुक्षयः ख भूमि जल संश्रितान्सूक्ष्मांस्त्रासयंते। जन्तून्समुत्त्रासयंति, इमं लोकं समन्ततः पर्यटन्निहतमेषां श्रामण्यं ध्वस्तमेषां ब्राह्मण्यं नास्त्येषां धर्मो न विनय इत्यनेकप्रकार प्रतिहत चेतसः शासनमेवापवदन्ति."**

"*Bahujana chittâ nurakṣaṇa tayâpa-vâda pariharam chechchhatah Sâsanasya mahâ mate mânsa ma-bhaksyam Kripâtmano bodhisattvasya, tadyathi mahâmate bhavanti loke śâsanâpa-vâda vaktàrah Kinchit tesâm Sramaṇyam kato vâ bràhmaṇyam yannâ maite pûrvarsi-bhojanâ-nyapâsya kravyâdâ evâmi sâ hârâh paripurṇa kuksayah khe bhumi Jala sanśritan suksmânstrasayanto Jantun samuttrasayanti imam lokam samantatah paryaṭan nihatamesâm srâmanyam dhvastamesâm brahmaṇyam nâstyesâm dharmo na vinaya ityaneka prakâra pratihata chetasah śâsana mevâpavadanti.*"

"A compassionate Buddha, who is mindful of protecting the mind of others and careful not to allow any ill-fame to spread, should maintain flesh to be un-eatable. O wise man, there are in this world persons who speak ill of the Preaching. They say that they, who having rejected the food fit for the saints of the old time, eat like the meat-eaters, give pain to the small creatures living in sky, earth and water, roam hither and thither troubling them; what kind of monk-hood and Brahman-hood they have got, their monk-hood is destroyed, their Brahman-hood is made impure; they do not possess piety nor conduct. Thus people say many sorts of ill words."

**"मृतशव दुर्गंध प्रतिकूल सामान्यादपि महामते मांसमभक्ष्यं बोधिसत्वस्य, मृतस्यापि महामते मनुष्यस्य मांसेदह्यमाने तदन्य प्राणिमांसे च न कश्चिद्गंधाविशेषः, सममुभय मांसयोर्दह्यमानयोर्दौर्गन्धमतोपि महामते शुचि कामस्य योगिनः सर्वं मांसमभक्ष्यं बोधिसत्वस्य."**

"*Mrita śava durgandha prati kūla sâmânyâdapi mahâ mate mânsa mabhaksyam bodhisattvasya, mritasyâpi mahamate mânsyasya manse dahyamane tadanya-prânimânse cha na Kaśchid gandhaviśesah, sama-mubhaya mânsayordahya mânayor dourgondhamatopi mahâ mate suchi kâ masya yoginah sarvam mânsa mabhaksyam bodhisattvasya.*"

"O wise man, there is bad and unbearable smell in the flesh. like that of a corpse, even for this reason, the flesh is not eatable by a Buddhist. If the corpse be burnt and also any other flesh be burnt, there would be no difference in their bad smells, therefore a Buddha monk wishing purity should not eat any flesh."

"योगाचाराणां–विद्याधराणां—विद्यासाधन मोक्षविघ्नकरत्वान्महायान संप्रस्थितानां कुलपुत्राणां कुलदुहितृणां च सर्व योगसाधनान्तराय करमित्यपि समनुपश्यतां महामते स्वपरात्म हितकामाय मांसं सर्वमभक्ष्यं बोधिसत्वस्य."

"*Yogâchârânam Vidyâdharâṇâm Vidyasâdhana-moksa vighna Karatvâm mahâyâna samprasthitânâm Kulaputrânâm Kula duhitrinâm cha sarva yoga sâdha-nântarâya Kula mityapi samanu paśya tâm mahâ mate svaparâtma hitakâmâya mânsam sarva mabhaksyam bodhisattvasya.*"

"Because it is obstructive to the saints and the students in their efforts for liberation and knowledge, therefore the followers of the Great Path, the family sons and daughters fully know it to be obstructive in all the efforts for meditation. O wise man, all the flesh is not, therefore, eatable by a Buddhist who is desirous of having spiritual benefit to himself and to others."

"क्रिमिजंतु प्रचुरकुष्टानिदानकोष्ठश्च भवति व्याधिबहुलं न च प्रतिकूलसंज्ञां प्रतिलभते, पुत्रमांसभैषज्य वदाहारं देशयंश्चाहं महामते कथमेवनार्यजनसेवित मार्यजन विवर्जितमेव मनेकदोषावहमनेकगुह्य विवर्जितमनृषि भोजनप्रणीतं मकल्प्यं मांसरूधिराहारं शिष्येभ्योऽनुज्ञापयामि."

*Krimijantuprachura kusṭha nidâna kosthaśchá bhavati vyâdhi bahulam na cha pratikūlasanjnâm pratilabhate putra mânsa bhaisajya vadâhâram desayanṣchâham mahâmate katha meva nârya janasevita mârya jana vivarjitanṛise bhojana praṇitam makalpyam mânsa rudhirâhâram sisyebhyo anujnapayâmi.*

"The flesh-eater is prone to many kinds of diseases such as worms, many insects, leprosy, belly-pains etc. O wise man, I am preaching eating flesh as taking the flesh of one's own son. How can I order my disciples for eating flesh and blood, which are served by the savages, prohibitable by gentlemen, full of many defects, devoid of any benefits, unfit to be taken by the saints and totally rejectable ?"

**"अनुज्ञातवान् पुनरहं महामते पूर्वर्षि प्रणीतभोजनं यदुत शालि यव गोधूम, मुद्गमाष मसूरादि सर्पिस्तैल मधुफाणित गुडखंड मत्सापिंडिकादिषु समुपद्यमानं भोजनं कल्प्यामिति कृत्वा."**

*Anujṇâtavân punaraham mahâmate pûrvarsi praṇitabhojanam ya dutâ sâli yava godhuma mudga mâṣa masurâdi sarpis taila madhu phâṇita guḍa khanḍa matsa pindi kâdisu samupadya-mânam bhojanam kalpyamiti kritva.*

"I have ordered, O wise man, for the fit food which has been prescribed by the saints of old time such as food prepared from rice, barley, wheat, pulses of *moonga*, *urad*, and *masura* etc., ghee, oil, milk, raw sugar, *guda*, sugar, coarse sugar etc."

"भूतपूर्वं महामते अतीतेध्वनि राजाभूत् सिंहसौदासो-नाम स मांसभोजनाहारातिं प्रसंगेन प्रतिसेवमानो रसतृष्ण ध्यवसान परमतया मांसानि मानुष्याण्यपि भक्षितवान्, तन्नि-दानं च मित्रमात्य ज्ञाति बन्धुबर्गेणापि परित्यक्तः प्रागेव पौर-ज्ञानपरैः स्वराज्य विषय परित्यागाच्च महाद्व्यसन मासादित-वान् मांसहेतोः."

*Bhûtapūrvam mahâmate atitedhvani râjâbhut sinha saudâso nâma sa mânsa bhojanâ hârâti prasangena pratisevamâno rasa trsna dhyavasâna parataya mânsâni mânuṣyâ ṇyapi bhaksitavân tannidânam cha mitrâ mâ tya jnâti bandhu-bargeṇâpi parityaktah prâgeva pour-ajana paraih svarâjya viṣaya parityâgâchcha mahad vyasana mâsâditavân mânsa hetoh.*

" O wise man, there flourished in old times *Raja Sinha Saudaso.* He became too much covetous of meat-eating. He used to eat the human flesh owing to heavy desire for it. He was therefore abandoned by his friends, ministers, caste people and others. Before this, he was dethroned and banished out of his country by the citizens. He suffered great miseries on account of flesh."

*Note.* This statement about *Saudaso* is written in the same way in the *Padmapurana* of the Digambar Jains.

"इहेव च महामते जन्मनि सप्तकुटीरकेपि ग्रामे प्रचुर मांस लौल्यादति प्रसंगेन निषेवमानामानुष्य मांसादा घोरा डाका

**व डाकिन्यश्च जायंते, जाति परिवर्ते च महामते तथैव मांस रसाध्यवसानतया सिंहव्याघ्रद्वीपिवृकतरक्षुमार्जार जम्बूकोलूकादिप्रचुर मांसादयोनिषु विनिपात्यन्ते.**"

*Ihaiva cha mahâmate janmani saptakutirakepi grâme prachura mânsa laulyâdati prasangena nisevamânâ mânusamâsâdâ ghorâ dâ kâ va etâ kinyaścha sanjâyante Jâti parivarte cha mahâmate tathaiva mânsa râsadhyavasâna tayâ sinha vyâghra dupi Vrika taraksu mârjâra jambukolu kâdi prachura mânsâda yonisu vini pâtyante.*

"Even in this very life, O wise man, they, who are addicted to too much flesh-eating, on account of great greed become eaters of human flesh, voracious and demonlike. On change of birth, on account of their greed for flesh they are fallen in flesh-eating genii of lion, tiger, wolf, hyena, cat, jackal, owl etc."

"**यदि च महामते मांसं न कथंचन केचनभक्षयेयुर्नतन्निदानं घातेरन् मूल्यहेतोर्हि महामतेप्रायः प्राणिनो निरपराधिनो बध्यन्ते स्वल्पादन्य हेतोः कष्टं महामते रसतृष्णायामति सेवितां मांसनि मानुष्याण्यापि मानुषैर्भक्ष्यन्ते किंपुनरितर मृगपक्षि प्राणासंभूत मांसानि, प्रायो महामते मांस रस तृष्णातैरिदं तथा जाल यंत्रमाविद्धं मोह पुरुषैर्यच्छाकुनिकौरभ्रुक कैवर्तादयः खेचर भूचर जलचरानप्राणि नोऽनपराधिनोऽनेकप्रकारं मूल्य हेतोर्विशसन्ति.**"

*Yadicha mahâmate mâmsaṁ na kathanchana kechana bhaksa yeyur na tannidânam ghâteran mulya hetor hi mahâmate prâyah pranino niraparâdhino badhyante svalpâdanya hetoh kastham mahâ mate rasa trisnâ yâmiti sevitam mansani manusyanyapi mânusavibhaksyante kimpunaritara mriga paksi prâne sambhūta mansani prâyo mahâmate mânsarasa trisnartairidam tathâ tathâ jâla yantra mâviddham moha purusair yachchhâ kuni kaurabhraka kaivartâdayah khechara bhūchara jalacharân prânino naparâ dhino nekaprakâram mulya hetor viśasanti.*

"O wise man, neither flesh should be eaten nor murder should be done on that account; mostly for the sake of money, harmless living beings are killed; very few on account of other cause. It is painful that for the great desire of flesh, even men eat the human flesh, what to speak about the flesh of animals and birds etc. Mostly for the sake of deluding persons pained by the desire of eating flesh, killers of birds, lambs and fish through their nets and machines kill birds, deer, fish etc., harmless creatures to gain money."

"न च महामतेऽकृतयमकारित मास्वकल्पितं नाम मांसं कल्प्यमस्ति यदुपायानुजानीयं श्रावकेभ्यः, भविष्यति तुपुनर्महामतेऽनागतेऽध्वनि ममैव शासने प्रव्रजित्वा शाक्यपुत्रीयत्वं प्रतिज्ञानानः काषायध्वजधारिणो मोह पुरुषां मिथ्याबितर्कोपहतचेतसो विविधविनय विकल्प वादिनः सत्कायदृष्टियुक्ताः रसतृष्णाद्यवासितास्तां तां मांसभक्षणहेत्वाभासां ग्रंथयिष्यंति, मम च भूताख्यानं दातव्यं मनस्यन्ते तत्तदथोत्पत्ति निदानं कल्पायित्वा वक्ष्यन्ति, इयं अर्थोत्पत्ति रस्मिन्निदाने भगवता

मांसभोजन मनुज्ञातं कल्प्यामिति प्रणीतभोजनेषु चोक्तं स्वयं च किल तथागतेन परिभुक्तमिति, न च महामते कुत्रचित्सूत्रे पतिसेवितव्यामिति अज्ञातं प्रणीत भोजनेषु वा देशितं कल्प्यमिति."

*Nacha mahâmate akritkamakârita masankalpitam nâma mânsam kalpyamasti yadupâdâyânujâniyam śravakebhyah bhavisyati tu punar mahâmate anâgate-adhavani mamaiva śâsane pravrajitva sakyaputriyattvam pratijânânâh kâsâya dhvaja dhariṇo moha purusâ mitthyavitarkopa hatachetso vividha vinaya vikalpa vâdinah satkâya dṛisti yuktah rasa tṛisṇa dhyavasitâstâm tâm mânsabhaksana hetvâbhâsâm grantha yisyanti mama châbhūtâ khyânam dâtavyam mansyante tattadarthotpatti nidânam kalpayitva vaksyanti iyam arthotpatti rasmin nidâne Bhagavata mânsa bhojam manujnâtam kalpyamiti praṇita bhojanesu chaktam syayum cha kila tathagatena pari bhuktamiti na cha mahâmate kutra chit sutre prati sevîtavyamitya nujnâtam pranita bhojanesu va desitam Kalpyamiti.*

"O wise man, there cannot be any flesh eatable, which may be undone, not caused to be done or not supposed to be done ; on account of which I may order it for the disciples. In the future time, there will occur in my order some, who having adopted the conduct of monk and having pledged to follow the order of the *Sâkyaputra* and having put on the flag of red clothes will be deluding and addicted to bodily pleasures. They will have many false notions in their minds and declare different rules of conduct. They will be desirous of taste and shall compile books giving false arguments for flesh-eating. They will maintain that which I have never told. They will tell matters in support of flesh-eating. They will say that I have ordered it for this reason, that I have counted it among the eatables and that Bhagavan has himself eaten flesh. But, O wise man, I have never ordered flesh in any *sutra*, nor told it to be eatable nor counted it among good eatables."

**"नहि महामते आर्यश्रवकाः प्राकृतमनुष्याहार माहारन्ति कुतएव मांसरुधिराहार मकल्प्यम्, धर्माहारा हि महामते मम श्रावकाः प्रत्येक बुद्धबोधिसत्त्वाश्च नामिषाहाराः प्रागेव यथा-गताः, धर्मकाया हि महामते तथागता धर्माहारस्थितयो नामि-सकाया न सर्वाभिषाहारस्थितयोवान्त सर्वभवोपकरण तृष्णैष-णावासना सर्वक्लेश दोषवासनापगताः सुविमुक्त चित्तप्रज्ञाः सर्वज्ञाः सर्वदर्शिनः सर्वसत्वैकपुत्रक समदर्शिनो महाकारुणि-काः, सोऽहं महामते सर्वसत्वैक पुत्रकसंज्ञी सन् कथमिव स्वपुत्र मांस मनुज्ञास्यामि परिभोक्तुं श्रावकेभ्यः कुतं एव स्वयं परि-भक्तुम्, अनुज्ञातवानस्मिन् श्रावकेभ्यः स्वयं वा परिभुक्तवानिति महामते नेदं स्थानं विद्यते."**

*Nahi mahâmate âryaśrâvakâh prâkrita manusyâ-hâra mâharanti kutaeva mânsarudhirâhâramakalpyam, dharmâhârâhi mahâ mate mama srâvakâh pratyeka buddha Bodhisattvaścha nâ misâ hârâh prâgeva tatha-gatâh Dharma Kâya hi mahâmate tathâgatâ Dharmâ-hâra sthitayo nâmisakâyâ na sarvâmisâhâra sthitayo vântasarva bhavopakarana trisnaisanâ vâsanâ sarva klesa dosa vâsanâpagatâh su-vimukta chittaprajnâh sarvajnâh sarva-darśinah sarvasattvaika putraka sama darśino mahakârunikâh soham mahâmate sarvasattvaika-putra ka sanjni san kathamiva svaputra mânsa manuj-nasyâmi paribhoktum śrâvakebhyah kuta eva svayam paribhoktum, anujnatavânasmin Sravakebhyah svayam vâ paribhukta vâniti mahâ mate nedam sthânam vidyate.*

"O wise man! *Arya Sravakas* do not even take the natural human diet, how can they eat the rejectable flesh and blood? My disciples are followers of Truth and so are the self-intelligent ones and other Buddhists. They are not flesh-eaters. Such were the *Tathagatas* in the former times......*Tathagatas* have Truth as their body, they live on Truth, they do not support their bodies with flesh. They never take any flesh. They have given up desire for all the worldly objects. They are free from all the defects causing misery. They are full of unattached discrimination, all-knowing, all-perceiving. They look towards all the creatures like their sons. They are very compassionate. Similarly I look towards all the creatures as my sons how can I order my disciples to eat the flesh of my sons and how can I eat it. There is no question of this that I ordered my disciples for it and that I have myself eaten it."

*Note.* The same chapter has some verses in the end ; a few are given here :—

मद्यं मांसं पलांडुंच न भक्षयेयं महामुने ।
बोधिसत्त्वैर्महासत्त्वै भाषद्‌भिर्जिनपुंगवैः ॥ १ ॥
मांसानि च पलांडूश्च मद्यानि विविधानिच ।
गृंजनं लशुनंचैव योगी नित्यं विवर्जयेत् ॥ ५ ॥
लाभार्थं हन्यतेसत्वो मांसार्थं दीयते धनं ।
उभौतौ पापकर्माणौ पच्यते रौरवादिषु ॥ ९ ॥
हस्तिकस्ये महामेधे निर्वाणांगुलिमालिके ।
लंकावतारसूत्रेच मयामांसं विवर्जितम् ॥ १६ ॥
यथैव रागो मोक्षाय अंतरायकरोभवेत् ।
तथैब मांस मद्याद्याः अतंरायकरो भवेत् ॥ २० ॥
तस्मान्न भक्षेयन्मांसं उद्वेजनकरं नृणां ।
मोक्षधर्म विरुद्धत्वदार्यणां मेष वै ध्वजः ॥ २४ ॥

*Madyam mânsam palânduncha na bhaksayeyam mahâmune,*
*Bodhisattvair mahâsattvair bhasadbhir Jina pungavaih*
*Mânsâni cha palanduscha madyâni vividhânicha,*
*Gṛinjanam laśunam chaiva yogi nittyam vivarjayet* 5
*Lâbhârtham hanyate sattvo mânsârthan diyate dhanam,*
*Ubhautau pâpakarmâṇau pachyete rouravâdisu* 9
*Hastikaksya mahâmeghe nirvâṇânguli mâlike,*
*Lankâvatarâsutre cha mayâ mânsam vivarjitam* 16
*Yathaiva rago moksâya antarâyakaro bhavet,*
*Tathaiva mânsa madyâdyâ antarâya karo bhavet* 20
*Tasmânna bhaksaye n mânsamudveja nakaram ṇṛi ṇam,*
*Moksadharma viruddhattvâdâryâṇâmesa vai dhvajah* 24

O wise man ! The conquerors have said that wine, flesh and onions should not be eaten by any Buddhist or great Buddhist. 1.

A monk should always abstain from flesh, onion, many kinds of intoxicating liquors, garlic, and turnip. 5.

He, who kills any creature for money and he, who pays money for it—both of them are evil-doers and shall fall in the *Rourava* etc., hells. 9.

I have prohibited flesh in the following scriptures (1) Hasti kaksya, (2) Mahâ megha, (3) Nirvânânguli mâlika (4) and Lankâvatârasutra. 16.

Just as attachment is obstructive to liberation, so is flesh, wine etc. obstructive to *nirvâna*. 20.

Therefore flesh, which is fearful to the creatures and is contrary to the conduct for liberation, should not be eaten. This is the flag of the *Arya people*. 24.

*Note.* This Lankavatâra sûtra is also very old. It appears to me that when the Pali sutras were at first compiled in Ceylon in the first century A. D. and flesh-eating was supported therein through any argument then this sutra appears to have been written in answer to that. This Lankavatâra sutra explicitly prohibits any Buddhist from taking any flesh. The saying of those persons who declare that they do not themselves kill the creatures, they only buy flesh from the market and so they are not guilty of any injury is contradicted in this sutra. When they pay money in change of flesh, then they are in fact indirectly promoters of killing. The butchers and fishermen kill the animals on this understanding that their flesh is sold and is used by the people. When they are getting money for the sake of flesh, they go on continually killing the animals.

Really they, who buy flesh, are the inducers of killing the dumb creatures. Those monks who say that they accept what is given to them only in alms, that they do not suppose of having flesh and therefore they are not guilty of killing animals, even if they accept and eat flesh, should deeply consider on their arguments. It is a rule that whatever is accepted by anyone is approved by the same. Accepting flesh proves approval of that food. This approval of flesh by the monks produces this conviction in mind of the donor-layman that there is no harm in eating flesh, when our worshipful monks accept and eat it. Thus the laymen remain flesh-eaters, and are obliged to induce the killers to kill the animals for flesh. Just a monk if supplied with the flesh of a man or a dog, refuses to accept it, because he does not approve of it, similarly he should not accept any kind of flesh. Then only he will be free from any kind of sin of killing animals. When flesh is accepted in alms, it is countable among the eatable foods; while it is altogether rejectable, as has been ordered in ***Lankavatâra Sutra***. Suppose any patriot has a mind to use country-made clothes and has a pledge not to use foreign-made clothes on the conviction that if foreign made clothes would be used and sold here, this country will starve for want of industry. If such a patriot monk is supplied with a foreign cloth for which he has not himself made any effort, nor he has induced others to make it, nor he has any notion of its making, he would not accept it, because his approval and his acceptance would be detrimental to the interests of the country he loves. Similarly acceptance of flesh is to give support to the practice of killing dumb creatures. In Ceylon I found some monks eating flesh on the ground that it is eatable because they were not guilty of killing the creatures in any way, while I saw some monks who do not eat it. But this belief, that if they do not kill animals nor cause to kill them, nor suppose to kill them then they would not be guilty of any injury if they accept flesh in alms, is prevalent in Ceylon, Burma, Siam and other countries where there are larger numbers of Buddhists. But in my opinion, this belief is not right, because the sellers of flesh in the market kill lambs, goats, fowls, fishes only for their sake. They sell it for money which is paid by the buyers. Therefore the buyers cannot be free from the sin of killing the dumb creatures.

In Vidyalankara College, Kelaniya, I saw a Chinese layman Mr. Wong Mow Lam, 19 Hard Road, Shanghai who was studying there. On consulting with him, it was known that this *Lankavatâra Sutra* is believed to be the authoritative book by the Buddhists of China and Japan and that all the Buddhist monasteries never use any flesh there. The laymen of those countries also believe it to be rejectable, although some eat it while others do not eat it. The followers of Tioist do, as a rule, not eat any flesh. They are pure vegetarians. It appears to me that Ceylon being an island where people generally use fish, the Pali Scriptures when compiled, have prescribed a way for the monks to accept it in alms, if it was given. At the very time this Lankâvatâra Sutra appears to have been written, which prohibits every follower of Buddhism from eating flesh or fish of any kind. The Buddhists in general should pay regard to this sutra and should try to check the prevalence of fish or flesh eating. The monks as a rule should not accept it and then they should preach to laymen to give up flesh-eating. Flesh-eating, no doubt, is a cause for the killing of dumb creatures."

Some description of AHIMSA in *JAIN SCRIPTURES*:

(1) *Samayasâra* says:—

**अज्झवसिदेण बंधो सत्तेमारेहि माव मारेहिं ।**
**एसो बंधसमासो जीवाणं णिच्छय णयस्स ॥ २७४ ॥**

*Ajjhava sideṇa Bandho satte mârehi mâva mârehim*
*Eso bandha samâso Jivâṇam ṇichchhaya ṇayassa* 274

" Bondage (of karmas) will be caused by the intention (of injury), whether the creatures may be killed or not. This is the brief of bondage for the souls from the correct stand-point."

(2) *Tattvârtha Sutra* says:

**प्रमत्तयोगात्प्राणव्यपरापणं हिंसा ॥ १३–७ ॥**

*Pramatha yogât prâṇa vyaparopaṇam ḥimsa* 13/7

"Destruction of (subjective and objective) vitalities through passionate activities of mind, body and speech is *injury* or *himsa*."

Subjective vitalities are the qualities of soul such as Knowledge, bliss and peacefulness. Objective or material vitalities are ten. Immobile one-sensed beings have four, two-sensed have six, three-sensed, seven; four-sensed, eight; five-sensed irrational, nine; and five-sensed rationals have ten. These are explained in the second chapter of this book (p. 94-95).

(4) *Puruśârthasiddhiupâya* describes *himsa* fully. Let us quote some verses:—

**यत्खलु कषाययोगात्प्राणानां द्रव्यभावरूपाणां ।**
**व्यपरोपणस्यकरणं सुनिश्चिताभवति सा हिंसा ॥ ४३ ॥**
**आत्मपरिणामहिंसनहेतुत्वात्सर्वमेव हिंसैतत् ।**
**अनृतवचनादि केवल मुदाहृतं शिष्यबोधाय ॥ ४२ ॥**
**अप्रादुर्भावः खलु रागादीनां भवत्याहिंसेति ।**
**तेषामेवोत्पत्तिर्हिंसेति जिनागमस्य संक्षेपः ॥ ४४ ॥**
**कृतकारितानुमननैर्वाक्काय मनोभिरिष्यते नवधा ।**
**औत्सर्गिकी निवृत्तिर्विचित्ररूपापवादिकीत्वेषा ॥ ७६ ॥**
**धर्म महिंसारूपं संश्रण्वंतो पि परित्यक्तु ।**
**स्थावर हिंसा म सहास्त्रासाहिंसांतेपि मुंचंतु ॥ ७५ ॥**
**स्तोकैकेन्द्रिय घाताद्गृहिणां सम्पन्न योग्य विषयाणां ।**
**शेषस्थावर मारण विरमणमपि भवति करणीयम् ॥ ७७ ॥**

*Yat khalu kaṣâya yogât prânânâm dravya bhâva rūpâṇâm,*
*Vyaparopaṇasya karaṇam suniśchitâ bhavati sâ himsâ* 43
*Atmapariṇâma himsana hetutvât sarvameva himsaitat,*
*Anṛitvachanâdi kevala mudâ-hṛitam śisya bodhaya* 42
*Aprâdurbhâvah khalu râgâdînâm bhavatya himseti;*
*Tesâ mevatpattir himseti Jinâgamasya sanksepah—* 44
*Krita kâritânumananair vâkkâya manobhirisyate navadhâ,*
*Autsargiki nivrittir vichitra rūpâ-pavâ dike tvesâ* 76
*Dharma mahimsâ rūpam sanśrânvantopi ye parittyaktu*
*Sthâvara himsá masâ hastrasa himsâm tapi munchantu* 75
*Stokaikendriya ghâtâd grihinâm sampanna yogya Visayânâm,*
*Seṣa sthâvara mâraṇa viramaṇa mapî bhavati Karaniyam* 77

" Destruction of objective and subjective vitalities through passionate activities of mind, body and speech is really *Himsa*." 43

" On account of the destruction of soul's (pure) thought-activity, there is *himsa* in all the (sinful) actions speaking false-hood etc., (sins) have only been exemplified for the knowledge of the students." 42

" Non-arising of attachment etc., is verily *Ahimsa*, while their arising is *himsa*—this is the summary of the Jain scriptures." 44

" Doing, causing others to do, and consenting for doing and each through mind, body and speech is ninefold (himsa) ; total freedom from this is real *Ahimsa*, while the exceptional is of many sorts." 76

" Having thus heard the doctrine of *Ahimsa*, they, who are unable to refrain from injury to immobiles, should at least give up the injury to mobiles." 75

" The house-holders possessing useful property may even injure the immobiles as least as possible ; they should also refrain from causing injury to other immobiles." 77

It should be noted that the monks and those laymen who take the vow of not performing any engagements are careful in pertecting both mobiles and immobiles ; while the laymen engaged in different pursuits cannot give up occupational (*ârambhi*) injury ; they can refrain from intentional (*sankalpi*) injury.

Intentional injury is useless killing such as animal sacrifice, hunting, killing for meat-eating, teasing creatures for sport, pleasure etc.

Occupational injury is of three kinds :—

(1) Professional (*Udyami*) injury caused in following the justified six kinds of professions :—(1) Military,

(2) writing (3) agriculture (4) trade (5) industry and (6) arts.

(2) *Household-work* (*Graharambhi*) *injury*—caused in preparing food, clothes, etc., digging wells, constructing houses, gardens etc.

(3) *Defensive* (*Virodhi*) *injury*—caused in defending oneself, one's family, property, country etc. from those who attack and do not give up their evil intention in spite of all other possible means. It is caused for saving oneself from plunderers and thieves, in giving punishment to the culprits, in making wars with the enemies.

Althougn ordinary house-holders cannot give up three kinds of occupational killing, yet they try to be saved from it as far as possible. They always, deal with kind hearts. Saints are vowful in following *Ahimsa* in full,—it is why they walk after seeing the ground, they do not walk at night, they do not tread on the grass, nor pluck leaves etc. from trees.

(5) *Sravakâchâra* by Amitagati says :—

**हिंसाद्वेधाप्रोक्ताऽरंभानारंभजत्वता दक्षैः ।**
**गृहवासतोऽनिवृत्तो द्वेधापि त्रायते तां च ॥ ६ ॥**
**गृहवास सेवन रतो मंदकषायः प्रवर्तितारंभाः ।**
**आरंभजां स हिंसां शक्नोति न रक्षितुं नियतम् ॥ ७-६ ॥**

*Himsâ dvedha proktârambhâ nârambha jatvato daksaih,*
*Grihavâsato nivritto dvedhâpi trâyate tâm cha 6*

*Griha vâsa sevana rato mandakasâyah pravartitarambhâh,*
*Ârambhajâm sa himsam sa knoti na raksitum niyatam* 7/6

" Injury has been said to be of two kinds, occupational and non-occupational by the learned; He, who is homeless, protects himself from both of them. A house-holder engaged in house-hold duties, although having mild passions cannot as a rule refrain from occupational injury."

No doubt, intentional killing is due to strong passions in comparison to occupational killing where the passions are mild. A house-holder is obliged to do it.

*Flesh-eating*—A follower of *Ahimsa* must not eat flesh.

(6) *Purusârthasiddhiupâya* says :—

**न विना प्राण विघातान्मांसस्योत्पत्तिरिष्यतेयस्मात् ।**
**मांसं भजतस्तस्मात्प्रसरत्यनिवारिता हिंसा ॥ ६५ ॥**
**यद्पि किलभवति मांसं स्वयमेव मृतस्य महिष वृषभादेः ।**
**तत्रापि भवति हिंसा तदाश्रितनिगोतनिर्मथनात् ॥ ६६ ॥**
**आमास्वपि पक्वास्वपि विपच्यमानासु मांसपेशीषु ।**
**सातत्येनोत्पादस्तज्जातीनां निगोतानाम् ॥ ६७ ॥**

***Na vinâ prâṇa vighâtân mansasyotpattiriṣyate yasmât,***
***Mânsam bhajatastasmat prasaratya-nivârita himsâ*** 65
***Yadapi kila bhavati mânsam svaya-meva mritasya mahiṣa vriṣabhâ-deh***
***Tatrâpi bhavati himsâ tadâ śrita nigotanirmathanâṭ*** 66

*Âmâsvapi pakvâsvapi vipachya-mânasu mânsapeśiśu,*
*Sâ tatyenotpâda stajjâtinâm nigotânâm* 67

"Because it is not possible to produce flesh without killing the vitalities, therefore he, who eats flesh, is unavoidably liable to do injury." 65

"Although there is flesh of bullocks and buffaloes etc. dying by themselves, yet there is injury by killing microbes and germs that originate in that flesh." 66

"There is continual coming into existence of microbes of the sort of the flesh in the pieces of flesh whether they may be raw, cooked or being cooked." 67

*Note.* That is the reason why the flesh in any case is bad-smelling.

*Wine drinking.* The same book says:—

**रसजानां च बहूनां जीवानां योनिरिष्यते मद्यं ।**
**मद्यं भजतां तेषां हिंसा संजायतेऽवश्यम् ॥ ६३ ॥**

*Rasajânâm cha babunâm Jivânâm yonirişyate madyam,*
*Madyam bhajatâm teşâm himsâ sam-jâyate vaśyam* 63

"As wine is the nucleus of many microbes originating in the liquor, therefore there is unavoidable injury to these by one who drinks it." 63

*Not eating at night.* The same book says:—

**रात्रौ भुंजानानां यस्मादनिवारिता भवति हिंसा ।**
**हिंसा विरतैस्तस्मात्यक्तव्या रात्रिभुक्ति रपि ॥ १२९ ॥**
**अर्कालोकेन विना भुंजानः परिहरेत्कथं हिंसां ।**
**अपि बोधितेः प्रदीपे भोज्यजुषां सूक्ष्मजंतूनाम् ॥ १३३ ॥**

*Râtrau bhunjânânâm yasmâdanivâritâ bhavati himsâ*
*Himsa virathi stasmât tyakatavyâ Râttribhuktirapi* 129
*Arkalokenavinâ bhunjânah pariharet katham himsâm,*
*Api bodhitah pradipa bhojyajusâm suksma jantunâm* 133

"Because there is unavoidable killing when eating at night, therefore they who avoid *himsa* should also give up eating at night. How can a partaker of food avoid injury to creatures in the absence of sunlight ; if lamp is lighted, many tiny creatures will fall in the eatables."

*Note.* From the statement of the Buddhist scriptures given in this Chapter it is evident that for the sake of following *ahimsa* one is required to protect both mobile and immobile creatures, to walk after seeing the ground, not to trample on grass, and not to eat at night. Similarly the Jain scriptures also declare.

If the Buddhists try to prevent the prevalence of flesh-eating, then Buddhism may really shine forth in its true nature; because the words of Lord Goutama which teach friendship towards all the creatures cannot prove that his preaching approved flesh-eating or that He himself would have taken flesh. The learned Buddhists should consider this point quite impartially.

# CHAPTER VI.

## WHY JAINISM AND BUDDHISM ARE THE SAME?

Goutama Buddha left home in his age of twenty-nine. He devoted six years in practising many kinds of austerities. At his age of thirty-five he decided his path and preached his first sermon at Benares. During these intervening six years, he followed a conduct resembling that of Digamber (naked) Jain Saint also. Lord Buddha has himself described it. Vide—*Majjhim Nikaya mahâ siha nâda sutta twelfth.*—In this sûtra *Goutam Buddha* in his old age describes the events of his life to his disciple *Sariputra*. The pali words are :

"अचेलको होमि....हत्थापलेखनो....नाभिहतं न उद्दिस्स कतं न निमंतणं सादियामि ; सो न कुंभीमुखा पटिगण्हामि न कलोभिमुखा पटिगण्हामि, न एलकमंतरं न दंडमंतरं न मुसलमंतर, न द्विन्नं भुंजमानानां न गब्भिनिया, न पायमानया, न पुरिसंतरगताय, न संकित्तिसु, न पथ सा उपट्ठितोहोति, न पथ मक्खिका संड संडचारिनी, न मच्छं न मांसं न सुरं न मेरयं न थुसोदकंपिवामि, सो एकागारिको वाहोमि, उकालोपिका, द्वागारिको होमि, द्वालोपिको सत्तागारिको वा होमि सत्तालोपिको ...एकाहं प आहारं आहारेमि, द्वीहिकंपि आहारं आहारेमि.... सत्ताहिकंपि आहारं आहारेमि—इति एयरूपं अद्धमासिकंपि परियाय तत्त भोजनानुयोगं अनुयुत्तो विहोरामि...केस्स मस्सु

लोचको विहोमि केस मस्सु लोचनानुयोगं अनुयुतो......याव उदविन्दुम्हिपि मि दया पच्चपट्ठिता होमि...माहं खुद्दके पाणे विसमगते संघातं अपादेस्संति."

गाथा.

सो तत्तो सो सीनो एकोभिंसनकेवने ।
नग्गो न च अग्गं आसीनो एसनापासुतो मुनीति ॥

"*Achelko homi...hathâpalekhano...nâbhihatam na uddisa katam nanimantanam sâdiyâmi; so nâ kumbhi mukhâ patiganhâmi na Kalopimukhâ patiganhâmi, na elakamantaram na dandamantaram na musala mantaram, na dvinnam bhunjamânânâm na gabbhanujâ na pâya mânaya na purusantaragataya, na sankittisu, na yatha sa uptthito hoti, na yath makkhikâ sanda sânda chârini na machchham na mânsam na suram na merayam na thusodakam pivâmi, so ekâgâriko vâhomi eka lopika dvâgâriko homi dvâlopikâ sattâ gâriko vâ homi sattu lopiko,—ekâ ham pa âhâram âharemi, dvihikam pa âhâram âhâremi,—sattâhikampi âhâram âhâremi—iti eyarupam addhamâsikam pi pariyâya bhatta bhojananuyogam anuyatto vihorâmi,...Kessa massu lockako vi homi Kesa massu lochanânuyogam anu yutto...yova uda Vindumhi pi me dayâ pachchapatthita hote—mâham khuddake pâne visama gate sanghâtam âpâdessanti.*

*Gâtha*

*So tatto so sino eko bhinsanake vane nuggo na cha aggim âsino esanâpasuto muniti.*

" I went without clothes......I licked my food from my hands. I did not eat food brought in, nor that prepared on my account, nor I accepted invitations for it. I took no alms from pot or dish. I took no food within a threshold, or through window-bar or within the pounding place, nor from two people eating together—nor from a pregnant woman, nor from a woman suckling a child, nor from one in intercourse, nor from food collected here and there, nor food where a dog stood by, nor from place where flies were swarming, nor fish, nor flesh, nor drink fermented, nor drink distilled, nor yet sour gruel did I drink. I ate from just one house, and just one morsel from that, or else I ate from two houses only and just two morsels thence......or I ate from seven houses only and just one morsel from each house. I took food only once a day or once in two days—or once in seven days, even to intervals of half a month......I plucked out hair and beard and kept thepractice up; even to a drop of water was charity established in me; thus :—" may I not be guilty of violence in harming tiny living beings (therein) scorched, frozen and alone in fearsome forest, dwelling naked, no fire to warm bent on the meditation is the sage."

*Note.* Whatever practical conduct of a sage is described above agrees with no other but the conduct of naked (Digambar) Jain Saints. Among the Digambar Jains there is an old Prakrit work on conduct of saints called *Mûlachâra* by Battakera ; it describes the similar practices. Even now-a-days also Digambara Jain Saints follow the same rules. Below I quote some verses in support of the above practices from this authoritative book. *Mûlachâra* says :—"

पंचय महव्वयाहं समिदी ओ पंच जिणवरुदिट्ठा ।
पंचेवींदिय रोहो छप्पिय अवासया लोचो ॥ २ ॥
अच्चेलक मण्हाणं खिदिसयणमदंत घसणंच्चेव ।
ठिदि भोयणेय भत्तं मूलगुणा अट्ठवीसदु ॥ ३ ॥

*Panchaya mahavvaya im samidi o panch a Jiṇavaruddi tthâ,*
*Pancha vindiya roho chhappiya-avâsayâ locho* 2
*Achchelaka manhâṇam khidi sayaṇa madanta ghasaṇam cheva*
*Thidi bhoyaṇeya bhattam mûlaguna at thavisadu* 3

A saint should follow the following twenty eight *root-duties*—

5 Great Vows of non-injury, truth, not taking what is not given, chastity and non-possession.

5 Careful dealing in walking, speaking, eating, handling things and excretions.

5 Control of five senses.

6 Daily important duties of repentance, renunciation, equanimity, prayer, obedience and abandoning bodily attachment.

1 plucking hair by hands.

1 not having any clothes.

1 not to bathe.
1 sleep on ground.
1 not to rub teeth.
1 to eat standing.
1 to eat only once a day.

28

*Locha—hastena mastaka keśa smasrûnam apanayanam, i.e.*, to pluck the hair of the head and beard by hands. This practice is specially observed by the Jain monks. It was followed by Goutam Buddha also.

Buddha remained *achelaka.*

*Mûlachâra* says about it :—

**वत्थाजिणवक्केणय अहवा पत्ताइणा असंवरणं ।**
**णिब्भूसण णिग्गंथं अच्चेलक्कं जगदिपूज्जं ॥ ३० ॥**

*Vatthâ Jiṇa vakke ṇaya ahavâ pattâinâ asamvaraṇam*
*Nibbhasaṇa nigganthaṃ achchelakkam Jogadi pajjam 30*

" Not to cover the body with clothes, skin, bark or leaves etc., not to wear ornaments, not to have attachment is the duty of *achelaka.* It is worshipful in the world."

The same book also describes eating from one's hands in standing posture.

**अंजलिपुडेण थिच्चा कुड्डाइ विवज्जणेण समपायं ।**
**पदिसुद्धे भूमितिये असणं थिदि भोजणं णाम ॥ ३४ ॥**

*Anjali puḍena thichchâ kuddâi vivajjanena samapâyam,*
*Padi sudde bhûmitiye asanam thidi bhojanam nâma 34*

" Leaving support of any wall etc., standing and keeping feet on parallel lines on pure ground to eat with hands is food in standing position."

A saint does not eat food specially prepared for saints as said in the same book—

**जावदियं उद्देसो पासंडोत्ति य हवे समुद्देसो ।**
**समणोत्तिय अदेसो णिग्गंथोत्तियहवे समादेसो ॥११-७-६॥**

*Jâvadiyam uddeso pá sandatti ya have samuddeso*
*Samanottiya âdeso nigganthottiya have samâdeso 11. 7/6*

" Whatever food is prepared for any saint, *sramana* or *nirgrantha* is *uddiṣta.* It should not be eaten by a Jain saint."

So it is said in the third verse of the 6th Chapter. Goutam Buddha also did not take such food when he was a naked saint.

A Saint takes food from not more than seven houses as said therein :—"

**उज्झहिं तिहिं सत्तोहिं वा घरेहिं जदि आगदं दु आचिण्णं ।**
**परदो तातेहिंभवे तव्विवरिदं अणाचिण्णं ॥ २०–६ ॥**

*Ujju him tihim sattehim vâ gharehim jadi âgadum du âchinnam*
*Parado tâtehin bhave tavvivaridam anâchinnam 20/6*

" The food brought from three or seven homes in one line is eatable, but not brought from more homes."

Goutama Buddha did not eat food from more than seven houses, when he was a naked saint.

Goutam Buddha did not eat food served by a pregnant woman as enjoined in *Mûlachârâ*.

अतिबाला अतिबुड्ढा घासत्ती गब्भिणी य अंधलिया ।
अंतरिदा व णिसण्णा उच्चत्था अहव णीचत्था ॥ ५०-६ ॥

*Ati bâlâ ati buddhâ ghâsatti gabbhini su ya andhaliya*
*Autaridâ va nisannâ uchchattha ahava nichatthâ* 50/4

"(Saints do not take food from) a child-woman, very old woman, a woman when eating, a pregnant woman, a blind woman, woman sitting in back of a wall, sitting high, or sitting very low."

*Note.* Goutam Buddha did not take food given through window-bars.

He did not accept dirty sour gruel or *thusodka*, which is prohibited in *Mûlâchâra*.

तिल तंडुल उसणोदय चणोदय तुसोदयं अविद्धत्थं ।
अण्णं तहाविहं वा अपरिणादं णेव गिण्हिज्जो ॥ ५४ ॥

*Tila tandula usanodaya–chanodaya tusodayam avid-dhattham*
*Annam tahâviham vâ aparinadam neva ginhijjo* 54

"Washing water of *Tilas*, rice, grams and husks and hot water which is not altered in colour etc., should not be taken."

Goutama did not take food from a woman suckling a child, as is prohibited in *Mûlâchâra* :—

लेवण मज्जण कम्मं पियमाणं दारयंच णिखविय।
एवं विहादिया पुण दाणं जदि दिंति दायगादोसा ॥५२-६॥

*Levana majjana Kammam piyamânam dârayamcha nikha viya*
*Evam vihâ diyâ puna dânam jadi dinti dâyagâ dosô*
*52/6*

"It is wrong on the part of a donor, if any woman serves food while smearing the ground, bathing, suckling a child and leaving it."

About taking food from the hands it is said in *Mûlâchâra Anagara bhavana chapter,*

असणं जदि वा पाणं खज्जं भोजं चलिज्जपेज्जं वा
पडिलेहि ऊण सुद्धं भुंजंति पाणि पत्तेसु ॥ ५४ ॥

*Asanam jadi vâ panam khajjam bhojam challijja pejjam va*
*Padi lehi una suddham bhunjanti pâni pattesuh.* 54

"The saints eat from the hollow of their hands the pure food eatable, drinkable, tastable, lickable etc., after properly seeing it."

Thus the Jain scriptures prove that the conduct followed by Goutama Buddha while he was a naked monk was nothing but the conduct of a naked Jain Saint.

From the Pali scriptures of the 1st century A.D. at Ceylon it is evident that Goutama Buddha in his 35th year *i.e.*, 6 years after he left his home preached his sermon on the middle path.

*Buddha Charya* Page 23 (referring to Samyutta Nikâya 55.2.1 and Vinaya Mahâvagga) says :—

" I heard thus " once the Exalted One was walking in the forest Risipattana of Benares. There he addressed *Pancha Virgiya* monks thus :—" O monks, the saints should not serve these two extremes :—First is this : to be addicted to sense-enjoyments, a path served by savages and fit for the low and vulgar village people and full of misuses ; the second is this :—to give pain to body, full of misuses, served by non-learned and miserable monks, leaving these two extremes *Tathagata* has searched after the *middle path*, which gives right view and produces Knowledge. It is for peace, discrimination, full knowledge and *Nirvana*. That middle path is the eight-fold path of liberation, right view etc.

This was the first sermon of the Buddha. It shows that nakedness and all other sufferings along with it were either considered by him to be difficult or unnecessary and therefore He proclaimed a path which was neither difficult nor easy He, who is not a follower of the Nirgrantha, may say that Goutama Buddha, thinking the conduct of nakedness to be difficult and unnecessary, ordered his monks to put on necessary clothes ; while a follower of the Nirgrantha cult, who has belief that the natural condition of the body is necessary for a saint for the success of Self concentration. It is why Lord Mahavira and His predecessors followed it. It is a help in austerities. No difficulty will be felt by one who has practised it. Natural bliss can be enjoyed only by deep self-absorption. Goutama found it difficult for him and he thought it better to adopt the middle path of Sravakas or laymen. The rules of conduct which are applicable to the Brahmachari sravakas were followed by him and preached to others.

According to the Digambar Jain scriptures, a Brahmachari Sravaka of the 7th stage can have two or three or necessary clothes, can dine where he is invited, can sleep on simple cots etc. This sort of conduct was adopted and preached by Goutam Buddha. I saw this sort of practical conduct among the Buddhist monks of Ceylon. According to Digambar Jain scriptures the middle path has eleven stages. One who is on the last stage has a loin cloth only on the body. A layman in 11th stage while keeping one short cloth and one loin cloth is called a *Kṣullaka* and one who has only one loin cloth is called an *ailaka*. They do not accept invitations, but go out for alms like the saints. Leaving this controversial point whether Goutama found the conduct of nakedness unnecessary or difficult, it is proved from the Pali books that He preached to monks to have necessary clothings and this conduct very aptly agrees with that of the Swetambar Jain Saints of India, who also maintain that there is no necessity for putting aside all the clothes for a monk in his efforts for *nirvana*. Perhaps this might have been the idea of Goutam also in adopting the easy mode. Buddhist monks take food once a day, before twelve noon, do not eat at night nor at improper time, nor break bows of trees and stay at one place in rainy season. All these rules of conduct are the same as those of a Jain Saint.

The internal philosophy of self is the same in Jainism and Buddhism as has been described in the previous chapters, only the external conduct of the Buddhists does not agree with that of the Digambar Jain Saints while it agrees mostly with that of Svetambar Jain saints. As the Svetambar saints keep pots to collect alms, so the Buddhist monks do. They eat by alms as well as by invitations, while the Svetambar saints do not accept invitations. Their accepting invitations agrees with that of the Digambar Jain Brahmachari sravaks of 7th degree. While Buddhist monks use vehicles and trains for journey like the Digambar Jain Brahmacharis, the Svetambar Jain monks do not use any vehicle, but walk on foot.

As regards the mode of concentration, there does not seem to be any difference between the Jain and Buddhist saints.

## IDOL WORSHIP AMONG THE JAINS AND THE BUDDHISTS.

The idols of Buddha resemble the Jain images as regards the contemplative mode. While Digambara Jain images are quite naked in standing *Kâyotsarga* or sitting *Padmâsana* or *half padmasana* and the Svetambar ones are in the same position, but with the sign of a loin cloth, the Buddha images have generally two clothes one under the waist and another upon the shoulders. The position is the same standing or sitting; some images have their hands like the Jain ones, some have one hand on the lap and one on the breast, or one or both the hands on legs, or in standing posture one hand lying down and one hand raised as if in preaching. Buddha images are constructed in lying posture also in the condition of Goutama Buddha in his last moments just before attaining nirvâna, which is a special feature with them. I had occasion to see Buddha images and temples at Ellora, Ajanta, Sanchi, Benares, Nasik, Bombay, Taxila etc., in India and in some places in Ceylon. In India I found almost all the Buddhist images made of stone, while those found in Ceylon are made of stone and also of a particular kind of nice clay. Clay images are constructed very nicely and with different colours of the bodily limbs. Such beautiful images are not seen in India. Here their images made of stone are generally of one colour like those of Jain images.

The Buddhist images seen by me at Kandy, Anuradhapura, Dambal, Kelaniya and Colombo at Ceylon are very meditative and attractive. They are placed on high plat-forms in the same way as in Jain temples. I saw in Ceylon the Buddhists worshipping their images just like the Jains worship their images. They make obeisance, bow and pray like the Jains and use generally flowers for worship and burn incense and light candles. Everything is put in front of the images nothing is put over them. Among some Digambar Jains and mostly among the Svetambar Jains, the mode of worship has considerably changed. They put flower etc., over the images and some cover them with flowers altogether. The Svetambar Jains even decorate their images with ornaments etc. There is no such decoration for the Buddhist images. They keep them very clean. Among the Digambar Jains of Northern India called the *Tera Panthis*—the images are kept more clean ; they do not put flowers etc., over them. The expression of unattachment is thereby properly kept. I attended in Ceylon two great Buddhist fairs, one on the birth-day of Buddha or *Vaisakha sudi 14*, and the other on *Jetha Sudi 14*, commemorating the day of the landing in Ceylon of Asoka's son Mihinda. I saw thousands of men and women bare-footed paying hearty homage to their images like the Jains. There was simplicity in the women, who were seen going on pilgrimage with pure flowers etc. If any one asked them where they were going, they would answer that they were going for *Vandana* or paying homage. As it is customary for the Jains to bath their images daily, this custom was not found prevalent among the Buddhists. In many places, they put glasses before the images, to prevent dust. I did not see uncleanliness, or wetness in their shrines.

## EACH SOUL IS RESPONSIBLE FOR ITS ADVANCEMENT.

The Jains and the Buddhists both believe that no God can give us pleasure or pain, or get us liberation. One can be liberated by one's own efforts.

" *The Doctrine of the Buddha* " by Grimm Page 29 " Liberation from suffering cannot be realized through any kind of grace especially not by the help of some personal God, but exclusively by our own strength and by personal action."

Just as the Jains worship the images of the worshipful *Arhats* and the perfect *Siddhas* or their meditative images for the sake of purification of their thoughts, so the Buddhists have the similar practice of the worship of Buddhas and their images.

The Jaina Scriptures Say :—

1. *`Samâdhi Sataka.*

**नयत्यात्मानमात्मैव जन्म निर्वाण मेव वा ।**
**गुरुरात्मात्मनस्तस्मान्नान्योऽस्ति परमार्थतः ॥ ७५ ॥**

*Nayatyâtmânamâtmaiva Janma nirvâna meva vâ*
*Gururâtmâtmanastasmânnânyosti paramârthatah* 75

" The self can lead itself to the wandering or to the *Nirvâna*, therefore the self is the teacher of the self, there is no other from the real point of view."

2. *Purusârtha Siddhiupaya.*

**सर्व विवर्तोत्तीर्णं यदा स चैतन्य मचल माप्नोति ।**
**भवति तदा कृतकृत्यः सम्यक् पुरुषार्थ सिद्धिमापन्नः ॥११॥**

*Sarva vivartottirnam yadâ sa chaitanya machala mâpnoti*
*Bhavati tadâ kritakrityah samyak purasârtha siddhi mâpannah*

" When he, after crossing over all the impure conditions, attains the steadfast self-realization; then he becomes content after having succeeded in the right efforts for *nirvana*."

3. *Svayambhu Stotra* :—

न पूजयार्तस्त्वयि वीतरागे न निन्दयानाथ विवांतवैरे ।
तथापि ते पुण्यगुण स्मृतिर्नः पुनातु चित्तं दुरितांजनेभ्यः ॥ ५७ ॥

*Na pujâyarthastvayi vitarage na nindayâ nath vivânt baire,*
*Tathâpi te punya guna smritinah punitu chittam duritanja nebhyah* 57

" O non-attached Lord, you have no regard for your worship, ; O Lord devoid of enmity, neither you have any concern with your censure ; still when we remember your pure qualities, our minds become free from the dirt of sins."

All the compounds, molecules and created things are destructible :—

The Jains and the Buddhists both believe that the compound or created things or worldly conditions are destructible and fleeting.

" *The Doctrine of the Buddha* " by Grimm.

Page 59.—Impermanent are all the compound of existence. Painful are all the compound of existence

(Theravad Gatha) *277–278* *Budda Charya* Page 541 Maha pari-nibban-sutta S. N. 2.3. (16).

The last words of Goutam Buddha were :—

" Well ! monks, I speak to you, all the created things have the nature of decay ; perform (life-object) carefully. These are the last words of the Thathâgata."

Buddha Charya P. 518 Chanda Sutta (S.N. 45-2-3).

On hearing of the death of Sariputra, Goutam Buddha says :—" Anand ! That which is created is all to be destroyed. It is impossible to check its destruction. Threfore, O Anand, make itself an island, make itself a refuge, walk, having no other shelter."

The Jain scriptures say the same thing :—

*Jnânârnava* says :—

**वस्तुजातमिदं मूढ प्रतिक्षण विनश्वरं ।**
**जानन्नपि न जानासि ग्रह कोऽय मनौषधः ॥ १४-२ ॥**

*Vastu jâtamidam mudha prati-ksana vinaśvaram,*
*Jânanapi na jânâsi graha ko-ya manausadhah* *14/2*

" O Ignorant, all the objects are decaying every moment, knowing this, why do not you understand. Have you been caught hold of by a ghost, for which there is no remedy."

**मनोज्ञ विषयैः सार्द्धं संयोगाः स्वप्नसन्निभाः ।**
**क्षणादेव क्षयंयांति वंचनोदुत बुद्धयाः ॥ ४५-२ ॥**

*Manojna visayaih sârdhum sanyogâh svapnasannibhâh*
*Ksanâ deva Kṣayam Yânti banchanoddhuta buddhayah*

*45/2*

" Association with agreeable objects is like seeing a dream ; they, cheating the intellect, soon disappear."

**घनमालानुकारिणि कुलानि च बलानि च ।**
**राज्यालंकार वित्तानि कीर्तितानि महर्षिभिः ॥ ४१-२ ॥**

*Ghana mâlâ nukârini kulâni cha batani cha*
*Rajyâlankara vittani kirtitani maharsibhih 41/2*

" Families, powers, kingdom, ornaments, and property are fleeting like the group of clouds. So have the great sages said.

**ये चात्र जगती मध्ये पदार्थाश्चेतनेतराः ।**
**ते ते मुनिभिरुद्दिष्टाः प्रतिक्षण विनश्वराः ॥ ४६-२ ॥**

*Ye châtra Jagati madhye padârthâ-schetane tarâh*
*Te te munibhiruddhistâh prati ksana vinasvarâh* 46/2

" Whatever conscious and unconscious objects are seen in this universe, are fleeting every moment. The saints have said so."

**गगन नगर तुल्यं संगमं वल्लभानां**
**जलद पटल तुल्यं यौवनं वा धनं वा ।**
**सुजनसुत शरीरादिनि विद्युच्चलानि**
**क्षणिक मिति समस्तं विद्धि संसार वृत्तम् ॥ ४७-२ ॥**

*Gagana nagara tulyum sangamam Vallabhânâm*
*Julada patala tulyam yauvanam va dhanam va,*
*Sujana suta śarîrâdini vidyuchchalâni*
*Ksanikâ miti samastam viddhi sansâravrittam* 47/2

" Association with the dear ones is like a city in the sky ; youth and riches are like a group of clouds ;

Relatives, sons and bodies etc. are like lightning. Know all the worldly phenomena to be transitory."

THE UNIVERSE IS WITHOUT BEGINNING AND END.

The Jains and Buddhists both agree that this universe is without beginning and end and that no personal God is its creator. Vide "*The Doctrine of the Buddha*" by Grimm. *Page 90.* "Without beginning or end, ye monks, is this round of re-birth (sansara). There cannot be discerned a first beginning of beings, who, sunk in ignorance and bound by thirst ceaselessly transmigrating again and again run to a new birth. Five, in number, Sariputra, are the fates that may befall after death: namely, the passage into hell-world, the animal kingdom, the realm of *Preta*, the world of men and the abodes of Gods."

*Page 94.* "Among these five fates ultimately only the last one, the abode in heaven-world, could be desirable. But according to the Buddha, this one is just as much subject to the great law of transmigration, as the abode in the four other ones."

*Page 96.* "Running down from birth to death, from death to birth, you have shed on this long way truly more tears than water is contained within the four great oceans."

*Page 106.* How can human insight bear the thought of a god who ought to be the sum of infinite goodness, wisdom and power, creating beings whom he knows to be condemned in an over-whelming majority to eternal damnation to hell. What would we think of a father who would send his child into the world, knowing for certain that it would later on commit "voluntarily" a crime that would be punished with life-long imprisonment. Is it conceivable that the same God who orders men to overlook and to forgive every offence, acts himself in quite a different manner, inflicting eternal punishment even after death."

*Note.* The Jain scriptures also teach the same thing that this universe is eternal and no God is the creator of it.

*Jnânârnava says* :—

**अनादि निधनः सोऽयं स्वयं सिद्धोप्यनश्वरः ।**
**अनीश्वरोऽपि जीवादिपदार्थैः संभृतो भृसम् ॥ ४-११ ॥**

*Anâdi nidhanah so yam svayam siddho pya naśvarah*
*Aniśvaropi jivâdipadârthaih sambhrito bhrisam* 4/11

"This universe is without beginning and end, itself existing, eternal, without being created by God, and full of substances, soul, etc."

**यत्रैते जन्तवः सर्वे नानागतिषु संस्थिताः ।**
**उत्पद्यंते विपद्यंते कर्मपाश वशंगताः ॥ ६-११ ॥**

*Yatraite jantavah sarve nânâgatisusansthitâh*
*Utpadyante vipadyante, karmapâsa vasamgatâh* 6/11

" Here the beings existing in different conditions of existence take birth and die under the influence of *karmic* nets."

*Note.* The Jain scriptures speak of four conditions of existence namely hell, sub-human, human and celestial. Preta or Ghost, etc. counted as fifth fate in Buddhism is included in the celestials. The Ghosts etc. have abode in the under-neath part of the universe, while the heavenly celestials live in the upper part. So there is no real difference if the *Pretas* are counted as separate.

*Mûlâchâra says* :—

लोओ अकिट्टिमो खलु अणाइणिहणो सहाव णिप्पण्णो ।
जीवाजीवेहिं भुडो णिच्चो तालरुक्खे संताणो ॥ १२२-८ ॥

*Loô akittimo khalu anâi nihâno sahâva nippanno,*
*Jivâjivehim bhudo nichcho tâla rukke santhâno* 122/8

" This universe is verily uncreated, without beginning or end, existing by nature, eternal, having figure like a palm tree and is full of souls and non-souls."

तत्थानु हवंति जीवा सकम्मणिव्वत्तियं सुहं दुक्खम् ।
जम्मणमरण पुणब्भव मंणतें भवसायर भीमे ॥ २५-८ ॥

*Tatthanu havanti jivâ sakamma nivvattiyam saham dukkham*
*Jammana marana punabbhava mananta bhavasâyare bhime 25/8.*

"There the beings experience pleasure, pain, birth, death, re-birth owing to the results of their own karmas in this fearful and endless world-ocean."

## THE PHILOSOPHY OF SYADVADA OR MANY-SIDED-NESS.

In the old Pali scriptures the doctrine of Syadvâda is found in many statements, just as it is existing in the Jain scriptures. One substance has many controversial natures which are viewed and stated from different points of view. It is for that reason that a substance is called *Anekânta* or having many natures at a time, just as a young man has many relations at one time. He is son with reference to his father, he is father with reference to his son, he is uncle with reference to his nephew, he is nephew with reference to his uncle. Thus a man can have many relations from different aspects at one and the same time. But they cannot be described by one word at one and the same time. When one relation will be described, others cannot be described although they are present there. In order to state a fact in its correct stand-point, the doctrine of Syadvâda is meant. *Syât* means, "from some stand-point," Vâda means "to state," thus Syadvâda means, 'to say a thing from some stand-point.'

Let us give an example. A man dies and is born as a horse. Now the being in the horse is the same as was in the man as well as not the same as it was in the man.

Both statements are controversial, but they are correct from both the different stand-points. If we look to the real being, then the same being which was in human condition has now its existence as a horse, but if we look with reference to change of condition, we must say that the condition of horse is quite separate from that of man. Thus we may say that from some points of view they are the same, but from another point of view they are not the same. Both the statements are correct.

Buddhistic literature states the thing in the same way.

"*The Doctrine of the Buddha*" by George Grimm.

*P. 104.* "There a reasonable man reflects thus; if some of these dear recluses and Brahmans teach personal continuance I cannot see it, and if other dear recluses and Brahmans teach there is no personal duration, neither do I perceive this. But if, without having seen or perceived it, I now decide in favour of one of these doctrines and say:—This one is only true and the other teaching is foolish; then this would not be well done. For we may easily trust to some thing that is hollow and empty and wrong, and we may fail to trust to some thing that is right and true and real. And thus who seeks for truth, if he is a reasonable man, will not draw readily the one-sided conclusion: 'only this opinion is true, and the other opinion is foolish', but to gain insight into these statements, it is of importance to to regard their content (M. N. I. P. 420 II. P. 270).

The Jain Saint *Kunda Kunda Acharya* says in *Panchâstikaya* the same thing.

मणुसत्तणेण णट्ठो देही देवो हवेदि इदरो वा ।
उभयत्त जीव भावो ण णस्सदि ण जायदे अण्णो ॥ १७ ॥

*Maṇusatthaṇeṇa nattho dehi devo havedi idaro vâ,*
*Ubhayatta jiva bhâvo ṇa ṇassadi ṇa jâyade aṇṇo* 17

"This being is destroyed with reference to human condition, and is born a celestial or another, but in both the existences, the soul-substance is the same, it is neither destroyed nor newly born."

Thus from the point of change of condition they are different; but from the point of the real being, the yare the same.

SAINTS CALMLY ENDURE SUFFERINGS.

As the Jain Saints are required to endure twenty-two sufferings calmly, so the Buddhist literature also speaks on the point for the Buddhist monks.

"*The Doctrine of the Buddha*" by George Grimm.

*Page 325.* This is a monk who bears cold and heat, hunger and thirst, wind and rain, mosquitoes, wasps, vexing crawling beings, malicious and spiteful words, painful feelings of the body striking him, violent cutting, piercing, disagreeable, tedious, life endangering, he patiently endures. He is entirely free from greed, hate and delusion, dis-joined from mis-conduct, sacrifice and gifts, service and greetings, he deserves as the holiest state in the world.

"Those who cause me pain and those who cause me pleasure, towards all of them I behave in the same way; affection and hate I know not, in joy and sorrow, I remain unmoved: in honour and dishonour, everywhere I am the same. This is the perfection of my equanimity." (Charujâpitaka III 15).

The Jain saint is required to endure twenty-two sufferings as is said in *Tattvârtha sutra* :—

**मार्गाच्यावन निर्जरार्थं पषिषोढव्याः परीषहाः ॥ ८-९ ॥**

**क्षुत्पिषासा शीतोष्ण दंशमशकनग्न्यारतिस्त्रीचर्या निपया सय्या क्रोश वधयाञ्चा लाभ रोग तृणास्पर्श मलसत्कारपुरस्कार प्रज्ञा ज्ञाना दर्शनानि ॥ ९-९ ॥**

*Márgâ chyavana nirjarârtham pari ṣoḍhvyâh pari ṣa hâh 8/9*

*Kṣyut pipâsâ sitoṣṇa danśa maśaka nâgnyaratistricharya nisadyâ sayyâ krośa vâdhayâchnalabha roga triṇa sparsa mala satkara puraskara prajna jnânâdarsanâni 9/9*

" With a view not to fall from the Path of liberation and to shed off karmas what one patiently endures are *pariṣahas*. They are twenty-two and are as follow :— (1) Hunger (2) thirst (3) cold (4) heat (5) mosquitoes etc., (6) nakedness (7) dissatisfaction (8) woman (9) walking (10) sitting (11) sleeping (12) malicious words (13) beating (14) begging (15) not gaining (16) disease (17) touch with thorny shrubs (18) dirt (19) honour dishonour (20) knowledge (21) ignorance (22) disbelief.

The Jain Saints are required to observe equanimity. *Sâra Samuchchaya* says :—

निन्दास्तुतिसमंधीरं शरीरेपि च निस्पृहं ।
जितेन्द्रियं जितक्रोधं जित लोभ महाभटं ॥ २०३ ॥
रागद्वेष विनिर्मुक्तं सिद्धि संगमनोत्सुकम् ।
ज्ञानाभ्यास रतं नित्त्यं च प्रशमेस्थितं ॥ २०६ ॥
एवं विधं हि यो दृष्ट्वा स्वगृहांगणमागतं ।
मात्सर्यं कुरुते मोहात् क्रियातस्यन विद्यते ॥ २०७ ॥
समः शत्रौ च मित्रेच समो मानापमानयोः ।
लाभालाभे समो नित्त्यं लोष्टकांचनयोस्तथा ॥ २२० ॥
सम्यक्तभावना सुद्धं ज्ञानसेवापरायणं ।
चारित्राचरणासक्तम क्षीण सुख कांक्षिणं ॥ २२१ ॥
ईदृशं श्रमणं दृष्ट्वा यो न मन्येत दुष्टधीः ।
नृजन्म निष्फलं सारं संहारयति सर्वता ॥ २२२ ॥

*Nindastuti saman dhiram sarirepi cha nispraham,*
*Jitendriyam jitakrodham jita lobha-mahâ bhaṭam* 203
*Râgadveṣa vinir muktam siddhi sangama notsukam,*
*Jnânâbhyâsaratam nittyum nitttyamcha praśame sthitam* 206
*Evam vidham hi yo dṛiṣtva svagrahangaṇa magatam*
*Mâtsaryam kurute mohat* kriyâ *tasya na vidyate* 207
*Samah satrau cha mitru cha samo mânâpa mânayoh,*
*Lâbhâlabhe samo nittyam lostha kânchana yostathâ,* 220
*Samyaktu bhâvanâ suddham jnâna-sevâ parâyaṇam,*
*Châritrâ charanâ sakta maksina sukha kanksinaṃ* 221
*Īdrasam sramanam draṣṭva yo na maṇyet a duṣṭadhih*
*Nra janma nisphalam sâram samhara-yati sarvathâ* 222

"One who is unmoved by censure and praise, patient, unattached even to his body, has control over senses, has conquered anger and has vanquished the great warrior greed, devoid of affection, and hatred, anxious of getting perfection, always engaged in pursuit of knowledge, for ever stead-fast in passionlessness—such (a saint) comes to the court-yard of his home, seeing him, he who has malice through delusion is devoid of conduct. One who equally treats enemy and friend, is unmoved by honour and dishonour, always the same in gain or loss, equally sees a clay-piece and gold, has pure meditation of right belief, engaged in service of Knowledge, well disposed to pursuit of conduct, and anxious of having eternal bliss—such a saint—he who seeing him does not honour him has a wicked conscience. He totally destroys his useful human birth, making it unprofitable."

## LAYMEN CANNOT GET NIRVANA.

As long as home life is not abandoned, and saint life is not adopted in order to have pure self concentration, so long one cannot have ***Nirvâna***, cannot end the miseries of the world. This fact is emphasized in the Digambar Jain Scriptures and also in the Buddhist-literature.

"*The Doctrine of the Buddha*" by George Grimm.

*Page 399.* "There is no house-holder whatever, O Vachha, who, not having left off house-hold ties, upon

the dissolution of the body, makes an end of suffering." (M. I. P. 483).

*Page 416.* "Cramped and confined is house-hold life, a den of dirt. But the homeless life is as the open air of heaven. It is hard to live the holy life in all its perfection and purity while bound to home. Let me go forth to homelessness." (M. I. P. 267).

The Jain book *Jnânârnava* says:—

न प्रमाद् जयं कर्तुं धीधनैरपि पार्यते ।
महा व्यसन संकीर्णे ग्रहवासेऽति निन्दिते ॥ ९ ॥
शक्यते न वशीकर्तुं ग्रहिभिश्चपलं मनः ।
अतश्चित्त प्रशान्त्यर्थं सद्भिस्त्यक्ताग्रहे सथितिः ॥ १०-४॥

*Na pramâda jayam kartum dhidha nai rapi pâryate,*
*Mahâ vyasana samkirne grahavâseti nindite* 9
*Sakyate na vasi kartum grahibhischapalam manah*
*Ataśchita prasântyartham sadbhis-tyaktâ grahe sthitih*
10/4

"Even the wise men cannot conquer the passions in house-hold life which is censurable and is full of many calamities. This wavering mind cannot be controlled by the house-holders, therefore the home life has been abandoned by the gentlemen for bringing peace to to the mind."

## SAINTS SHOULD MEDITATE IN SOLITARY PLACES.

"*The Doctrine of the Buddha*" by George Grimm.

***Page 350.*** "Whoso once has experienced this state within himself, is lost to the turmoil of the world,

even if he again awakes to it: " His mind inclines to solitude, bends towards solitude, sinks itself in solitude, to him this is highest blessedness." (M. I. P. 306)

SACRED BOOKS OF THE EAST. VOL. X.

Dhammapada Ch. XXI.

*Page 305.* " He alone, who, without ceasing, practises the duty of sitting alone, sleeping alone, he subdues himself, with rejoice in the destruction of all desires alone, as if living in a forest."

THE JAIN SCRIPTURES ALSO DESCRIBE THE BEAUTY OF SOLITARINESS.

**अभवच्चित्त विक्षेप एकांते तत्त्व संस्थितः ।**
**अभ्यास्येदभियोगेन योगीतत्त्वं विजात्मनः ॥ ३६ ॥**

*Abhavachchitta viksepaekânte tattva sansthitih,*
*Abhyasyedabhiyogen yogi tattvam nijâtmanah*

" A meditating saint should practise contemplation of one's own self being steadfast in the true principle with efforts in a solitary place where the mind may not be disturbed.

*Jnânárnava says :—*

**रागादिं बागुराजालं निकृत्याचिन्त्य विक्रमः ।**
**स्थानमाश्रयते धन्यो विविक्तं ध्यान सिद्धये ॥ २-२७ ॥**

***Râgâdi bâgurâjâlam nikritya chintya vikramah,***
***Sthâna mâsrayate dhanyo viviktam dhyana siddhaé 2/27***

"A qualified saint having unthinkable valour, hrowing away the net-work of attachment etc. takes helter in a solitary place for success in self-concentra-ion."

Those who want to arrive at Truth should study the old literature of Jainism and Buddhism. I believe that they will have to conclude that the philosophy of both the systems is one and the same. One who vishes freedom from miseries must follow the eight-fold path of Buddhism or the three-fold path of Jainism. The teaching of both is to be dependent on one's own self, and to practise self-concentration with firm belief and knowledge in order to gain Liberation or Nirvâna.

The Jains and the Buddhists should mutually understand each other's literature and be friendly knowing that their philosophies have emanated from one COMMON SOURCE.

Bibliotheca Indo-Buddhica Series No.7

# A Comparative Study of Jainism & Buddhism

SITAL PRASAD

Sri Satguru Publications
A Division of
Indian Books Centre
Delhi, India

Published by
Sri Satguru Publications,
Indological and Oriental Publishers
A Division of
Indian Books Centre
40/5, Shakti Nagar,
Delhi-110007
India

Email: ibcindia@vsnl.com
Website: http://www.indianbookscei

First Edition : Madras 1932
Reprinted : Delhi, 1985, 2003

ISBN 81-7030-82-7

Printed at Chawla Offset Printers, Delhi 110 052